The
CHRISTIAN
APPROACH
to
CULTURE

Emile Cailliet

THE CHRISTIAN APPROACH to CULTURE

> Don't let the world around you squeeze you into its own mould, but let God re-mould your minds from within, so that you may prove in practice that the Plan of God for you is good, meets all His demands and moves towards the goal of true maturity.
>
> Paul

The Letter to Rome, 12:2

ABINGDON-COKESBURY PRESS

NEW YORK • NASHVILLE

THE CHRISTIAN APPROACH TO CULTURE

Copyright MCMLIII by Pierce & Washabaugh

Library of Congress Catalog Card Number: 52-13754

SET UP, PRINTED, AND BOUND BY THE
PARTHENON PRESS, AT NASHVILLE,
TENNESSEE, UNITED STATES OF AMERICA

To Christian workers everywhere,
and to those conscientious seekers after truth,
men of good will and of honest mind, who have
come to the candid admission that they have
lost their way in the wilderness of the con-
temporary world

E. C.

PREFACE

IN the beginning God . . ." The four opening words of our Bible constitute the charter for all sound thinking. It is not enough to rely on the ingenious answers uncovered from past experience or on the great scientific advance of our own age for the solution to our problems. Neither is a resorption of the various disciplines of culture into theology to be advocated here. The way to sanity and to a genuine knowledge and understanding of the world of nature and of man is to take into account the entire landscape of reality and to survey it in the light of Scripture. If a Christian pattern of truth can be re-established, we shall have found again the one essential frame of reference for a pertinent appraisal of God's quest for man and of man's quest for truth down to our own time.

Looking at the world today, the Christian philosopher comes to the realization that the basic questions which are on the minds of our contemporaries are age-old problems. Hence the Christian approach to culture should enable a thoughtful man to understand how and why these questions came to be raised, how and why the resulting formulations so often missed the mark. Here then he may profit from past performance.

Combining the resources of an adequate culture and of a mature religion, the Christian philosopher will reap the fruits of a timely interaction between the two. Christianity will provide orientation and control, suggesting the right moves and pointing to danger signs along the way. Culture will afford a keener penetration and a firmer appropriation of truth already held while providing at all times access to fresh information which may be turned into nuggets of gold.

This design is implied in the title of this book and points to our method. By "the Christian approach to culture" I do not mean strictly a consideration of what happened when Christianity came to grips with the secular order. What I have in mind is to view cultural manifestations with Christian eyes. As soon as this is done, however, it becomes obvious that such an approach must of necessity involve the further consideration of the ways in which any conclusion reached affects the approach itself. In other words, the approach immediately becomes a conversation with culture. It would be a strange thing to deal with culture without ever learning anything from culture. When the Christian philosopher views a certain cultural pattern from his own vantage point, appraising the data at hand according to his own frame of reference, and thus tries to make out the meaning and relevance of his observations, the immediate outcome hardly constitutes anything more than a working hypothesis, one which may be sound and "well taken," yet a working hypothesis just the same. The reason for this may be readily seen: the knowledge of faith is no substitute for that of the specialist in his field, or of the man of culture in his cultural circle. As soon as the answer of either of them is forthcoming, the conversation is likely to take some unexpected turn. The Christian philosopher then is bound to reconsider his question, to reformulate it with an eye to the fresh information just made available to him. And so the exchange proceeds in an atmosphere of mutual respect and understanding.

However considerate toward culture his method may be, the Christian philosopher constantly keeps in mind that the way to knowledge and understanding originates in him who is the Principle and the End, the only one, therefore, who can give meaning to the world of nature and of man. Only he, Originator of the design and Lord of all, can finally map the way for us.

E. C.

CONTENTS

V. THE CHRISTIAN APPROACH TO CULTURE

PART I

The Christian Point of View on Culture

CHAPTER ONE

CHRISTIANITY and CULTURE

IN HYPATIA, Charles Kingsley tells of a young Greek intellectual of Jewish extraction who has come to see and hear Augustine, the famous scholar whose name is on every lip. Having spent some time on the inscription of a psalm, Augustine presently allegorizes it. The plain truth is that he makes it mean something which it never did mean in the mind of the psalmist, and which undoubtedly it could never mean, for the preacher has based his interpretation on a mistranslation at the very outset. He now makes puns on the Latin version and playfully derives the meaning of Hebrew words from Latin etymologies. And so the young Greek intellectual is left to wonder about the learning for which Augustine is so famed. But then there appear in the preacher's reasoning a few practical hints. An organic texture looms up amid allegories and overstrained interpretations. Finally there emerges the landscape of a reality seen to depend for its existence upon a living, present God. By now our Greek brother really is puzzled but nevertheless glows with Hebrew pride. Could this be *the* landscape of reality? What if Augustine were right after all? What if his hints were to the point? But more, what if Augustine were right in going even further than Philo of Alexandria? What if this same Jehovah, Wisdom, Logos, call him what they might, were actually the true God and not merely the god of a favored race or one favored class of minds? Whereupon there flashes into the mind of the young Greek intellectual the possibility

13

that that strange story of the cross of Calvary might not be so impossible after all.[1]

Yes, what if . . . ? These questions are our questions down to this day. They refer to the truths that matter most to us in the last analysis, so that they really come first.

Each one of us needs an understanding of reality which will enable him not only to *do* the truth, but further to claim and appropriate whatever has been well said with a view to securing even more relevant knowledge.

Preliminary Reservations

This much, however, must be made clear from the beginning: while the biblical pattern of truth provides for our essential needs, it was never meant to answer our scientific questions, still less to play up to any cultural interest we may happen to have. We may with interest and profit study traces of folklore in the Old Testament. In so doing we may greatly contribute to our knowledge and understanding of the Old Testament. Yet the Old Testament was never designed as a source book for the study of folklore. Or again, we may be fascinated by tracing the development of great ideas within the various books of the Bible once they are recast according to chronology, and thereby add to our apprehension of the Bible. Yet, however legitimate and praiseworthy such a study, it can never constitute a guide to understanding the Bible as Bible. The divine Library as such constitutes the history of a single continuous community. It was the consciousness of this continuity under the living Lord of history which led this same community to identify and preserve the books which make up the Library. The Book of books is not a museum piece. It is not a textbook. It is not even an anthology of great literature. The plain fact is it does not belong to a realm, if by realm a class is meant. The Bible is not in a class. It constitutes a class by itself. In the last analysis it is therefore beyond explanation, since to explain is to put in a class. The Bible is the living record of God's disclosure of himself and his purpose in calling forth the com-

[1] Chapter 21.

14

munity of his people, and of the resources made available by him for those who would "live themselves into" that community, thus becoming his children in Jesus Christ, our Lord. Such, then, being the nature of the Book, it becomes clear that we must turn to it first of all to ascertain those features of the landscape of reality which matter most to us. By the same token, it also becomes clear that we should not expect the Book to answer questions pertaining to scientific speculation or cultural interest, however legitimate or praiseworthy. It is a fact, moreover, that Scripture is hardly ever found to provide that which man can find or produce by himself. A man is called upon to be a laborer together with God. Applied to the life of the mind, this means that there is ample initiative left to man for interpreting and "filling in" the landscape of reality.

Before any further step toward this purpose is taken, however, we should realize that no Christian approach to culture is safe which does not begin by disengaging Christian truth from the cultural forms in which it has been embedded throughout the ages. The Christian *challenge* to culture constitutes the prolegomenon to any Christian approach to culture. Since the process involved is of necessity most laborious, however, the preceding proposition need not be strictly interpreted in terms of chronology. Let us understand it as a matter of priority pointing to the spirit of our method.

Need a Christian Be Concerned with Culture?

Some will want to go still further and ask, Why should a Christian be concerned with culture at all? Far from being irrelevant, this question is one of long standing. Ever since evangelical Christianity came to grips with Hellenism, it seems to have harbored a deep-seated prejudice against secular culture in general, and science in particular.

Let us bear in mind that when Jesus began his ministry some 360 years had already elapsed since Alexander the Great had conquered Palestine, a mere district of the civilized world soon to be brought under his rule. This corresponds roughly to the period between the age of Shakespeare and our day. Not that the assimilation of Greek

15

ways had run a perfectly smooth course, as witnessed by the uprising of the Maccabees after 165 years of occupation. Yet such resistance was mostly in vain. Even the Maccabees became Hellenized. So in a measure did the exclusive Sadducees and Pharisees. Their cunning ways of arguing with Jesus unmistakably betrayed the infiltration of even their schools with Hellenistic methods of dialectics.

The process of assimilation of the Hebrew-Christian tradition to Greek views throughout Christianity began to spread through a Hellenized world. The usual method of integration on the part of theologians was to incorporate religious notions into systems of scientific and philosophical doctrines, then, by means of allegorical interpretation, to point out in the resulting formulation aspects of the same divine revelation. Thus Philo of Alexandria (30 B.C.–A.D. 50), a Jewish theologian of Neoplatonist inspiration, read Greek thought back into Mosaic teachings. Since Plato must have learned from Moses, he thought it was only natural to make use of Greek philosophy for a spiritual interpretation of Scripture. The resulting trend reached its climax with the gratuitous elaborations of the Gnostics, whose theological metaphysics made a mockery of Holy Writ as well as of the recent apostolic tradition.

To all this there was a strong reaction on the part of evangelical Christianity, a reaction essentially expressed in an exclusiveness which would henceforth provide a safeguard for the cause of the gospel through many a crisis. What was seen to be at stake at this point on the side of the early church was the unique character of the salvation offered in Jesus Christ, with the corollary that the Christian message was exclusive of any other. In the words of J. Gresham Machen, "What struck the early observers of Christianity most forcibly was not merely that salvation was offered by means of the Christian gospel, but that all other means were resolutely rejected. The early Christian missionaries demanded an absolutely exclusive devotion to Christ. Such exclusiveness ran directly counter to the prevailing syncretism of the Hellenistic age." [2] This is correct. The way in which Paul, then a prisoner in Rome (ca.

[2] Christianity and Liberalism (New York: The Macmillan Co., 1923), p. 123.

60-62), was inspired to write his letter to the Colossians is a good case in point. One of his visitors who came for counsel and help was Epaphras, minister of the church at Colossae in the Roman province of Asia. Trying as they were to bridge the gap between Christianity and forms of gnosticism of Platonic inspiration, his people had come to the point where they identified Jesus with one of the intermediaries between the divine Being and this material world. Such views led them on to seek a higher spiritual realm by means of ascetic practices while discarding the Christian way deemed by them to be an inferior way. In his letter, therefore, Paul was inspired to insist on the all-sufficiency of Jesus Christ as the Mediator, to the exclusion of all other mediators and apart from ascetic practices henceforth exposed as perfectly worthless. It was in such a situation that he wrote the famous passage so often isolated from its context and made into a pretext: "Beware lest any man spoil you through philosophy and vain deceit, after the tradition of men, after the rudiments of the world, and not after Christ" (Col. 2:8).

Henceforth opposition to brazen departure from the faith became keener on the part of Christians. The classical illustration of the protest uttered by an aroused evangelical conscience is the case of Tertullian (*ca.* 165-220), who became known as the prosecutor of paganism. What indeed had Athens to do with Jerusalem? No more disputation was wanted after possessing Jesus.[3] *Credo quia absurdum* (I believe because it is absurd); *Certum est, quia impossibile est* (It is certain, because it is impossible)—these and similar slogans became badges of a genuine evangelicalism. Even such masters as Lactantius (*ca.* 260-330) and Jerome (*ca.* 347-420) were thus induced to forego their first love for letters. Lactantius banished Homer as one writing of human rather than divine things, and as such unable to give information relating to the truth.[4] Jerome managed to rule out the three outstanding representatives of Latin literature at one blow: "How can Horace go with the psalter, Vergil with the gospels, Cicero with the apostle?" he asked in one of his

[3] *On the Prescription Against Heretics* 7.
[4] *Divine Institutes* I. 5.

17

letters.[5] Science shared the fate of philosophy and classical literature. For example, astronomy and cosmology were dismissed by
Ambrose of Milan (340-397) as presumptuous manifestations of
heathenism.[6] Similar dismissals were echoed throughout the ages by
such eminent churchmen as Bernard of Clairvaux (1091-1153) and
many of the Reformers, of whom Luther was the most outspoken
with his indictment of natural reason as "the bride of the devil."

We are likely to come still closer to a right apprehension of this
same situation if we see the background against which the preceding statements were made. Hellenistic philosophy increasingly shared
in the degeneracy of the age. More and more divorced from practice,
it became a rhetorical type of disputation where one would argue for
victory rather than for the sake of truth. In the overcrowded colleges of the Hellenistic world, students loved such intellectual gym-
nastics as do our debating teams today. Augustine well characterized
this later period of Hellenistic philosophy in his recollection of
schools of rhetoricians "alive with the din of crowds of students." [7]
The teachers themselves were perfectly satisfied to live the life of
itinerant preachers in long robes, honored in society, petted by great
ladies, and assigned to privileged quarters (*filosophi locus*). Yet it
was obvious to everyone, according to Lucian, that the man who
preached in the morning behaved later in the day "in exactly the
opposite way to his sermons." He went on preaching all the time
about temperance and moderation, for instance, until he was "so
dead-drunk that the servants had to carry him out." [8]

Here, then, is found the fundamental contrast between the dominant culture and early forms of Christianity. While a degenerate
Hellenism preached in an imperative mood a philosophy which
proved as vain as it was obviously deceitful, Christianity began by
telling in a glowing indicative mood a story that actually worked,

[5] *Letter* 22. 29.

[6] *On Belief in the Resurrection* II. 86.

[7] *De utilitate credendi* 7.

[8] Edwin Hatch, *The Influence of Greek Ideas and Usages upon the Christian
Church* (London, Edinburgh: Williams and Norgate, 1891), p. 42.

however foolish it might seem to the ancient world. Truly "the foolishness of God is wiser than men" (I Cor. 1:25).

The divorce between Christianity and *such* a culture became more marked when Greek philosophic and political thought was blended with the native Latin tradition to form the Roman classical tradition, *Romanitas,* forever associated with emperor worship and the apotheosis of power. As such it was at opposite poles from what Augustine was to call the *City of God.* I take the liberty of referring the reader to the superb treatment of this subject by Professor Charles Norris Cochrane of University College, Toronto.[9] Following the Greco-Roman tradition from Augustus through Theodosius, the author describes the various fortunes of a culture whose spirit was at bottom incompatible with the spirit of Christianity. He brings out the inconsistencies of the classical Augustan formulation, as well as the futile attempts made by Constantine to rejuvenate it by means of an impossible syncretism. After the Julian reaction we witness the last desperate efforts of Theodosius to salvage whatever was left of *Romanitas* by trying to constitute its shadow the guardian of the Christian faith. What is actually seen to take place, however, is the crumbling of a pagan civilization which bore its stumbling block within itself from the very beginning. On the ruins of this monument of ancient classical inspiration arises the imposing edifice of a Christian civilization under God. In Augustine we finally perceive "the full meaning of the Evangel as it presented itself to the mind of the fourth century and, therewith, the measure of the revolution in attitude and outlook which resulted from the impact of Christianity upon the Graeco-Roman world." [10]

It is fair to say, therefore, that what is actually witnessed in and through a vast period of Christian civilization is not so much the conflict of Christianity and culture *as such,* as the exclusiveness of a Christianity on the defensive whenever it is confronted by such an antagonistic culture that the triumph of the latter would imply the

[9] *Christianity and Classical Culture, A Study of Thought and Action from Augustus to Augustine* (London, New York, Toronto: Oxford University Press, 1944).
[10] *Ibid.,* p. 399.

destruction of Christianity. Further proof may be seen in the fact that the normal contrast as viewed by Professor Cochrane is that of the self-assertive *civitas terrena* versus the *civitas Dei* characterized by its "adhesion" to God, the source of all truth.[11] It is the normal contrast because it is the collective expression of the contrast between the natural man and the child of God. It is noteworthy that in this normal climate Cochrane develops the most serene view of "*Nostra philosophia*" [12]—the Augustinian view of a Christian culture under God. The Augustinian motto of such a culture, far from repudiating reason, suggests that the Christian is the only genuine rationalist: *Nisi credideritis, non intelligetis*[13] (If you will not believe, you shall not understand).

Contrary to legend, then, Augustine is far from the idea of a universe corrupted in its nature. With him we behold "man himself, *opus ejus tam magnum et admirabile,* whose intelligence, dormant in the infant, progressively awakens and develops until it produces all these arts lit up with the prodigal splendours of intelligence and invention." [14] Even Bernard of Clairvaux, who was named before among the despisers of culture, praised man as *celsa creatura in capacitate majestatis.*[15] As for the Jansenist Pascal, he repeatedly stated in his *Pensées* that thought constitutes the greatness of man, that all of man's dignity consists in thought.[16]

For the present it is not necessary to say more about this. It has become sufficiently clear that whatever tension may exist between the ideas of Christianity and culture per se, we are far from the notion of mutually impervious characters. Neither need we leave the argument at this point.

[11] *Ibid.,* pp. 489-501.

[12] *Ibid.,* pp. 399-455.

[13] In fact a translation of the Septuagint version of Isa. 7:9*b*. See Alan Richardson, *Christian Apologetics* (New York: Harper & Bros., 1947), p. 233.

[14] Etienne Gilson, *The Spirit of Mediaeval Philosophy* (New York: Charles Scribner's Sons, 1936), p. 123. The entire sixth chapter on "Christian Optimism" deserves careful attention with reference to the Christian approach to culture.

[15] *In Cant. Canticorum,* sermo 80, art. 5 (quoted by Gilson, *op. cit.,* p. 117).

[16] Cf. Sec. 6 in Brunschvicg ed., esp. fr. 347.

A Bygone Age of Christian Leadership

In a day when obscurantism and defeatism are seen once more to raise their ugly heads in the holy place, those concerned with the resulting plight of our Christian civilization may well pause to consider what actually happens to culture when Christianity takes the lead.

Let us therefore heed the testimony of such a Roman Catholic scholar as Christopher Dawson, whose Gifford Lectures for 1948-49 were devoted to *Religion and the Rise of Western Culture.*[17] The author's previous series of Gifford Lectures (for 1947) presented essentially a closely reasoned study of the nature of religion and culture in their various relationships through the distant civilizations of China, India, and Egypt; of Mexico and Africa; as well as through the ancient civilizations of Greece and Rome. His main thesis was that the culture of a man or society remains a closed book to those who fail to approach it with a deep understanding of its religious undergirding—a position similar to that taken by T. S. Eliot in *The Idea of a Christian Society*[18] and in his *Notes Towards the Definition of Culture.*[19]

In this new series of lectures the field of investigation shifts from the cultures of a non-European world and those of a remote past to our own Christian culture. The significance of the Western development once brought out, the author finds its religious origins in a new spiritual community, the one which arose from the ruins of the Roman Empire owing to the conversion of the Northern barbarians to the Christian faith. During the seven hundred years which elapsed between the decline of classical civilization and the rise of European universities in the twelfth century, the tradition of Latin culture and the patterns of a new Christian outlook on life were preserved and fostered in the monasteries. "The monks were the apostles of the West and the founders of medieval culture." [20] A

[17] New York: Sheed & Ward, 1950.
[18] New York: Harcourt, Brace & Co., 1940.
[19] New York: Harcourt, Brace & Co., 1949.
[20] Dawson, *op. cit.*, p. 43.

whole chapter (ch. iii) is next devoted to a history of a Western monasticism which proved to be inseparable from the temporal institutions on which it depended for its existence. Thus we are led to a consideration of the wider context of religion and culture in Western Europe, more particularly to the development of monarchical institutions and the idea of kingship during the Dark Ages, from 400 to 1000. In spite of the adverse conditions of the ninth century, we now witness the survival of a Christian view of life whose unifying ideal spreads over to the North in the eleventh and twelfth centuries. Organically related to the conversion of Scandinavia, a second Christendom appears along the Viking trade routes to the East. The sixth chapter, devoted to the Byzantine tradition and the conversion of Eastern Europe, is particularly rich in new insights into the origins of an anti-Latin and anti-Western tendency in Russian national tradition. Politicians could read such pages with profit, had culture still anything to do with politics.

Reverting to Western Europe proper, the author proceeds with a striking parallel between the breakdown of the Carolingian Empire and the feudal secularization of the church. Once again, however, the infinite capacity of Christianity to create new organs for spiritual regeneration asserts itself. Born of a purely monastic and ascetic movement, the reform will ultimately affect every aspect of Western civilization. A series of chapters (chs. viii-x) presents a masterful succession of frescoes depicting a culture born of the church: the feudal world and its courtly culture, with special reference to chivalry; the medieval city coming to its own in a new spirit of Christian fellowship strikingly illustrated in *communes* and guilds; last but not least, the medieval tradition of a Christian culture coming to its own in school and university. These luminous frescoes make a Christian's heart leap for admiration and gratitude. This, the reader concludes, is what Christianity can do once it is allowed to become the inspiration of culture and society. And it seems most natural to see the author ultimately assign the crisis of medieval culture to the slackening of that same spiritual, creative inspiration which allowed a Christian age to attain unity and genuine leadership.

In this volume of Catholic inspiration the Catholic point of view is reduced to a minimum. Some of the reasons for this are obvious. The treatment deals with the period when the church was one and does not go beyond the fourteenth century. Besides, a high sense of intellectual honesty at the service of a sober, yet exacting, scholarship never allows a sense of partisanship to mar the development. But more, even mistakes are also brought out. There are errors, there is wrong timing, and there is sin. For example, there is the illuminating Chapter XI, which deals with the religious crisis of medieval culture in the thirteenth century, a section which contains admissions such as this: "The prophetic and evangelical vocation of the early Friars became subordinated to the demands of ecclesiastical power politics, and this produced a rift in the reforming movement from which medieval Christendom never recovered."[21] Again, while the chapter on "The Medieval City: School and University" hailed the *Divina Commedia* as the greatest literary achievement of the Middle Ages,[22] acknowledgment is made thirty pages further that it constitutes at the same time a most drastic indictment of the medieval church. At this juncture the author is frank to the point of bluntness. To him, "the great apocalyptic pageant of the concluding cantos of the *Purgatorio* expresses the revolutionary criticism of the spiritual Franciscans and Joachimites rather than the orthodox conception of the Papal theocracy" which was the ideal of Thomas Aquinas himself. No "solicitation of text" is to be feared on the part of this Oxford-trained scholar with whom it would be a pleasure to shake hands. As for modesty, "I do not propose to deal with [the rise of the modern scientific movement] in my present lectures; only a man like Pierre Duhem, who was at once a scientist, an historian and a philosopher, is capable of undertaking such a task."[23] If there is a Roman Catholic bias in the book, it is more likely to be found in omissions such as are involved in a rather one-sided view of Aristotle. But then, the reservation just made as to the intentional

[21] *Ibid.*, p. 262.
[22] *Ibid.*, p. 233.
[23] *Ibid.*, p. 16.

omission of the scientific aspects of the subject silences at this point the critic of good faith. Not only are such omissions admitted, but also they are pointed out and explained for perfectly good reasons.

The Catholic point of view, then, must be seen in the fact that here is a Christian lecturer and writer who thinks that he can use his time to better purpose than in spending the best of it vilifying a human intellect originally created in the image of God. What may a Christian thinker gain by burning bridges between the church and the lay world which is her own mission field?

The Wages of Isolationism

The second section of the present chapter has indeed led us to acknowledge that an open breach between Christianity and culture often expresses the inevitable stand of the Christian Church in the face of the onrush of destructive and demonic forces. It may even turn out to be Christianity's solution in our Western world during these ever more troubled times.

What must further be made clear, however, are the implications of such a solution. It means that evangelical Christianity cannot properly assume any constructive interest in cultural problems of the commonwealth upon which it depends for physical maintenance. It cannot provide a frame of reference for culture, and because it has no guidance to offer, it is led to insist more and more upon a dichotomy between the Christian faith and any cultural expression or manifestation either in word or in deed, whether it be in the sphere of education, social philosophy, or government. The massive effect of such corollaries is to stifle any sense of responsibility in citizenship, to paralyze any active participation in the constructive tasks of society. It amounts to a defiance of the most obvious, common-sense duties. Such effects, moreover, are already being felt, even in the realm of theology.

It is a significant fact, for example, that the books on theological subjects that really succeed in establishing contact with the reading public nowadays are those of literary men. The well-known work of popularization achieved by C. S. Lewis constitutes a fine example of this. More recently it took a Harvard man of letters, Perry Miller, to produce at long last the book which would do justice to the much caricatured Jonathan Edwards. Curiously enough the jacket of that book, calling attention to the intellectual strength and literary grace, thanks to which Edwards "has few if any peers among American writers," added this devastating remark: "If this was better understood once than it is now, the reason lies in the poor estate of theology at the present moment." It also appears from Professor Miller's masterly treatment that the revivalist who preached the famous sermon "Sinners in the Hands of an Angry God" refused to "compartmentalize his thinking." He was thoroughly familiar with the most varied aspects of the science of his time.

He is the last great American, perhaps the last European, for whom there could be no warfare between religion and science, or between ethics and nature. He was incapable of accepting Christianity and physics on separate premises. His mind was so constituted . . . that he went directly to the issues of his age, defined them, and asserted the historic Protestant doctrine in full cognizance of the latest disclosures in both psychology and natural science.[24]

We may well long for such Christian leadership in our day.

Our intellectual world is greatly confused, easily given to arrogance, and divided between the enticement of agnosticism and the fascination of substitute forms of religion. Communism constitutes the most virulent of these. So also our sense of responsibility seems too sensitive to changes of weather in public opinion. For such weaknesses, however, theologians and churchmen have themselves to blame first of all. Let them resume proper contacts with the world of culture in general, and with the scientific world in particular, and they will soon come to the realization that a sense of responsibility was largely wanting on their part, with the result that evangelical Christianity and culture became more and more estranged. One day Voltaire turned a street corner to be confronted with a procession led by a choir boy bearing the cross. Voltaire took off his hat, and as a passer-by wondered at it, the bareheaded wit explained: "You

[24] *Jonathan Edwards* (New York, Toronto: William Sloane Associates, 1949), p. 72.

see, it is like this—we greet each other, but we are not on speaking terms." The grotesque shadow of that scene still lingers on our horizon, at least as a suggestive symbol.

The exclusiveness we feel constrained to reprove no doubt saved the cause of the gospel from the evils of compromise through many a crisis. Seen in its true light, however, such isolationism was, and should have remained, part and parcel of a regime of exception. It is only too obvious that no one can give leadership who remains uncertain as to the essential implications of his Christian faith for his whole outlook on life.

At a time when our drifting civilization on the one hand is being challenged by futility, and on the other hand is strained to the uttermost by the rise of ideologies or even sheer intoxication of power, it is most imperative for us to reassess our cultural heritage and destiny in terms of the Christian frame of reference.

CHAPTER TWO

The VANTAGE POINT

To SEE what the One Church sees is the beginning of wisdom and the sure way to sanity. This thesis is likely to meet with severe opposition. The visible Church is divided, so hopelessly divided, in fact, that a publisher recently deemed it advisable to issue a guidebook to the various denominations in America.[1] Although it must be admitted that nowhere have Christian divisions multiplied more profusely than in this country, to deal with Christian denominations all over the world would have proved a much more demanding task. A divided church implies a divided testimony, that is, a multiplicity of angles of vision from which the much-vaunted Christian pattern of truth is being viewed. How then, one may ask, can the frame of reference postulated by the present method of approach be found? To be more specific still, the task at hand presupposes a vantage point. Is such a vantage point anywhere to be discovered, one that may be claimed to be *the* point? If so, where is it?

The relevance of this whole treatment is admittedly at stake in the face of such weighty objections and resulting questions.

The Challenge of Denominationalism

Let our starting point be the concise statement of the general epistle of Jude according to which we should "earnestly contend for the faith which was once delivered unto the saints" (Jude 3). Since

[1] Frank S. Mead, *Handbook of Denominations in the United States* (New York and Nashville: Abingdon-Cokesbury Press, 1951).

faith was once delivered, it may be argued, the statement of its contents is a closed book, and according to one of the last warnings of the Bible, "if any man shall add unto these things, God shall add unto him the plagues that are written in this book" (Rev. 22:18). It would help the reader little to point out that the immediate reference is to the book of Revelation. The perennial suggestion of the above line of argument is that the whole creed of the church is identical today with what it was in past ages.

That this is a wishful oversimplification of the problem becomes evident when we remember that there are in the United States of America some 255 Christian denominations and sects, practically all of them arising from an earnest interpretation of the faith "once delivered" to the saints. Such interpretations are obviously dependent upon the mental and social molds of the day of their formulation. As a result they may prove difficult or even impossible to understand for people unaware of, or unfamiliar with, the cultural climate in which they took shape. The Protestant method, moreover, invites the faithful to follow the Spirit speaking in and through Scripture.

For a more objective consideration of the difficulty involved here, the best approach would probably be a thoughtful study of the Library of Congress classification of subjects under "Religion," that is, with special attention to Class B, Part II, BL-BX. After a general consideration of religions, mythology, and free thought, the index proceeds under the headings "Judaism," "Mohammedanism," "Bahaism," "Theosophy," and so forth—and later, "Christianity." The following topics are encountered: Bible, Doctrinal Theology, Practical Theology—but then the BX section is made to cover the tremendous scope of "special denominations, sects, etc." There is the Apostolic church and there are the Oriental churches. From the Eastern church, the Greek church, Russia, other countries, we proceed through the Roman Catholic church to Protestantism in general, early Protestant sects, Anglican churches (Church of England, Church of Scotland, Church of Ireland, and so forth, Mexican and Reformed Episcopal churches). There follows the whole gamut of Protestant denominations: Adventists, Arminians, Baptists, Christa-

28

delphians, and so forth, in alphabetical order down to the Volunteers of America and the Wallon church. Surely there are in all the groups involved thoughtful men and earnest believers trying to do justly and to walk humbly with their God. We need not use as an argument that the most profuse multiplicity of Christian divisions is to be found in the smaller sects, that 95 per cent of the Protestants in this country may be brought together in less than ten groupings. The relevance of the small flock has never been a matter of size or statistics for Christian disciples.

We must face the fact of a divided church. A divided church suggests a confused outlook. A growing emphasis upon a private interpretation implies that the Christian landscape of reality remains open to constant contention.

The Fact of the Israel of God

Transcending the fact of denominationalism, however, there stands the far more impressive fact of a growing world-wide Christian community. The fifty-fifth Canon of the Church of England has defined this community as "Christ's Holy Catholic Church, that is, the whole congregation of Christian people dispersed throughout the whole world." Even the exclusive Roman church interprets the dogma "Outside the Church, no salvation" to mean that non-Catholics may actually be saved outside the visible body of the Church. What happens then is that they are joined invisibly to the Church by charity as well as by that implicit desire of belonging to the Mystical Body of Christ, which is inseparable from the explicit desire to do God's will.[2]

Let us further recall the all-important fact of continuity already brought out in our previous characterization of the Bible. It was insisted that the divine Library came into existence within the life of

[2] On this see Pius IX, *Allocution* of December 9, 1854, and clarification of the whole question in the revised edition of the Baltimore catechism: *A Catechism of Christian Doctrine, A Test for Secondary Schools and Colleges No. 3* (Copyright 1941 and 1949 by Confraternity of Christian Doctrine), art. 166, 167, 168 (pp. 128-31). It is noteworthy that this recent clarification was made in answer to the criticism of overzealous Roman Catholic teachers.

the historic "Israel of God." The reason for saying that the Bible testifies to the continuing embodiment of the people of God is that we received it from the people of God, whose sense of continuity it expresses and preserves. Or rather, the two realities, that is, the Israel of God and its ancestral record, are inseparable. This is amply confirmed by the liturgy of the Church. Christians worship with the singing of Hebrew psalms. Their prayers use the language and the categories of the whole Bible to exalt the Living God of the Covenant and his mighty salvation. They speak with infinite gratitude of the wonderful deliverance of "our fathers," the children of Israel, who were made to come out of their Egyptian servitude. Finally, to the confirmation of liturgy and prayer should be added the weighty consideration that the same word *ekklesia*, used in the earliest Greek version of the Hebrew Bible to translate the Hebrew *qahal*, referring to the children of Israel as a religious body, is used in the New Testament for the Body of Christ, which is the Church.

This last consideration is so vital in this matter of continuity that we should pause to consider it more closely at this point, where the New Testament takes over the witness of the Old so as to correct and fulfill its one-sidedness and its incompleteness in an awe-inspiring transfiguration.

When the student of classical Greek comes across the word *ekklesia* at the close of such a text as the account of the uproar of the silversmiths at Ephesus (Acts 19:23-41),[3] he need feel no surprise, for the reference there is simply to an assembly of people. Let us further notice that even in classical Greek this implies a weakened meaning. The etymological connotation of those "called forth" referred to a gathering of citizens called out to some public place for a civic purpose. What should strike the student of classical Greek, however, is the consistent use of the word with the definite article, namely *the ekklesia* (of God). Now the only analogy for this usage outside the New Testament is in that earliest Greek translation of the Hebrew bible known as the Septuagint. It is noteworthy that in

[3] The specific reference is to vs. 41, "And when he had thus spoken, he dismissed the assembly."

30

the Pentateuch, that is, in the first five books of the Hebrew scripture, there were two words to suggest a gathering, that is, *edhah* and *qahal*. Both were translated in the Septuagint by the Greek word *synagoge*. In the later books, however, this last word was reserved for the translation of *edhah*, *ekklesia* being used to render *qahal*. The added meaning was designed to emphasize the special vocation of those "called out" to become the *qahal of Jehovah*, the Lord's people. When the Jews had rejected the Messiah, it was necessary to draw the dividing line between *synagoge* and *ekklesia*, while emphasizing the corporate sense of those "called out," "called forth" to be the new Israel of God. Hence the special use of *the ekklesia*, the meaning of the word being further magnified to express a deep unity in actual dispersion, one greatly superseding the mere notion of gathering. And so we hear of "the *called-out* of God which is at Corinth, . . . *called* to be saints, with all that *call* upon the name of the Lord." [4] The very fact of this continuity of creative experience in the light of a revelation followed by the historian as far back as thirty-three centuries—that is, dating the Exodus from Egypt in the thirteenth century B.C. at the very latest—should carry a tremendous weight of evidence were this an attempt to "demonstrate" the reality here involved. That there is no such intention has become obvious by this time.

A perennial criticism of Roman Catholic inspiration may henceforth be seen to have hopelessly missed the point. To wonder at what Bishop Bossuet used to call "the variations of the Protestant churches" amounts to wondering why an organism everywhere identical in its nature and essential functions should undergo secondary modifications according to degree of development and geographic environment considered as a whole.[5] That this is the *sine qua non* condition

[4] I have followed in this consideration of *ekklesia* the interpretation of Sir Edwyn Hoskyns and Francis N. Davey, *The Riddle of the New Testament* (3rd ed.; London: Faber & Faber, 1937), pp. 20-25.

[5] Invaluable help, as far as method is concerned, may be derived from Wilhelm Schmidt, *The Culture Historical Method of Ethnology*, tr. S. A. Sieber (New York: Fortuny's, 1939).

31

of existence for any living organism needs no further demonstration from the scientific world.

While the One Church is not of the world, it is very much in the world. As a consequence, essential manifestations of its life are hardly separable from those manifestations studied by the human sciences, beginning with ethnology. There are on the human side of church life collective patterns of thought and behavior whose variations must be taken for granted. These patterns are deeply rooted in historic, ethnic, linguistic, and economic realities.[6] Institutions are being maintained, traditions are being handed down, and languages are being spoken, each one of them expressing, and accordingly molding further, depths of human experience in a given part of the world. As one of the results, the apprehension of truth in this or that "climate" of life and thought varies in ways which invite a comparative method of study. It is most natural, therefore, that we should find ourselves confronted with Continental theologies, English theologies, American theologies, and even the New England theology. A comparative approach in this field as in the field of scientific linguistics, for instance, should prove most fruitful. There is no doubt that it would considerably enrich our knowledge and understanding of the perennial reality we call the Church. Neither is it claimed that new ground is being broken by saying this. Canon Alan Richardson rightly reminded us in a recent book that "theology, in this modern scientific sense, has been operating as a science for rather more than a hundred years."[7]

What has been said is that such variations as may be observed throughout ages and societies in Church life and thought do not alter the fact of the identity of the Church in continuity. Or rather, as Josiah Royce might say in this case also, there are both "internal meaning" and "external meaning" in the reality we call the One

[6] On this see, for instance, Bronislaw Malinowski, "Culture," *Encyclopedia of the Social Sciences*, IV, 621-45, and *The Dynamics of Culture Change* (New Haven: Yale University Press, 1945).

[7] *The Gospel and Modern Thought* (London, New York, Toronto: Oxford University Press, 1950), p. 39.

Church. What matters is the stubborn and irreducible fact of that reality.

What must further be said is that the Israel of God, the Body of Christ, the Church—call it what we may—is not only a reality, but because it is the reality it is, it actually constitutes the core of our own reality in this world. Paul brings this whole matter to a head in his letter to the Ephesians, in which the oneness of the people of God in Christ is the keynote: "There is one body, and one spirit . . . one Lord, one faith, one baptism, one God and Father of all" (Eph. 4:4-6). Neither has anything been said with reference to denominationalism or its aftermath that makes a dent in the core of that reality.

Our Vantage Point

At this apex we would take our stand. This unshakeable position may in more than one way be reverently likened to that of the contemporary physicist securing the ideal C.S. (Coordinate System). Just as the laws of the field are invariant with respect to the Lorentz transformation, just as there exists only one ideal C.S. from which the laws of mechanics are universally valid, there is but one apex from which to view aright the landscape of reality. This apex is the ideal see of the One Church we call the Israel of God, the Body of Christ.

CHAPTER THREE

The OBSERVER'S REFERENCE

THE OBSERVER now called upon to occupy the ideal vantage point determined in the preceding chapter is one who takes his stand within the One Church we call the Israel of God, the Body of Christ. He is emphatically a committed man who knows in whom he has believed. His broad-mindedness in the consideration of cultural activities will never degenerate into laxity, and neither will his tolerance ever imply that his Christianity has lost its cutting edge. He is first and foremost a man of faith willing to show his colors at all times.

Basis for the Formulation

Of the observer's frame of reference it has just been said in effect that it proceeds immediately from the knowledge of faith. Yet this is more easily said than worked out in actual practice. What exactly is to be our basis for the formulation involved?

The most natural answer to this question would seem to be that Scripture itself is to be the measure. This sounds simple. In fact it proves to be too simple. No mechanical biblicism based on a dictation theory of verbal inspiration could ever claim relevance for such a task as is involved in the Christian approach to culture. While this biblicism was originally devised by culture as a way of understanding the Bible, a better informed reading of the Bible actually disqualified it as such, even in the consideration of its most earnest exponents. Both a better informed culture and a better informed Christian con-

34

science are at one in this. No Christian worth his salt would come out today with the assertion, for instance, that in I Sam. 15 a genuine test of loyalty to God is to be derived from the command, "Go and smite Amalek . . . and spare them not; but slay both man and woman, infant and suckling, ox and sheep, camel and ass." That would be a strange way of promoting the Christian approach to culture, nay, of getting a hearing in the world of culture! But without having recourse to such extreme arguments, have we, for example, to subscribe to outmoded world views or a literal interpretation of narratives in order to be loyal to New Testament Christianity? Or shall we, perhaps, use a materializing concordance method and clarify a passage in the Bible by placing it side by side with all passages seemingly referring to the same subject, without thought of chronology or cultural context? There is in fact, among hundreds of others, a book which has had a wide circulation that does exactly that. I refer to Torrey's *What the Bible Teaches*. The method adopted by this great evangelist was to bring together the material contained in Scripture, to scrutinize it carefully, and then to state in the most exact terms what was contained in it. The preface carried the admission that some of the resulting propositions "may appear new and even startling to many," but it made it clear that these propositions "fairly and exactly" stated the contents of the passages upon which they were based.[1] This was followed to the letter.

Since such literalism is out of the question for the elaboration of a frame of reference for the Christian approach to culture, the next suggestion in order may be, Why not proceed upon a *selection* of really "essential" passages? The answer is that this would lead to an unbearable arbitrariness, if not to absurdity. But more, the solution would imply an external and essentially legalistic notion of formal authority foreign to both Scripture and true scholarship.

A static eclecticism would fare no better. It would mean a slavish regard for forms and formulas to the detriment of essentially dynamic themes.

[1] R. A. Torrey, *What the Bible Teaches* (New York: Fleming H. Revell Co., 1898), p. 2.

35

Should we then try to elaborate a pattern of reference based on some form of ecclesiastical authority as is the case in the Roman Catholic Church? There would at least be in this plan the advantage of escaping the unlimited aberrations always to be feared on the part of an excessive individualism. Yet the democratic spirit inherent in the Reformed tradition is too strong to allow any hope in that direction.

Very well, some will say, let us count the votes. But this would only mean that we proceed from one form of external legalism to another. And it would be to a worse form, inasmuch as the voice of God is never to be identified with the voice of the people—unless such a voice be that of the Israel of God guardedly speaking from within the continuity of its experience. In such a context it was that the canon of Scripture slowly took shape, as was already pointed out in these pages. But of this hallowed, time-tested process, our current democratic methods may be said to constitute the counterpart.

The only mediation between the two preceding possibilities is the solution strongly suggested in the concluding words of the preceding chapter. The basis for the formulation of our observer's reference can only be found in the witness of the Israel of God. Admittedly the successive formulations involved in creeds and confessions are not meant to add new affirmations to the essential Christian faith, but rather they are meant to secure new insights into the whole content of that faith. The real task, as Karl Barth himself has fully realized, is for the One Church to test the truth and relevance of her peculiar language about God. In other words, the Church must periodically proceed to a critique of the agreement of her proclamation as "achieved and to be achieved by men with the revelation attested in Scripture." [2]

Hence the test of the knowledge of faith leads to a reassessment of the proclamation and teaching of the One Church, as seen from the ideal vantage point defined in the second chapter of this book.

[2] Karl Barth, The Doctrine of the Word of God, tr. G. T. Thomson (Edinburgh: T. & T. Clark, 1936), p. 284.

36

THE OBSERVER'S REFERENCE

The Climate of Faith

Any positive approach to this subject must further take into consideration the fact that all genuine revivals of Christianity and Christian thought have implied an immediate reference to the Christianity of the New Testament.[3] Bent on the center as we are in the present section, we see special significance in this perennial return to the Christianity of the New Testament.

The reference to the original Christology is essentially one to "the Father of our Lord Jesus Christ." Everything there is of God. But what kind of God? The *plain answer* is: the kind of God who was in Christ. Words fail man at this point, for the truth involved is so tremendous that our commonplace terms can be combined only into the most inadequate materializing concepts.

The reality they are striving to suggest is that in the Man Christ Jesus the very nature of God is made visible. In listening to him "we are brought face to face with *God,* and what we experience as the critical and momentous new thing is the direct and inexorable quality of the issue put before us—for or against God's will to reign!" [4] There is a luminous transparence disclosed at this point of history and of our own life history. In Jesus Christ and through him, *God.* How we understand the surrender of even the doubting Thomas, as he uttered the moving "My Lord and my God!" (John 20:28.)

There *is* light beyond the "vast black veil," uncertain no longer.[5] It is to this light that the direct reference leads us, at the very point where the great Doer of redeeming things breaks in upon our lives. As our groping and renewal comes to a glorious fulfillment in the splendor of that radiance, lo and behold, the Light of the world, the

[3] See for example the case as stated in *Kierkegaard's Attack upon "Christendom" 1854-1855,* tr. Walter Lowrie (Princeton University Press, 1944), esp. pp. 29-40, 59-60, 117-24, 142-43, 150-53, 168-69, 174-77, 193-98, 282-88.

[4] William Manson, *Jesus the Messiah* (Philadelphia: Westminster Press, 1946), pp. 209-10.

[5] Cf. James Thomson, *The City of Dreadful Night* (London: Reeves and Turner, 1880), st. xxi:

"None can pierce the vast black veil uncertain
Because there is no light beyond the curtain."

Christ! Turgenev might have been right when he visualized the face of Christ as a face like all men's faces. In Hazlitt's essay *Of Persons One Would Like to Have Seen,* Charles Lamb is imagined to make the comment that there is only *one* other Person. If Shakespeare were to come into the room, they would all rise to meet him. But if *that* Person were ever to enter, they should all fall down and try to kiss the hem of his garment.

It seems that the best introduction to the faith of the New Testament should be an attempt, however vain, to restore such a climate of warmth and light, of ardor and fervor. And by the way, both of these two words come from Latin terms suggesting a fire burning.

Yet the amazing thing is that in such a climate, at this focus where the Israel of God comes to its own in a fulfillment undreamed of, there is found a unanimity of testimony beyond our understanding. The modern mind is baffled in the face of it. It splits hairs over it. All this because the modern heart is cold. It has lost its first love. It is fatuous in its argumentative ways and instinctively recedes in the dark for comfort.

This much is sure. The faith of the One Church is there, in the glowing intensity of this unanimity. A little knowledge of the New Testament may incline a man to view it as a literary hotchpotch made up of all types of literary forms and specimens revealing a variety of themes. Yet a deeper study is bound to bring out not only the unity of the message, but the unanimity of first love, of which the message is already a materialization. Modern scholars, like sheep, have gone astray in this. They have missed the mark inasmuch as they have missed this unanimity. For this unanimity is there. To fail to see it and single it out for consideration is to fail to see *what is there.* The reason I seem to labor this point is that the point is in dire need of being so labored. There is a great difference between merely knowing things and seeing them the way they are.

The Outlook of Faith

Having restored the proper climate of biblical Christianity, let us now approach the testimony of Scripture with candor, that is to say, without even the preconceptions our present concern for culture may force upon us consciously or unconsciously.

Let us rather call to mind the witness of a great scholar and man of letters as he was confronted with this actual testimony of Scripture. Matthew Arnold, in the preface of his classic *Literature and Dogma,* freely admitted to his great belief in culture, that is, in "knowing the best that has been known and said in the world." Yet, having set out in this frame of mind to vindicate the Bible with all the scholarship and literary skill he could muster, he had to acknowledge that the religion of the Bible was not primarily, or even essentially, concerned with culture.[6] Matthew Arnold was led to insist:

If there be anything with which metaphysics have nothing to do, and where a plain man, without skill to walk in the arduous paths of abstruse reasoning, may yet find himself at home, it is religion. For the subject of religion is *conduct;* and conduct is really, however men may overlay it with philosophical disquisitions, the simplest thing in the world. That is to say, it is the simplest thing in the world as far as *understanding* is concerned; as regards *doing,* it is the hardest thing in the world. Here is the difficulty,—to *do* what we very well know ought to be done; instead of facing this, men have searched out another with which they occupy themselves by preference.[7]

And the author goes on to explain that this other preoccupation is essentially speculation in the realm of metaphysics, dealing with questions of origin, and so on.

What then forced itself upon this objective advocate of culture as he was confronted with Scripture was essentially this: the Book, beginning with the Old Testament, is not concerned with speculation, but with an all-important reality called righteousness. "In the way of righteousness is life; and in the pathway thereof there is no

[6] The question reaches even deeper. May biblical Christianity be said to be concerned with culture *at all?* The first chapter has already brought to light a basic tension between Christianity and culture. Ever since, resulting conflicts have been sensed to underlie our various problems. As the objection comes once more to the surface, I consider only its bearing upon the subject at hand. The issue is a crucial one, however, and as such will come up for discussion in chapter 5, "The Christian Landscape of Reality," in the section on The Ministry of Jesus.

[7] *Literature and Dogma,* I, 1.

death" (Prov. 12:28). "Righteousness tendeth to life" (Prov. 11:19). This principle of righteousness was such an object of attention to the Hebrew people that to keep it always in mind they actually wore the essential texts, "went about with them, made talismans of them."[8] The central text on this subject Matthew Arnold found in Micah's oft quoted verse, "He hath shewed thee, O man, what is good; and what doth the Lord require of thee, but to do justly, and to love mercy, and to walk humbly with thy God?" (6:8.)

Leaving Matthew Arnold at this point, let us ask ourselves if Micah's great pronouncement refers to morals only. Decidedly not, for morals have chiefly to do with the observance of a social code. They do not necessarily imply the "cleaning of the cup." Righteousness has to do rather with a new God-given direction of life, with a life henceforth under the control of and in line with his sovereign Will. It is basically *the* life meant for the Israel of God.

As we pass from the Old Testament to the New, this elemental theme remains unbroken. Jewish scholars like Klausner and Montefiore bring out the continuity. To Klausner, for example, all of the separate sayings of Jesus can be paralleled in other Jewish sources. Montefiore sets out to see whether there is anything quite new in the teachings of Jesus which no Jewish prophet or rabbi had ever said. His findings bring an impressive confirmation to what was stated in a preceding paragraph as to the *nature* of the God who was in Jesus Christ. What Montefiore singles out as the new distinctive feature appearing with and in Jesus is the picture of the shepherd going out into the wilderness to seek a lost sheep—that is, the "new figure" of a *seeking* God.

Taken as a whole, the critical consideration of the Old Testament may be said to point to the fact that while it is the word of God, it is not the *final* word of God. Not only do the various aspects of its truths remain unfinished, fragmentary to the point of appearing at times one-sided and even erroneous, but the main fact glaringly stands out that while the meaning of righteousness is clear enough, human attempts at righteousness are ultimately found to be self-

[8] *Ibid.*, I, 3.

defeating. Only in the seeking God who was in Christ reconciling the world unto himself does the prophetic, priestly, and kingly call of Israel to righteousness come to fulfillment.

Righteousness, then, is seen to come out of the earth to emerge in and through the stuff of history in the Man Christ Jesus. Salvation is from the Jews. Henceforth godlessness will go hand in hand with anti-Semitism. Yet the prefiguration of this self-defeating godlessness *also* was originally wrought out by the Jews, inasmuch as Judaism carried its stumbling block within itself. The Jews simply could not live up to the righteousness sprung out of the earth in the Man Christ Jesus. The best their own self-righteousness could achieve was to nail that incarnate righteousness to the cross, thus acknowledging defeat in the shedding of blood. And the eternal miracle of the cross is that righteousness came down from heaven there and then to vindicate forever the righteousness coming out of the earth in the form of the Suffering Servant.

No wonder the focus is one of light and warmth! It is the focus where the prevenient Doer of redeeming things breaks forth upon his Creation in judgment and renewal.

The God of Faith Is a Person

When Paul the apostle draws a contrast with regard to the point at issue, it is always one between natural man as uninspired by the divine Spirit and the spiritual man transformed by the grace of Providence. What he calls "flesh" is a metaphor for the lower, unredeemed part of human nature, such as even the "fleshly mind" of pagan inspiration. Man, therefore, is made "whole" only when the Spirit takes possession of the "old man" to transform him.

The same teaching looms up in the Old Testament. The Hebrew word *nephesh* may be translated "breath-soul." Yahweh shaped man from the dust of the earth and blew into his nostrils the breath of life, and so man became a *nephesh,* that is, an animated being. It should be understood that the word ranges all the way from physical breath up to high connotations of inner life. Thus Ps. 19:7 reads, "The law of Jehovah is perfect, restoring the *nephesh.*" Such an inner life, how-

41

ever, remains to the Hebrew mind associated with a psychical activity having its seat in the heart, the kidneys, the bowels, and other bodily organs. *Ruach,* on the other hand, was first used to refer to the heavy breathing of a man under strong emotion. Later it was used of the blowing of the wind as the breath of God "inbreathing" man, inspiring him. There are some fine shades of mind obtained from the "inspired" use of these two words, *nephesh* and *ruach,* as for instance in the reading of Isa. 26:9, "With my *nephesh* have I desired thee in the night; yea, with my *ruach* within me will I seek thee earnestly." Yet, even in such limited cases, the same basic distinction is present between the unredeemed part of human nature and the divine Presence coming over the natural "old man" to control him.[9]

Let us then reaffirm the lofty Bible teaching which led men of old to characterize it as good news. The constant implication of this good news is that the prevenient God who pours his Spirit upon all flesh is a Person. Yet the ancient church had to struggle hard to convey this notion, the main reason for the struggle being that the Greek language had no single term to express all we mean by "personality." In a letter to me Professor Bruce Metzger was kind enough to confirm this, pointing out that our own concept of personality is of a comparatively recent origin. On the other hand, in Italy the term "person" came into use through the defining influence of Roman law, making a distinction, shortly before the time of Cicero, between *persona* and *res.* What were the various attempts to define by several circumlocutions the mystery of the Trinity are set forth with a certain amount of fullness in Jules Lebreton's great work on the history of the doctrine of the Trinity.[10]

[9] I owe the best of this clarification to Harry E. Fosdick, *A Guide to Understanding the Bible, the Development of Ideas Within the Old and New Testaments* (New York: Harper & Bros., 1938), ch. 2 "The Idea of Man," esp. pp. 92-93.

[10] *History of the Dogma of the Trinity from Its Origins to the Council of Nicaea,* tr. A. Thorold (London: Burns Oates & Washbourne, 1939), Vol. I. On the notion of personality with reference to our subject, cf. Hans Rheinfelder, *Das Wort "Persona" Geschichte seiner Bedeutung* (Halle: Max Niemeyer Verlag, 1928); S. Schlossman, *Persona und Prosopon im Recht und im Christlichen Dogma* (Kiel und Leipzig: Lipsius & Tischer, 1906); Wilamowitz-Moellendorf, *Platon, sein Leben und seine Werke* (Berlin: Weidmann, 1948), pp. 607-14. Also R. Hirzen, *Sitzenbericht d. Wiss.* (1914), pp. 28 ff.

The word *persona* originally applied in a juridical sense to a possible party to a contract, and also to a character in a play, as in the phrase *dramatis personae*. What actually happened was this. During the Christological controversies of the fourth century the term *homoousios* (of the same "genus") was finally adopted to express the relation of God the Father to God the Son in order to accentuate the doctrine that the Son was not a "creature." So also the term was further applied to the Holy Spirit to placate those[11] who asserted that he was "severed from the essence of the Father." [12] This happened at the Council of Alexandria (362), presided over by Athanasius, who had written four letters *Ad Serapionem,* to prove that the Spirit is *coessential, consubstantial* with the Son, as seen from the work of sanctification. Yet should we say *coessential* or *consubstantial?* The one Latin word *substantia* had thus far been used to translate both *ousia* (as found in *homoousios*) and *hypostasis,* which laid emphasis upon the concept of an essential nature or modality. But then, this very emphasis led to a differentiation between the two Greek words concerned. As a result, it became necessary for the Latin translation to mark the difference. The word *substantia* could no longer suffice for both. It was made to translate *ousia* only, in preference to the better equivalent *essentia,* for the Latin *essentia* is just what the Greek *ousia* means; yet it jarred upon a Latin ear. What remained to be done, then, was to find a fresh Latin translation for the Greek *hypostasis.* This was found in *persona.* Hence the doctrine of a personal unity eternally existing in three eternal modes or functions, "neither confounding the Persons, nor dividing the Substance."

In case the reader wearies of such hairsplitting, or "Trinitarian

[11] Especially Bishop Macedonius of Constantinople, who declared that the Holy Spirit is a creature subordinate to the Son.

[12] The phrase is quoted from Athanasius, *Ad Antioch* 3. The Nicene Creed (325) said simply, "We believe in the Holy Spirit." Yet, if the Holy Spirit is a creature in contradistinction to the Godhead of Father and Son, we have a Diad instead of a Trinity. The doctrine of the Trinity came to expression at the Council of Constantinople in 381.

arithmetic" as Thomas Jefferson called it,[13] I should beg permission to plead for his patience. The notion of the personality of God matters most to the knowledge of faith. The main question for us in these pages is to see to what extent this knowledge of faith was integrated into Christian philosophy. The answer of course is that to the Scholastics it did not belong in natural theology (that is, philosophy) but in revealed theology, and this by virtue of the Thomistic formal distinction between truth of reason and truth of faith. Yet a theology of Augustinian inspiration made ample room for considerations which Thomism would set apart as pertaining to philosophy.

I single out for consideration in these necessarily brief pages Bonaventure's admirable short treatise entitled *De reductione artium ad theologiam*,[14] truly a jewel of medieval thought. Once the limitations of scientific knowledge are taken for granted, the work under consideration is found to express a view essential to the Christian approach to culture. To Bonaventure the way God *is* in the universe may be likened for the sake of understanding to the way the soul (that is, that which in us says "I") is in the body. By *artes* (the arts) the Seraphic Doctor meant philosophy in the broad acceptation of the term. As far as his short treatise is concerned, philosophy applied to secular knowledge embraces all culture, in accordance with the broad conception of Hugh of St. Victor[15] who was Bonaventure's favorite author.[16] In the light of the preceding principles Bonaventure took an uncompromising stand on the alleged autonomy of

[13] "When we shall have done with the incomprehensible jargon of the Trinitarian arithmetic, that the three are one, and one is three; when we shall have knocked down the artificial scaffolding, reared to mask from view the simple structure of Jesus; when, in short, we shall have unlearned everything which has been taught since his day, and got back to the pure and simple doctrines he inculcated, we shall then be truly and worthily his disciples; and my opinion is that if nothing had ever been added to what flowed purely from his lips, the whole world would at this day have been Christian." Quoted by T. C. Hall, *The Religious Background of American Culture* (Boston: Little, Brown & Co., 1930), p. 172.

[14] *On Reducing the Arts to Theology*. This treatise can be best studied in the edition carefully and lovingly prepared by Sister Emma Th. Healy and published by Saint Bonaventure College (New York, 1940).

[15] The reference is here to Hugh of St. Victor's *Eruditio didascalica*, Migne, P. L., 176, 741-848. The structure of Bonaventure's *De reductione artium ad theologiam* gives evidence that the author used Hugh's *Eruditio didascalica*.

[16] *De reductione artium ad theologiam*, ed. Healy, p. 35.

44

philosophy. To him no philosophy had a legitimate standing in the curriculum of studies if it disregarded revelation.[17] As for the verb *reducere* (to reduce), one of Bonaventure's favorite words, it meant for him to bring, or rather take back, things to God the Creator, who alone could provide their true meaning.

Bonaventure's method then was to refer all knowledge to a knowledge of the personal God of Scripture. This is in the main the method advocated in the present work.

This Person Is Not a Self-contained Absolute

Surely the seeking God revealed in Scripture is not to be thought of as a self-contained Absolute identified with his attributes, neither lacking anything nor wanting anything. Such an interpretation of Moses' *I AM* as *ipsum esse, actus purus* immediately impresses the Bible reader as involving a misplaced emphasis on the verb. A plain rhetorician knows that even in our relations with persons, the subject as a rule matters as much as, if not far more than, the verb. And this the exegesis of Exod. 3:14 in the light of recent research has amply confirmed. The matter involved in Moses' dealings with the God on the Mount was not essentially one of ontological speculation, but one of the personal identification.

It is precisely with reference to this last aspect that the Scholastic notion of an absolute God seems hardly adequate. This ab-solute God cannot be conceived as one entering into relationship with men, that is, if we keep in mind all that such a relationship involves in the context of the Hebrew-Christian revelation. How could the merciful and gracious seeking Shepherd of the sheep be an absolute God in the ontological sense of the word? Slow to anger and plenteous in mercy, we are told. "He will not always chide: neither will he keep his anger for ever." Surely the God of Israel who yearns after his children's souls would seem to be strangely confined even in the Thomist pure act of existing. So also does our idea of commitment to the living God of Abraham, Isaac, and Jacob differ profoundly from the concept of *theoria*, the pure contemplation of a contemplative

[17] *Ibid.*, p. 157.

self-contained Deity. The attitudes suggested by such a concept are necessarily aesthetic. They do not induce those who hold them to be on speaking terms with a supreme Existence.

As our observer is about to view the world of culture, then, let him admit that he does not hold the scholastic conception of the absoluteness of a self-contained Deity, nay, not even in its Christianized version as brought up to date by Neo-Thomism. This is said in the awareness that "absolute" may be predicated in a variety of senses. The main point at issue is the nonrelative, immutable type of absoluteness currently ascribed to God by philosophers and theologians of ontological persuasion. The reader may expect the present inquiry to keep this vital issue in the foreground.

This, Then, Is Our Reference

Our observer's ultimate reference is to a Christian faith expressing in the thought forms of his day the perennial witness of the Israel of God, which is the Body of Christ. This witness traces its ancestry through the Scriptures of the Old and the New Testaments, the tradition of the Apostles' Creed, the successive pronouncements of the great ecumenical councils, and the confessions of faith of the Reformed tradition down to our time.

The core of the faith to which our ideal observer stands committed is that the living God was in Christ reconciling the world unto himself. While the doctrinal statement of this faith should be as correct as the best-informed biblical scholarship can make it, the observer's emphasis should never be on strict conformity with the fallible man-made language used in its infirm formulation. The emphasis should rather be on a basic loyalty to the living catholicity of the Spirit-led Israel of God now speaking in terms of a contemporary grammar of concepts accessible to all men of good will.

It was said in the opening paragraph of the present chapter that the observer should be willing to show his colors at all times. This latter statement surely applies to me, however far I may be from attaining the ideal status of the observer under consideration. Let me therefore illustrate what I have been trying to say by suggesting

46

the type of contemporary statement of faith I have in mind, one "scriptural in tone, rooted in the evangelical tradition, brief and to the point, and couched in terms which are inclined to unite rather than to divide Christians." Such a declaration was recently presented to the American public by Professor Donald G. Miller on his return from a sabbatical leave of absence mostly spent among the Protestants of southern France. The statement, which follows in Professor Miller's translation, was adopted in 1938 by the Reformed Church of France in the awareness that previous stataments were in some measure outgrown and that the Church today must face the problems of this day:

At the moment when she confesses her faith in the sovereign God and in Christ the Savior, the Reformed Church of France deeply senses above all things the need of raising toward the Father of mercies the cry of her gratitude and her adoration.

Faithful to the principles of faith and of liberty on which she was founded, in the communion of the church universal, she affirms the perpetuity of the Christian faith, through its successive expressions, in the Apostles' Creed, the ecumenical creeds, and the confessions of faith of the Reformation, notably the Confession of Rochelle; she finds the source of it in the central revelation of the Gospel: God so loved the world that he gave his only begotten Son that whosoever believeth on him should not perish, but have eternal life.

With the fathers and the martyrs, with all the churches issuing from the Reformation, she affirms the sovereign authority of the Holy Scriptures, founded on the interior testimony of the Holy Spirit, and recognizes in them the rule of faith and of life.

She proclaims before the decadence of men, salvation by grace through faith in Jesus Christ, the unique Son of God, who was delivered up for our offenses and who was raised for our justification.

She places at the base of her teaching and of her worship the great Christian facts affirmed in the gospel, represented in her sacraments, celebrated in her religious solemnities, and expressed in her liturgy.

In obedience to her divine vocation, she announces to a sinful world the gospel of repentance and of pardon, of the new birth, of holiness, and of life eternal.

Under the action of the Holy Spirit, she shows her faith by her works: she works in prayer for the awakening of souls, for the manifestation of the unity of the body of Christ, and for peace among men. By evangelization, by missionary work, by battling against social ills, she prepares

47

the way of the Lord until there comes, by the triumph of her Master, the Kingdom of God and his justice.

To the One who is able, by the power which worketh in us, to do exceedingly abundantly above that which we ask or think, to him be the glory in the church and in Christ Jesus, from generation to generation, for ever and ever! Amen! [18]

[18] Donald G. Miller, "What We May Learn from French Protestantism," *The Presbyterian Outlook*, November 19, 1951, p. 7. Used by permission.

CHAPTER FOUR

The OBSERVER'S SITUATION

As our observer is about to view the various manifestations of culture from his vantage point in the light of the reference presented in the preceding chapter, he becomes increasingly aware of
the difficulties inherent in his situation. The fact was emphasized
that he is first and foremost a man of faith willing to show his colors
at all times. Yet human knowledge as a whole cannot be deduced
from the faith, still less reduced to any pronouncement of the faith,
however correct. The record will show that whenever such *theologism* was attempted, the result was to wrong both nature *and*
the faith. The immediate counterpart of this, however, may also be
readily seen. Whenever cultural activities claimed to be self-sufficient
and all-explanatory, such *secularism* wronged both the faith *and*
nature. The delicate character of the observer's situation is better
realized when we consider the further fact that he is both a man of
faith and a man of culture. One of the most direct implications of the
preceding chapter bears upon this point, namely, that Christianity
can never be identified with any specific culture, however Christianized that culture may be; nay, not even with the most "successful"
Greco-Judean expressions of Western culture. Such an equation
would amount to idolatry and could well constitute a new aggressive
form of cultural arrogance similar to that which has brought about
the bankruptcy of missionary endeavor in many parts of the world
today.

It would seem that the only way to steer clear of both the Scylla of theologism and the Charybdis of secularism is for the culturally informed man of faith to initiate a conversation between Christianity and a certain type of cultural pattern. Yet there are those who claim that such an attempt is likely to prove disappointing, not only because Christianity *qua* Christianity is not immediately concerned with culture *qua* culture, but because there is no real continuity between the notions of truth respectively involved—that is, between that which the world of men and affairs calls truth, and the truth which is identified with Jesus Christ. The faith, they further assert, is not to be integrated in any kind of *Glaubenslehre;* it is to be proclaimed. And then only the God who was in Jesus Christ can restore to natural man eyes to see and ears to hear, together with freedom to understand and to will aright. While pagan philosophers and even well-meaning scholastics settle down to their neatly drawn up tasks, our ideal observer would then seem to stand helpless on the border of two worlds, poised upon a dizzying mountain divide—on one side a secular order bereft of the true God; on the other the realm of the faith not to be reached save by the gracious intervention of the living Lord.

The Barthian Challenge

No one has ever challenged the relevance, validity, and even the advisability of Christian philosophy as has Karl Barth in our day. No one, that is, except some of his overzealous disciples to the point where Karl Barth had to insist with his well-known sense of humor that even he does not consider himself a Barthian. Nevertheless the Barthians we have with us.

But first a minimum background should be presented if we are to view the challenge in its proper setting. In the year of our Lord 1934 the closed corporation known as the theological world was startled by a loud "No" angrily riposted by Karl Barth to his repudiated disciple, Emil Brunner.[1]

[1] Karl Barth, "Nein! Antwort an Emil Brunner," *Theologische Existenz Heute,* vol. 14, 1934. The best available edition in English is to be found in the volume *Natural Theology,* comprising "Nature and Grace" by Emil Brunner, and the reply "No!" by Karl Barth, tr. Peter Fraenkel, with an introduction by John Baillie (London: Geoffrey Bles, The Centenary Press, 1946).

Barth's "Angry Introduction"—his own title—provides a firsthand version of the origin of the quarrel. Having "erred on the liberal side" until about 1916, he began to recover noticeably from the effects of his theological studies and the influences of the liberal-political prewar theology. To these the European conflict was now giving the lie. He came to the conclusion that theologians must learn again to understand revelation as grace, and grace as revelation. They must therefore turn away from all *theologia naturalis,* that is, from any philosophical approach to theology. Having followed him thus far, roughly until 1929, his disciple Brunner began openly to proclaim as the "other" task of theology the necessity of acknowledging a "point of contact" between God and whatever likeness to him may have been left in man after the fall. Whereupon Barth asserts, "I made it known that whatever might happen I could and would not agree with this." [2] What aroused Barth's ire further was that while proceeding with his "heresy," Brunner kept on showering him with love and praise, as if the matters which separated them were merely "false conclusion." Thus Barth felt that he had to reply with a "No" to the wandering Brunner, who had "joined the crowd." [3]

What this quarrel amounts to is that the idea of a total corruption of human nature strongly entrenched in Calvinism not only is being reaffirmed in our day, but is made to be far more radical than Calvin himself ever meant it to be. Calvin heeded Paul's statement to the effect that there is such a thing as natural, or general, revelation. "That which may be known of God is manifest in them; for God hath shewed it unto them. For the invisible things of him from the creation of the world are clearly seen, being understood by the things that are made, even his eternal power and Godhead; so that they are without excuse" (Rom. 1:19-20).[4] Calvin further used such obvious facts as the universality of belief in God, the existence of polytheism, and great achievements in the liberal arts to state his firm conviction

[2] *Natural Theology,* "No!", I, "Angry Introduction," p. 71.

[3] *Ibid.,* p. 73. To follow further episodes in this controversy and argue endlessly about the possibility of a "point of contact" between God and natural man have become the favorite, time-consuming hobby of theological students.

[4] Cf. Calvin, *Institutes,* I, 3; I, 5; in the 1559 ed.

that God has manifested himself, and continues to manifest himself, in the entire created world. He went as far as to say that the original revelation of God the Creator to man his creature would have been sufficient, had man stood blameless, *si integer stetisset Adam.* It remains a genuine revelation, a God-given endowment.[5] All this nothwithstanding, it must be admitted that to Calvin whatever vestige of the image of God may remain in fallen man is so perverted that it does not deserve the name of knowledge at all. Man's original corruption leaves him indisposed and disabled.[6] This admission is of course not to be construed in such extravagant terms as those of South's sermon on "Man Created in God's Image," which contained the famous sentence, "An Aristotle was but the rubbish of an Adam, and Athens but the rudiments of Paradise."[7]

The question before us, then, concerns the survival of any such vestige of the glory that was man. Can a man left to himself welcome the Christian revelation as answering a question he had raised in his own mind?

Brunner felt it necessary to reassert the possibility of a "point of contact"[8] between God and natural man, to insist that man is neither a stone nor a clod of earth, that he *does* have a capacity for speech, an "addressability" which makes him both receptive (*wortempfänglich*) and responsible (*verantwortlich*). It will shortly be seen that Barth could go far in granting that Christian truth had always been communicable in terms of coherent, reasonable speech, but only inasmuch and in so far as such language was a one-way proclamation proceeding from the Church. What concerned Barth in his controversy with Brunner was a "foolproof" tightening up and rewording of the Reformation doctrine of *sola gratia,* that is, salvation by grace

[5] *Ibid.* Cf. also Calvin's preface to his *Commentary on Genesis,* 23, 7.

[6] Cf. the Westminster Confession of Faith, 6, 4.

[7] Quoted by J. S. Whale, *Christian Doctrine* (New York: The Macmillan Co., 1941), p. 51.

[8] Emil Brunner, *Natur und Gnade* (Tübingen: J. C. B. Mohr, 1935), 5., pp. 18-20; *Man in Revolt,* tr. Olive Wyon (New York: Chas. Scribner's Sons, 1939), App. III, 7., pp. 536-41; *Revelation and Reason,* tr. Olive Wyon (Philadelphia: Westminster Press, 1946), pp. 77-80, in answer to Barth's *Kirchliche Dogmatik* (Zurich: Zollikon, Evangelischer Verlag), II, 1, 107-141.

alone. There is nothing in natural man to which the Word of God as such can address itself, except a heart that feels and a brain that functions. So God must in effect recreate and illumine natural man's nature, make it free to live in the truth, if the penitent is to receive the knowledge of faith as the only knowledge that matters to him. The gift comes from the Holy Spirit *with the capacity to receive it.*[9] One searches Barth's writings in vain for even the beginning of an appreciation of general revelation as a glimmer of truth remaining as a starting point in the heart and mind of man.[10] The Word which is not to be confused with the written word of the Bible, and which even a preacher shall never speak,[11] is the one source of all our knowledge of God. *"Gott wird nur durch Gott erkannt"* (God is only known through God) is the dominant theme throughout in Barth's works.

A mood of wonder and expectation greeted Barth's invitation to the lectureship established by Lord Gifford for the furtherance of a natural theology as a strictly natural science, "without reference to or reliance upon any supposed special exceptional or so-called miraculous revelation." But then the new Gifford lecturer opened the 1937 series with the candid assertion that the "science" that Lord Gifford had in mind "owes its existence to a radical error." Whereupon he reminded his audience that he was "an avowed opponent of all natural theology." [12]

The gist of the Barthian message and the burden of his bulky volumes are that man is a sinner and not an image-bearer. There is not to be found in him any likeness to God which may in any way *prepare* him to know God, or even to respond to God. Whatever is

[9] Cf. Calvin's seventh sermon on Eph. 1:17-18: "Ainsi il faut que Dieu besongne en nous et nous donne des yeux nouveaux pour comprendre ce qui est requis a notre salut."

[10] Unless a (weak) argument is taken from the *"Nebenlinie"* emerging for one brief moment in the *Kirchliche Dogmatik*, II, 1, 112 sq. But this must have been a slip on the part of Barth.

[11] Karl Barth, *The Word of God and the Word of Man*, tr. Horton (New York: The Pilgrim Press, 1928), p. 216.

[12] Karl Barth, *The Knowledge of God and the Service of God According to the Teaching of the Reformation*, tr. Haire and Henderson (London: Hodder and Stoughton, 1938), pp. 3, 5-6.

to effect this in him, if God so elects him, must be a divine renewal amounting to a new creation. Even the gentle, levelheaded John Baillie has to admit that "this is a piece of theological radicalism, in comparison with which that of William of Ockham appears harmless." [13]

If Barthianism Were True

It must be readily admitted that the truth of propositions cannot be ultimately appraised in terms of their practical consequences. Nevertheless, while declining to accept a pragmatic view of truth as a canon of the correct use of reason, we are urged by Jesus himself to judge a tree by its fruits.

In a constant awareness of our debt to Karl Barth for having restored the high notion of the honor and sovereignty of God, we may well wonder about some of the corollaries of his own views with reference to the burning issues of the day. He likes to insist that he never expects to find in natural man anything already "there" to correspond to the Word of God. The bearing of such a notion on our own subject is only too obvious. Let us therefore pause at this point.

We are told that Karl Barth produced a sensation at the 1948 World Council Assembly in Amsterdam by stating that the theme of the conference, "Man's Disorder and God's Design," was upside down. Besides, he added, the two shall never meet. He went on, exposing the Amsterdam procedure as "a Christian Marshall Plan." A bishop of a Western diocese of the Protestant Episcopal Church then remarked, "If I believed that, I'd leave Amsterdam and go fishing. I would not bother to bait a hook or wet a line, but would set my skillet on the shore and start frying, grateful to God for undeserved blessings if a fish jumped in, admitting that as a poor sinner I was getting what I deserved if I went hungry."

The issue at stake is brought to a head in a more realistic vein by Karl Barth's aloofness from the conflict between East and West on the part of the Church. I refer to his short work on *The Church Be-*

[13] John Baillie, *Natural Theology*, p. 54. For Baillie's more comprehensive critique of Karl Barth, the reader may turn to his luminous treatment of *Our Knowledge of God* (New York: Charles Scribner's Sons, 1939), pp. 17-27.

tween East and West.[14] Our challenge to Stalinism[15] appears to Barth as one of power politics, pertaining to what he calls "the natural history of the world." He insists that a strict neutrality on the part of the Church constitutes the only and last chance of Protestant survival. Christianity should not open itself to the suspicion of having any part in the most unholy cause of Occidental capitalism. In taking sides between East and West, as we are bidden to do, Barth concludes that we could only make ourselves "the doubtful interpreters of certain Western opinions which are politically murky and contestable." The small volume reveals throughout a most indulgent attitude toward sovietism. The religious character of the Stalinian ideology would seem to escape Barth completely. To him, obviously, the whole drama unfolds on the level of natural man. Or rather, as he puts it, it belongs in "the natural history of the world."

Not only does such an attitude make for a deplorable isolationism, leaving the field to the wildest ideologies, but it continues to befuddle the best minds and to restrain many a seeker of good will. But according to Barthianism there is no such thing as a useful quest for God on the part of natural man. An insidious laziness helping, moreover, such a radicalism constitutes an inducement to neglect purely "secular" knowledge, not to say anything of the main current of Christian classics. Perhaps it is better not to insist on these things. Yet one can hardly help calling to mind Hawthorne's Reverend Mr. Dimmesdale, "a young clergyman, who had come from one of the great English universities, bringing all the learning of the age into our wild forest-land." [16] Neither need one refer to fictitious characters, however true to life. Hundreds of names suggest themselves. Methodists, for example, would immediately suggest the Oxford-trained pioneer John Wesley, who from childhood reasoned everything. His successful logic—chopping at the service of his Lord—would make light of the new theological defeatism. Nay, we may well remember that Calvin himself never shunned his cul-

[14] *Die Kirche Zwischen Ost und West* (Zurich: Zollikon, 1949).
[15] On this see Part IV, chap. 3.
[16] *The Scarlet Letter*, ch. 3.

55

tural task, and we gratefully acknowledge the part played by such men as Reinhold Niebuhr in reviving that genuine Christian concern today.

A Radical Form of Theologism

It would be a grave misunderstanding to characterize the Barthian attitude as a revolt against reason. What we have is rather a new radical form of theologism. In a recent popularization of his views Barth insists that faith means knowledge, and that the word "knowledge" means what it says. He points out in this connection that the saying, "Despise only reason and science, man's supremest power of all," was uttered not by a prophet, but by Goethe's Mephistopheles. Theology, Barth insists, is no mere talk or babbling. It is concerned with a proclamation revealed and demonstrated in the human *nous* (mind) as meaning, as truth to be learned. As such it involves *ratio* (reason) in which human *ratio* may also be reflected and reproduced. What has been apprehended of old is to be apprehended again. *Vernunft* (reason's faculty of apprehension) comes from *vernehmen* (to apprehend, to grasp). Those were always unpropitious periods when *gnosis* (knowledge) was separated from *pistis* (faith).[17] This is a precious clarification. And Karl Barth goes further still. He admits that while the language of the Church should have priority when the proclamation is made, it is often advisable for the Church to use a paraphrase in the language of the market place, nay, even in that of the newspaper, to assure a better communication of the truth. Better still, a direct concern for the responsibility of the Church with regard to culture finds expression in such texts as Karl Barth's lecture on *Evangelium und Bildung* (*The Gospel and Culture*). The thesis set forth in these pages is that the Church is called upon to formulate and to erect standards for the whole of secular creative activity from the standpoint of the knowledge of faith.

On the other hand the Barthian implication throughout is that

[17] Karl Barth, *Dogmatics in Outline,* tr. G. T. Thomson (New York: Philosophical Library, 1949), pp. 22-23.

the proclamation of the Church absorbs all knowledge worthy of the name. As Emil Brunner points out, Barth makes the Word of revelation "the sole and sufficient source of *all* truth and of *all* knowledge of truth. Thus over against extreme rationalism, which proposes to solve all problems of knowledge exclusively by the autonomous reason, there is here set up an equally exclusive and radical fideism which, alongside the Word of revelation does not recognize any second, independent source of knowledge for any sphere of life." Whereupon Brunner proceeds to ask, "Can anyone seriously maintain that all questions in mathematics, physics, biology, and astronomy are 'answered in the Word of God'? Does anyone seriously contend that in the future, instead of turning to Euclid for geometry, to Galileo for physics, to Lyell for geology, we must turn instead, for everything, to the Holy Scriptures?" [18]

Barth's radical theologism is brought to a head in a dichotomy between heaven, the realm characterized as *invisibilia* in the Nicene Creed, and earth, the realm characterized in the same Creed as *visibilia*. The first realm is said to be that of the creation inconceivable to man, the second that of creation conceivable to him. The immediate corollary of the above dichotomy is that any attempt to combine the two, nay, even to interpret the second in terms of the first, must be guarded against. Christians should beware of any entanglement with the world picture (*Weltanschauung*) whether ancient, modern, or contemporary. Such "philosophico-metaphysical" comprehensive views can only mean trouble for an all-sufficient knowledge of faith. "We Christians are once for all dispensed from attempting, by starting from ourselves, to understand what exists, or to reach the cause of things and with or without God to reach a general view." [19]

As Karl Barth sees it, then, theology alone is responsible for the truth concerning God, man, and human destiny. To philosophy is abandoned the task of analyzing scientific methods and of relating the temporary conclusions of the various branches of scientific

[18] *Revelation and Reason,* p. 378.
[19] *Dogmatics in Outline,* p. 60.

knowledge. A united world view may well emerge as a result of the philosopher's effort, but the theologian has already disclaimed any responsibility for, or even interest in, such a view. In case the reader should believe that this last sentence is emphatically an over-statement, let him consider still another quote from Karl Barth. "So my advice would be, that if you are faced with any such general view, you should bracket it, even if it should be called a *Christian Weltanschauung.*" [20] No wonder a recent book quite friendly to Karl Barth contains the admission that, while a large group of con-temporary philosophers are quite satisfied with Barth's assignment, they return his compliment "by consigning all that he stands for to the realm of the meaningless." [21]

A perfect deadlock seems to have been reached at this point. Even a philosopher of good will like Dorothy Emmet feels con-strained to conclude a chapter on "Revelation and Faith" with the reluctant remark: If the theologian insists, "as certain of the ortho-dox do insist, that faith can only properly be said to be present when the power to submit to revelation has been supernaturally created in us, then those who know themselves impelled to follow the inner call of one of the growing points of the spirit in creative thought and work must go their way without the blessing of theol-ogy." [22] And she goes her way, as it were, in the awareness that the deadlock inherent in Barthianism may prove a costly one indeed. As a rule, the verb "to abandon" calls for a complement that will answer the further question, Abandon to whom?

It is at such a place that one is tempted to question the optimistic statement with which Descartes opened his *Discourse on Method:* "Good sense is, of all things among men, the most equally dis-tributed."

Christian Philosophy Is

According to etymology, philosophy is the love of wisdom. Thus

[20] *Ibid.*

[21] James H. Cotton, *Christian Knowledge of God* (New York: The Macmillan Co., 1951), p. 130.

[22] *The Nature of Metaphysical Thinking* (London: Macmillan & Co., 1945), p. 145.

Pythagoras (sixth century B.C.) coined the word by calling himself a lover of wisdom, a philosopher. His reference was to both the quest for wisdom and the wisdom sought. In this connection each one of us is a philosopher. Each one of us actually has an outlook on life, a world view of his own, which motivates him whether he realizes it or not. Just as Molière's *parvenu* had spoken prose for forty years without ever being aware of it, each one of us has his own way of looking at the world, that is, his own philosophy. It is therefore obvious that we need waste no more time in justifying the relevance of philosophy than the relevance of the nose, which, for better or for worse, protrudes in the middle of our face. I am intentionally trivial on this because triviality becomes the order of the day when people depart from common sense.

Common sense, then, would have everyone realize that Christian philosophy appears whenever and wherever a Christian begins to think. The possible alternatives to this could only be either a thinker who was not a Christian at all, or a Christian who did not think at all. And then it should be of uttermost concern to the Church to have people think as Christians, and to see to it that Christians actually think, and do think as Christians.

But should a Christian purposely shun philosophy, others would step into the realm thus abandoned and proceed to provide contemporaries with non-Christian views of reality. There springs up a wild growth of ideologies promising a harvest of bitter fruits, as was the case in Germany when an exclusive evangelical Lutheranism abandoned the field to Hitler.

Does it matter at all that there have been, and that there still are in the secular order, Christian men and women who think as Christians? Or should the protagonists of the wildest ideologies be given a free hand, whether they advocate sacrificing little children to Moloch or little Koreans to Stalin? Must we believe that the best way to serve the Creator is to ignore his Creation, while holding the lowest estimate of the possibilities of the human intellect? Here, for instance, is a brother who, after having laboriously worked for truth, finds himself constrained to admit the existence of what

59

he calls a supreme being, an absolute nature, an utterly free power, or an ultimate being towering over everything. Shall we greet him with the terse, Barthian comment: "This absolute and supreme being, this ultimate and most profound, this 'thing in itself,' has *nothing* to do with God"? [23] Shall we say further, as an eminent Barthian once said to me, that the Socrates of the *Apology* actually knew nothing of God? That neither did the aging Epictetus as he was entreating his disciples to show him one whom he characterized in such a way as to approach the Christ, and this at the very time when the Crucifixion had just taken place?

The irony of it all is that nothing is more philosophical than the series of fallacious arguments used in establishing such folly. It is fair to conclude this admittedly unpleasant part of our development with this fragment remaining from one of Aristotle's lost works: "You say one must philosophize. Then you must philosophize. You say one should not philosophize. Then to prove your point, you must philosophize. In any case, you must philosophize."

No one philosophizes more, yet to a worse purpose, than the Christian bent upon convincing infidels that they waste their time and effort whenever their mind is bent upon the ultimate.

Delicate Position of the Christian Philosopher

Having steered clear of the Scylla of theologism, we should further heed the Charybdis of secularism. While certain cultural manifestations would seem at first to be self-sufficient and all-explanatory, that is, remote from God, others are clearly not so. Supposing, for instance, we were passing from the realm of the natural sciences to that of the human sciences (*Geisteswissenschaften*); a certain degree of uneasiness might well disturb our self-assurance, especially as we came to grips with ethicoreligious realities.

Emil Brunner has given full expression to the increasingly difficult character of the task confronting the candid student whose consideration draws closer and closer to the things that are God's. He has finally formulated his views into a law which has since become

[23] *Dogmatics in Outline,* p. 23. (Italics mine.)

60

his guiding principle for all problems that concern the relation between the Christian and the world. This he called "the law of the closeness of relation."

The nearer anything lies to that center of existence where we are concerned with the whole, that is, with man's relation to God and the being of the person, the greater is the disturbance of rational knowledge by sin; the farther away anything lies from this center, the less is the disturbance felt, and the less difference is there between knowing as a believer or an unbeliever. This disturbance reaches its maximum in theology and its minimum in the exact sciences, and zero in the sphere of the formal.[24]

Hence, explains Brunner, while it would seem meaningless to speak of "Christian mathematics," it is important to distinguish the Christian conceptions of freedom, the good, community, and still more the Christian idea of God, from all other conceptions.

This statement of Brunner's "law of the closeness of relation" brings into full view an element which any Christian philosopher worth his salt will never minimize, namely, the actual disharmony brought about in natural man by his rebellious estrangement from God by his sin. Christian epistemology may even be characterized by saying that it remains constantly aware of the resulting disturbance in the realm where the intellect is affected by a will in bondage. It is precisely because this is the case that the disturbance brought out by Brunner's law is increasingly felt in those areas of knowledge where the human ego becomes ever more tensely involved. There is here far more at stake, therefore, than the difficulties encountered as one proceeds from natural to revealed theology.

Let it be remembered in all humility at this point, however, that our observer is first and foremost a Christian who remains in the world without being of the world. He has been made whole again. A man in Christ, he has eyes to see and ears to hear, together with freedom to understand and to will aright. The time-tested view applies to the man of faith he is, namely, that the faith remains the best way of assuring the very rationality of reason. Precisely because

[24] *Revelation and Reason,* p. 383.

the Christian is the only genuine rationalist under God's high heaven, he may authoritatively claim all truth that has been well expressed.[25] By the same token he will understand and truly appraise the increasing difficulties of the man of culture who comes to grips with ethicoreligious realities, closer to "that center of existence where we are concerned with the whole." The Christian philosopher may thus truly prepare the path of the man of culture toward the light. He can only do this, however, if he is otherwise qualified and adequately prepared.

The Christian philosopher may only claim a privileged position inasmuch and in so far as he has "the advantage of believing," [26] that is, as his mind has been freed from the distorting influence of a perverted will, illuminated by revelation upon the deeper issues involved in philosophical problems. While this constitutes an immeasurable privilege, this same privilege is not to be construed as implying a higher grade of intelligence.[27] In other words the intellect of the Christian philosopher belongs to the rank and file of intellects. The reason this must be said is that an extreme theological view seems to suggest that enlightened minds are altogether in a class by themselves, a fact which neither current observation nor even a candid look at *Who's Who* would substantiate.

The Christian philosopher should, most emphatically, familiarize himself with the great achievements of secular culture while specializing in at least one realm of investigation. This is precisely the type of approach advocated by Max Planck with reference to scientific research:

Anyone desirous of obtaining a scientific view of the world must first acquire a knowledge of the facts.

To-day the individual student can no longer form a comprehensive view of every department of science and in most instances he must take his facts at second-hand. It is all the more important that he should be master of one trade and have an independent judgment on his own

[25] Cf. Justin Martyr's famous statement to that effect: "Whatever has been well said belongs to us Christians" (*Second Apology*, 13).

[26] Cf. Augustine, *De utilitate credendi* (*On the Advantage of Believing*).

[27] To be specific, I(ntelligence) Q(uotient).

62

subject. Personally, as a member of the philosophical faculty, I have always asked that candidates for a philosophical doctorate should give evidence of special knowledge in one given special science. Whether this department belonged to the natural sciences or to the intellectual sciences is not important: what is important, is that the candidate should have acquired by actual study an idea of scientific method.[28]

Our ideal observer would make his own, at this point, Nels Ferré's incontrovertible principle that "in order to be the human ultimate, Christianity must be no less than man's highest practical ideal." [29] There was not so long ago a time when the philosopher could be satisfied with proclaiming edifying generalities, very much in the manner of those itinerant professors in long robes who flourished in the Hellenistic world in the days of Thrasycles. They also practiced the art of refined extemporary lectures. A studied diction made of their sermons pieces of vocal achievement. In the middle of the last century a young scientifically minded philosopher, Hippolyte Taine, who had just suffered unfair treatment on the part of academic authorities, retaliated by drawing up what he called an ideal biography of the most illustrious representative of the day. Victor Cousin, the author of the oft-revised eclectic treatise *On the Truth, On the Beautiful, On the Good,* was thus said to have been born in the nineteenth century only through some uncanny trick of fate. Did not this eloquent philosopher, whose chair was a throne, thunder over his audience in the manner of a great seventeenth-century king of the pulpit? Why, he seemed to hold God in his hand. He was inebriated by his own words, and the phantasmagory of his images troubled even the certainty of his vaunted inspiration. How easy it was, even in the middle of the nineteenth century, to image a grand lady of the great Louis' court almost converted by such unctuous display! [30]

The days when philosophy could be satisfied with eloquent

[28] *The Philosophy of Physics* (New York: W. W. Norton & Co., 1936), p. 107. Used by permission.

[29] *The Christian Faith* (New York: Harper & Bros., 1942), p. 3.

[30] Hippolyte Taine, *Les Philosophes classiques du XIXe siècle en France* (1857), pp. 198-202 in Hachette ed., Paris.

generalities, uninformed by the knowledge made available through the specialist, are definitely over. Granted that the Church may well exult in the galaxy of her great doctors down to our day and age, the plain fact is that Christian scholarship does not always remain on a par with purely secular qualifications and achievements, especially in certain sections of the Church. This is the contention of such a witness as Erwin R. Goodenough, professor of the history of religion at Yale University. Our children, he claims, "are either turned over to a clergy whose inferiority is often too painfully obvious even to youngsters, or they are allowed to grow up quite pagan." [31] Even to imply that the knowledge of faith can be a substitute for either mental acumen or cultural equipment is simply preposterous. Neither should there be any need for pointing out such obvious realities.

Now that all this has been made clear, let a sense of proper jurisdiction be restored between the knowledge of faith and secular knowledge. The knowledge of faith proceeds from the light of the Holy Spirit speaking in Scripture through the mediation of the One Church. It enables the members of the Body of Christ to appraise the ground, goal, and spiritual value of created things, more especially the meaning and relevance of their own existence. Secular knowledge proceeds from the intellection of the natures and properties of created things, and of the laws by which they are governed.

Since we live, and move, and have our being in the world of sense experience, the two great aspects of knowledge just considered may be said to be active in the Christian philosopher as they are, in various degrees, in "every man that cometh into the world." This, however, does not mean that he should expect the observation, induction, and patterns of clues of the scientist to map out and actually retrace creative processes in their actuality.

This universe is teleological and truly sacramental. It expresses a profound and ultimately unfathomable finality. Its potentialities suggest at every turn a meaning born of Omnipotence. There is "causality" in it in the sense that it is, in every one of its constitutive

[31] *Religious Tradition and Myth* (New Haven: Yale University Press, 1937), p. 11.

64

elements, a receiver of existence; also in the sense that, as a whole, it is oriented by Him who created it and maintains it in existence. Yet the "causality" thus implied in God's agency may well have little in common with the constructions placed upon its apparent manifestations by the uncouth patterns of clues of the scientist.

A fruitful conversation may therefore be initiated between the Christian philosopher and the representatives of culture as between partners under God's high heaven. In a new awareness of their respective condition, moreover, they are henceforth in a position to bring to light the reasons which used to make issues between them so irritating and fruitless. The Christian philosopher in particular realizes that his task is not to sit in judgment on anyone, but rather to appraise cultural manifestations in their themes as well as in their deepest intentions with a view to renewal and rebirth

Admittedly the task of our ideal observer is a difficult one. He is a man "knowing the time" (Rom. 13:11) in which he lives, the *kairos* appointed by the living God, who was in Christ reconciling the world unto himself. This time of the Israel of God is a strange time indeed.[32] Everything is accomplished and yet everything remains to be done. One waits for what is to come and yet everything remains hidden. The greatest service that the Christian philosopher can render in this situation is to bear witness to what he sees when he looks at the world of men and affairs in the light of the faith.

Let therefore the presentation of the Christian landscape of reality constitute a meeting ground between the Christian philosopher and the representatives of culture in the light "which lighteth every man that cometh into the world" (John 1:9).

[32] On this see Paul S. Minear, *Eyes of Faith* (Philadelphia: The Westminster Press, 1946), pp. 97-113, and Roger Mehl, *La Condition du Philosophe Chrétien* (Neufchatel: Delachaux & Niestlé, 1947), pp. 198-99.

CHAPTER FIVE

The CHRISTIAN LANDSCAPE
of REALITY

THE view underlying this Christian approach to culture is that there can be no genuine sanity for the man who does not see things as they really are. This does not mean merely one element here or there, one pinned, as it were, upon the landscape devised by a certain culture, as a true slogan may be pinned on one's lapel. It means the landscape of reality as a whole, the landscape that the One Church actually sees when she looks at the universe of nature and of man—God created, God upheld at every moment, God bathed in its integrality. Again, this means that as the "passing show" of time unfolds under our very eyes, carrying us along in the successive mobility of particular events, seeing the Christian landscape of reality means seeing God as the Supreme Ruler of history, including our own life history, either willing or permitting everything that comes to pass. To us Christians this created universe is a great signaling station. It is our task to make out its meaning and to proceed upon this same meaning at all times.

A Temporal Order Against a Background of Impermanence

Before proceeding with the task at hand, however—nay, throughout the entire discussion—an all-important reservation should always be kept in mind: whatever is stated about this temporal order should be apprehended against a background of impermanence. Our status here on earth is that of pilgrims, *viatores, peregrini.* The true

66

pattern of life for the man of God was set by Abram the Hebrew. Alexander Maclaren saw great significance in his designation of Hebrew as found in Gen. 14:13. He pointed out that it is "in plain English, a nickname, and it means, probably, as the ancient Greek translation of Genesis gives it . . . 'The man from the other side,' the man that had come across the water." [1] This is why he elected to live in a tent. Commenting upon his situation, the Epistle to the Hebrews states that he dwelt in tabernacles because he looked for a city.

The dominant note of the true landscape of reality, therefore, is that however fascinating the present temporal order may be, however alluring, it is but a temporal order. [2] We should not be "taken in" by it, nor give our hearts to it beyond the point of no return. Our ultimate rule should not be that of conformity to its values. We should never take our citizenship in the village Morality. This is one of the essential specifications of what J. B. Phillips called *Letters to Young Churches*. It is also, as he insisted in his "Translator's Preface," one of the most needed emphases in our day: "Today when all the emphasis is thrown upon making the most of life, and even Christianity is only seriously considered in many quarters because of its social implications, this point of view is comparatively rarely held." [3]

Yet this is not saying enough. The main point is that it is only against this background of impermanence that it becomes possible to "do the truth." "The heavenly life alone lends reality to all schemes of earthly amelioration; the life beyond which alone gives value to this; the eternal, the immortal, the invisible, which alone makes it worth while to lift mankind from the mire of selfishness and corruption. . . . Only as we live within the circle of the Ascended Glory shall we really be able for work here." [4]

[1] *Expositions of Holy Scriptures* (Grand Rapids: Eerdmans, 1938), I, 93.

[2] The argument is excellently stated in John Baillie, *And the Life Everlasting* (New York: Charles Scribner's Sons, 1933), ch. 8, "Strangers and Pilgrims," pp. 306-43.

[3] New York: The Macmillan Co., 1947. P. xiii.

[4] F. J. E. Raby in *Theology*, May, 1940, as quoted by J. S. Whale, *Christian Doctrine*, p. 184.

Not to see the landscape of reality in this otherworldly context is just not to see what is there. It is to see everything the wrong way and, as a result, to miss the mark. The main reason that quite a large number of scholars have misunderstood Jesus' attitude toward culture is precisely that they have missed the mark at this point.

A Clue to the Ministry of Jesus

The reason Jesus impressed the secular order by his exclusiveness, if not by his hostility toward even the culture of his day in its Jewish nature, is that he came primarily to proclaim a kingdom which is not of this world. Culture *qua* culture was not within the perspective of his mission. Any concern for culture that may appear as the aftermath of the apostolic preaching must be a *derived* interest. The wonder of it all is that even within this fundamental restriction, and even quite apart from the actual salvation wrought out in those who were and continue to be added to the Israel of God, this world of men and affairs has been wonderfully transformed for having been the abode of the man Christ Jesus.

There is in the first instance evidence of an exclusiveness on the part of Jesus which singled out the Jewish people for attention. His ministry seems to have been limited to the Jews until the moment came when he despaired of the whole religious economy of the nation during his last days on earth. It was too late, however, for him to proceed upon this awareness. And so it was that his whole activity may be said to have been confined to his own countrymen, as he himself asserted to the Syrophoenician woman: "I am not sent but unto the lost sheep of the house of Israel" (Matt. 15:24).[5] He sent his disciples out on a mission with the explicit mandate that they were not to go into the way of the Gentiles, nor into any city of the Samaritans, but rather "to the lost sheep of the house of Israel" (Matt. 10:5-7). Besides, the disciples received the promise that they would judge—that is, govern—the twelve tribes of Israel, the suggestion being at this point that there would be only Jews in the Kingdom (Matt. 19:28). But more, there is no record of any

[5] Cf. Mark 7:24-28.

missionary tour into Gentile country. Jesus never left Jewish territory, except to find solitude or to escape Herod's hostility. As for the great command to go, teach, and baptize all nations (Matt. 28:19), it is reported as having been given by Jesus *after* his resurrection.[6] Goguel, whom we are following in this paragraph, further points out that when Jesus, in the days of his flesh, spoke of Gentiles who would be admitted into the kingdom,[7] his words sounded "more like warnings to the Jews than like promises to the Gentiles." [8]

To this exclusiveness which singled out the Jewish people for attention Jesus added the exclusiveness of the otherworldliness of his gospel. Not only was the kingdom of God restricted in the main to the Jews, but this kingdom was not even of this world. Jewish scholars, and more especially Klausner, have seized upon the manifestations of this attitude to show to what extent Jesus not only ignored the cultural order, but only remembered it to throw aside all its requirements. Therefore it is an understatement to say that he does not belong to civilization. To all practical purposes, according to Klausner, he was a peril to civilization, even in its Jewish form of a truly theocratic culture.

In the special realm of ethics a group of scholars led by Albert Schweitzer has insisted that the strenuously eschatological character of Jesus' teaching left no room for truly constructive views. Since the time before the end was to be so short, the teachings of Jesus were merely in terms of an "interim ethic." The radicalism and otherworldliness of this ethic, in fact, should suffice to show that it belongs to another order only, namely, to the future kingdom. Paul Ramsey, who otherwise brings out the perennial validity of the teachings of Jesus, nevertheless feels constrained to admit that "there are crucial teachings of Jesus whose meaning has been so decisively affected by his kingdom-expectation that they can be torn from their context only at great peril of complete misunder-

[6] For a fuller discussion of this limitation of the ministry of Jesus, see Maurice Goguel, *The Life of Jesus,* tr. Olive Wyon (New York: The Macmillan Co., 1945), pp. 321-23.

[7] For instance, in Matt. 11:20-24; 8:11-12.

[8] Goguel, *op. cit.,* p. 323.

standing or with exceeding carefulness to conserve their original meaning." [9]

It is a further fact that it was partly on their own cultural grounds that the Jews rejected Jesus, and this has remained true down to our day. This attitude, moreover, has provided throughout the ages a rather exceptional meeting ground between Jews and Gentiles. The whole history of Western and Oriental culture bears witness to this. Christianity has again and again been exposed by Hellenists, Romans, and moderns as sheer barbarism, contempt for the values of civilization, intolerance toward the most sacred institutions and traditions of men. Following upon the systematic indictments of Nietzsche on the one hand and of Marx and Engels on the other, the whole ideological trend in our day is based on the assumption that while the devitalizing "opium of the people" can only lead to stagnation and decay, Marxism truly provides a view of life making for the richest cultural pattern.[10]

In his substantial book on *Christ and Culture*, Richard Niebuhr presents a methodical consideration of the various manifestations of the impact of the Christ upon culture. Having stated the problem, he frankly acknowledges the first immediate aspect to be the one we have just surveyed, namely, that of "Christ against culture." The climax of this aspect is reached with Tolstoy's rejection of culture, likened to that of Tertullian. "But there was one man who in his own way and under the circumstances of his own time and place stated the radical position as vehemently and consistently as Tertullian. That man was Leo Tolstoy." [11] The interesting thing, however, is that the scholar's methodical consideration of the evidence at hand causes him to restrict this exclusiveness to expressing only *one* of

[9] *Basic Christian Ethics* (New York: Charles Scribner's Sons, 1950), p. 35. Sections II and III of the first chapter cover the various aspects of the problem most thoroughly ("The Kingdom of God in the Teachings of Jesus" and "In What Way, Then, Are the Teachings of Jesus Valid?"). It is essential to the development here to remark that these two sections follow upon an opening section dealing with "The Righteousness of God."

[10] A good primer on this is Alexander Miller's *The Christian Significance of Karl Marx* (New York: The Macmillan Co., 1946). See Annotated Book List, pp. 110-11.

[11] New York: Harper & Bros., 1951. P. 57.

five essential attitudes. Thus he is led to proceed from "Christ Against Culture" to "The Christ of Culture," whom he follows from the Gnostics to present-day America. Part 4 shows what happens when a real synthesis is brought about between Christ and a church-centered culture. It is entitled "Christ Above Culture." Yet the tension reappears with the dualism so characteristic of the modern age, the result being that we now see "Christ and Culture in Paradox" (Part 5). Reverting then to the conversion motif of the Fourth Gospel and following it along the Augustinian trend, Richard Niebuhr points to "Christ the Transformer of Culture" (Part 6). The concluding Part 7 brings out the fact that all these characteristic views of Christ and culture contain truth. They correspond to existing attitudes which should, all of them, be taken into consideration when the Christian answer is formulated. Yet the author, who writes this last section under the sign of the Kierkegaard of the *Concluding Unscientific Postscript,* sees this final answer as that of a personal decision on the part of the existing individual.

We are grateful to Richard Niebuhr for a penetrating analysis which greatly facilitates our task. It has already become clear that once the Christian perspective has been restored, the impact of the gospel message upon the secular order, even in its derived forms, gives the lie to any sustained contention of exclusiveness.

With immediate reference to the restricted character of the earlier ministry of Jesus in particular, the contention of exclusiveness proves to be contradicted not only by the very nature of the gospel, but by the actuality of the apostolic preaching. The commission of the risen Lord to go, teach, and baptize all nations is but the prelude to the Acts of the Apostles. The missionary character of the early Church culminates in the conquest of the Greco-Roman world so beautifully pictured in the great fresco of Kenneth Scott Latourette. One is truly left to wonder with Arnold J. Toynbee at "the indomitable growth of this Galilean grain of mustard-seed" as "the propagators of the new faith deliberately 'turn to the Gentiles' and proceed to conquer new worlds for Christianity on ground far beyond the farthest limits of the Maccabeean kingdom." [12] Edward Gibbon in his *History of the Decline and Fall of the Roman Empire* ascribes this rapid development of the Christian Church to five main causes:

1. The inflexible and . . . intolerant zeal of the Christians, . . . purified from the narrow and unsocial spirit [of the Jewish religion].
2. The doctrine of a future life, improved by every additional circumstance which could give weight and efficacy to that important truth.
3. The miraculous powers ascribed to the primitive church.
4. The pure and austere morals of the Christians.
5. The union and discipline of the Christian republic, which gradually formed an independent and increasing state in the heart of the Roman empire.[13]

What Price Christian Leadership

What impresses the candid reader of Gibbon's great work is that it progressively reveals the secret of this irresistible power *on the cultural level* to have been that of Christian character. Repentance for their sins, and the laudable desire of supporting the reputation of the society in which they were engaged, rendered the lives of the primitive Christians much purer and more austere than those of their pagan contemporaries or their degenerate successors. Gibbon testifies that the Christians were insistent in their condemnation of pleasure and luxury and in their search after purity. As for the government of the primitive Church, it was based on the principles of freedom and equality.

This view has since been vindicated in such outstanding works as that of Ernst Troeltsch, *The Social Teachings of the Christian Churches.*[14] It has been extended by Max Weber to apply to the amazing fortune of Protestantism in general, and more especially to Calvinism. It was the power resulting from Christian character that made for industry and thrift. Once more the old Hebrew view that righteousness proves ultimately to be a blessing, even in the mate-

[12] *A Study of History* (New York and London: Oxford University Press, 1946), p. 99.

[13] Vol. I, ch. 15, in the Modern Library edition.

[14] Tr. Olive Wyon (New York: The Macmillan Co., 1931).

rial order, was vindicated. Such is the thesis of Weber's *The Protestant Ethic and the Spirit of Capitalism.*[15] His views on the subject proved so fruitful that they resulted in a vast literature in which I would single out R. H. Tawney's *Religion and the Rise of Capitalism.* The section devoted to Calvin strangely enough echoes Gibbon's views on the all-important factor of character in the rise of Christianity. For Calvinism

good works are not a way of attaining salvation, but they are indispensable as a proof that salvation has been attained. The central paradox of religious ethics—that only those are nerved with the courage needed to turn the world upside down, who are convinced that already, in a higher sense, it is disposed for the best by a Power of which they are the humble instruments—finds in it a special exemplification. For the Calvinist the world is ordained to show forth the majesty of God, and the duty of the Christian is to live for that end. His task is at once to discipline his individual life, and to create a sanctified society. The Church, the State, the community in which he lives, must not merely be a means of personal salvation, or minister to his temporal needs. It must be a "Kingdom of Christ," in which individual duties are performed by men conscious that they are "ever in their great Taskmaster's eye," and the whole fabric is preserved from corruption by a stringent and all-embracing discipline.[16]

From Gibbon to Weber and Tawney the same basic truth is suggested, namely, that the immediate contribution of Christianity to culture *as such* is that of a Christian character. It is an ethical contribution in line with the age-old biblical teaching of righteousness—that genuine righteousness which "tendeth to life" (Prov. 10:16). Once restored in redeemed individual souls, it truly radiates in and through whole communities, flashing upon them as it were the words of Isaiah, "Arise, shine; for thy light is come, and the glory of Jehovah is risen upon thee. . . . Thou shalt see and be radiant, and thy heart shall thrill and be enlarged" (60:1, 5). True

[15] Tr. Talcott Parsons (London: George Allen & Unwin, Ltd., 1930).

[16] New York: Harcourt, Brace & Co., 1926. Used by permission of the publisher. This quotation is taken from the 1937 ed. as published by The New American Library, Mentor Books, 1947-50, pp. 96-97.

civilization must be rooted in an uncompromising ethic. All other values are merely "added unto it."

While it is true, then, that the primary concern of Christianity is not for culture, its most immediate contribution to culture is in the realm of Christian character, which knows how to live for eternity in the midst of change.

How Christianity Breaks In upon Culture

To say that the landscape of reality should be viewed against a background of impermanence is to say that it is essentially "other-worldly," not that it is "utterly other." Christianity actually breaks in upon culture, even if this must be seen as the derived aspect of a primary concern, namely, the concern for the proclamation of the gospel. How then does Christianity break in upon culture?

The preceding section has already made it clear that the most immediate effect of the new transcendent constraint is to make the highest moral law articulate and to bring men into touch with "the supreme moral reality of the universe." [17] Thus Christianity's first point of contact with culture is the conscience of mortal man. As Matthew Arnold puts it, it *is* so! Try, and you will find it to be so! What a strange thing, then, to believe that Christianity has no concern for the secular order, while the actual truth is that it provides the *sine qua non* clue to all essential cultural values and activities! Reinhold Niebuhr brings out this basic truth with remarkable incisiveness:

The prophetic movement in Hebraic religion offers an interesting confirmation of the thesis that a genuine faith in transcendence is the power which lifts religion above its culture and emancipates it from sharing the fate of dying cultures. The prophets saved Hebraic religion from extinction when the Babylonian exile ended the Hebraic culture-religion with its center in the worship of the Temple. They not only saved the life of religion, but raised it to a new purity by their interpretation of the meaning of catastrophe, the redemptive power of vicarious suffering, and the possibility of a redemption which would include more than the

[17] L. H. Marshall, *The Challenge of New Testament Ethics* (New York: The Macmillan Co., 1947), p. 352.

74

fortunes of Israel. In somewhat the same fashion Augustine's faith dissociated Christianity from a dying world.[18]

Another merit of the preceding clarification is this. It reminds us that Christianity's impact upon culture cannot be adequately assessed unless it is viewed within the prophetic tradition, better still, within the perspective of the historical continuity of the Israel of God. It is a matter of record that only when Augustine himself reached an understanding of the Trinity did he come to a true assessment of the values involved in personality and culture. In his already considered study, *Christianity and Classical Culture*, Cochrane makes this point clearly. It was in the light of his new insights into the Trinity that Augustine revolted, not from nature, but from the pagan, naturalistic picture of a cosmology and an anthropology determined by their own exclusive laws. Only then was he enabled to "dissipate the nightmare." Only then was he in the position of helping to hasten the collapse of classical ideology, thus making room for the advent of what he called "Our Philosophy," that is, the Christian world view of the City of God. Yet, Cochrane insists, this transformation was brought about only after Augustine had "acknowledged as authoritative the formulation of Christian principles made at Nicaea." [19] The reason for this is easily seen. What came to formulation at Nicaea involved the *whole* revealed truth undergirding the Christian landscape of reality.

Let therefore the Christian landscape of reality be kept whole, and let us by the same token be protected from evil. Let us pause here, for there is a notion in the air about us that the glorious simplicity of the gospel implies that one need not spend much time in understanding one's religion. Besides, there are so many other demands placed upon our time! That the intelligence of things scientific is a complex matter that requires thorough preparation and sustained effort, everyone will readily grant. What an unbearable inconsistency, then, to take it for granted that the intelligence of the infinitely

[18] *An Interpretation of Christian Ethics* (New York: Harper & Bros., 1935), p. 30. Used by permission.
[19] Cochrane, *op. cit.*, p. 411.

higher realities, involved in the whole biblical outlook culminating in the Christ, may well become the subject of a barbaric over-simplification! As a result, for instance, one's spiritual life is at the mercy of any agnostic treatment which may claim any semblance of authority, the fluctuations of a secular knowledge of Jesus being a good case in point. Hence the scandal of a minister who seems to depend on the latest "scholarly" echo while proceeding with the preparation of his sermon. It would serve no useful purpose to say that a record of thousands of years should carry weight as he takes his place in the heavenly fellowship of the Israel of God.

Anyone who loses sight of the perennial context of the Christian landscape of reality loses sight of the landscape altogether. This is again true of the moderns who look at the landscape from the wrong end, as it were. In the manner of the oft-quoted old liberal Dr. H. A. L. Fisher in the opening pages of his *History of Europe,* they fail to discover in history any plot, rhythm, or pattern. These "harmonies" are concealed from them. Having been trained according to a man-made tradition to make themselves at home in a landscape in which the absence of God is taken for granted, they candidly declare that they cannot find any trace of God anywhere. Nothing looks more like a culture which has not yet found the God of Scripture than a culture which has lost him.

Once these corollaries are kept in mind, not only may the true landscape of reality come within sight, but as a result culture may be adequately viewed and interpreted. At this point the Christian historian corroborates the previously expressed awareness that the biblical notion of righteousness holds the clue to the fortunes of culture. A naïve belief in the natural goodness of man is not far from proving a very disastrous heresy,[20] for the Hebrew-Christian view of anthropology is also the key to a sound interpretation of history. Then, and only then, do the historical aspects of the landscape of reality unfold as a truly divine pattern where time is perceived as biblical time, that is, as meaningful duration. No one in our day has better suggested this historical aspect of the Christian

[20] Herbert Butterfield, *Christianity and History* (London: Bell, 1949), pp. 34-42.

landscape of reality than Oscar Cullman in *Christ and Time*.[21] Let not the title mislead the reader, for biblical Christianity is not confined to the Christ in this work, which may turn out to be an epoch-making treatment. The very fact that we designate time as B.C. and A.D. implies that time cannot be reduced to point C. What Cullman shows is that God the Creator called mankind into existence; then out of mankind he called a nation; out of that nation, a remnant; and finally out of that remnant the one representative man Christ Jesus. Thus, through representative substitution and calling, the Creator and Performer of redeeming acts directs the plot of history toward a triumphant climax.

This means that history is *oriented* as we have found the universe to be oriented. In other words, the time-space continuum we call the true landscape of reality is a meaningful pattern. And as was already suggested in the Preface, only he can guide us through the landscape who is the Lord of the hill and the Originator of the map.

This, Then, Is the Landscape

Our sovereign God, the Creator and Upholder of the universe, is at the roaring loom of events and reveals himself in his creation, in the very texture of history, and in the human soul. There is, therefore, a Christian view of nature and of human nature; there is a Christian outlook on history, including our own life history; there is a Christian approach to psychology and human relations; there is a Christian epistemology preparing the way for constructive Christian metaphysics.

Such views appeal to the scientist as a person, if the views are carefully defined. The scientist may pause even in his scientific capacity as his Christian friend proceeds to suggest deeper interpretations of available uncolored data, in such fields as history, psychology, and ethics, or as he submits further propositions on points where science has nothing to say because it never pauses to consider the deeper "why" issue—for instance, that ours is a *created* universe.

[21] Tr. F. V. Filson (Philadelphia: The Westminster Press, 1950).

Thus we would render unto Caesar the things that are Caesar's only to secure a firmer hold on the things that are God's.

While theology attempts to clarify the process according to which the light is being presented to the world, Christian philosophy should remain in the world without being of it, so as to prepare the path of the world toward the light. This movement to Zion is one of the great themes of Bible teaching from Isaiah to Bunyan. The author of *The Pilgrim's Progress* may actually be said to have summed up Christian philosophy in the briefest and yet most pungent form with Christian's oft repeated statement, "I am a man that am come from the City of Destruction, and I am going to Mount Zion."

The frame of the City may rise higher than the clouds, yet it is often hidden from view by partial—that is, false—perspectives arising from the experience of mortal man, especially from his failure to acknowledge the great Doer of redeeming things, and consequently to heed the divine Agency at work in this God-created, God-controlled-and-upheld universe of ours.

It is the part of the Christian philosopher to help restore the true perspective as he has been given eyes to see it. In doing this he will prepare a path for the theologian. At the same time he will be formulating and applying a good neighbor policy with the catholicity of science, through which the thinking of the world of men and affairs is mostly being framed nowadays. We need, therefore, no longer lend a semblance of truth to Whitehead's contention that any step forward on the part of science *ipso facto* brings about a panic on the part of the Church.

In many instances the Church and the lay world are no longer on speaking terms. A meeting ground must be prepared for them from which both perspectives, the God-centered as well as the man-centered, may be seen in their true implications. Thus the old invitation, "Choose you this day" (Josh. 24:15), will take on a new meaning for our contemporaries of good will.

Let us therefore emerge from the vanity of artifact, of pseudo-theories, and mere dialectical feats. Let our language recover, with a power pertaining to the reality of the things that *are*, a clarity of expression arising from the awareness of a well-assessed and scripturally thought-out integration of data.

Precisely because we look for a city beyond this wilderness, let us cast our lot with this matter-of-fact world temporarily assigned to our care, yet without being of it, learning its most perfect techniques while availing ourselves of the best information yielded by them. Let us boldly come out for a truly Christian approach to culture.

PART TWO

The Religious Relationship of Ancient Man with Reality

CHAPTER SIX

The DIM LIGHT of ANCIENT DAYS

JUST as there was an age when a diffuse sunlight contending with thick watery clouds kept alive with the promise of a coming dawn upon the primitive chaos, so a shadowy brightness cheers the student of early cultural patterns as he gropes his way through the dimness of ancient days.

To whatever excesses mankind may have attained in various ways of self-assertion, there is on every side evidence of a primitive revelation in the light of general revelation. Although collective notions are not found everywhere with equal clearness, their universality brings their massive testimony to the point of unanimity, whether it is found in the study of fossil men, archeology, cultural anthropology, history, or psychology.

What this means is that a candid study of the human situation even at the dawn of prehistory confirms the fact of a direct presence of God in the soul of man. This fact was particularly well brought out by the late Professor Cook Wilson to an Oxford society in the year 1897, in a paper which Professor John Baillie, in common with many other distinguished students of the religious life, considers one of the most important theological documents of our time. The conclusion of this document is that the fact that some people think they have no experience or knowledge of God is quite compatible with the notion of his direct presence in their consciousness. Or, as I once heard John Baillie put it, all men have some knowledge of God

83

and do in some sense believe at the bottom of their heart. What actually happens, sophistication helping, is that many a modern is prompted to deny this same belief with the top of his mind. This conclusion is my own, and I trust that any unprejudiced study of the record will lead men of good will to the same admission. Let this, then, be our clue and directing principle as we move into the world of culture. Let us have the constant awareness that the scholar's longing for truth, the artist's quest for beauty, the plain man's craving for justice, nay, the magico-religious practices of ancient man, must be considered in this context first of all if they are to be appraised truly.

Inseparable from this same context of general revelation there is also detected, on the other hand, a moral and spiritual plight which gives the lie to any man-made scheme of ideology. This remains true throughout the ages. It constitutes some of the earliest available data as soon as the knowledge of primitive man begins to make sense. However limited the technological equipment of our distant ancestors, their high degree of intelligence would seem to have given them access to far more power than their will was able to control. In this sense at least the Bible remains the best guide to understanding even the study of fossil men.

Disproportion of Man

A strange disproportion is sensed between the type of existence our distant ancestors led for hundreds upon hundreds of thousands of years and what seems to have been an intellectual endowment comparable to a great extent to ours. This is increasingly confirmed as the brain capacity of fossil men is interpreted in the light of all we learn about their life.

Man's earliest known features are made manifest through scanty bits of evidence, such as unmistakably human teeth in the Java or the Heidelberg jaws, and partly dislocated fragments of skulls such as were found among the rare remains of the Java or Pekin men.

What is of particular interest to us is the relatively large size of the brain housed in craniums whose age approaches the half million mark. The mysterious Piltdown woman who probably lived during the second interglacial period, maybe more than 350,000 years ago, has rightly been nicknamed by anthropologists "she of the big brain" —a brain as large as ours. As for the Neanderthals who were living in Europe between 100,000 and 50,000 years ago, and are known through an exceptionally large number of perfect specimens, they may well humble our pride. Their brain capacity was even larger than ours on the average. Few of us could match the 1,625 cubic centimeters of the middle-aged man at La Chapelle.

And yet during those hundreds upon hundreds of thousands of years the activity of this richly endowed man was monopolized by a quest for food. Bands of men would shift camp in pursuit of game, one band fiercely contending with the others. Their technological equipment remained rudimentary, crude choppers constituting its mainstay. The early Neanderthals must have "created a sensation" with their invention of a new way of chipping a stone tool. It was only toward the end of the Old Stone Age that points, scrapers, and knives materialized, reaching a high degree of perfection in the Neolithic Age some 10,000 or 15,000 years ago. Progress was then stepped up with the invention of the bow and arrow and the domestication by Azilian hunters of dogs for the detection and pursuit of game. All this put together looks to us a rather meager cultural result for hundreds of thousands of years of activity on the part of men endowed with an intellectual equipment very much like our own.

How, then, are we to explain this first aspect of a disproportion which admittedly calls for a much more thorough analysis? The immediate answer is not far to seek on the part of most of us who, incidentally, never invented anything and should therefore be modest as we approach the problem. Although those of our distant ancestors who can be traced with any certainty were probably as intelligent as we are, one of their main troubles was that they lacked the most elementary "labor-saving devices." And so it is that they could not devise anything like our "accelerated programs." Not only did they lack the most elementary security—and this in itself is very important—but they had nothing to start with, and there was nobody from whom they could learn anything. This is why no Robinson

Crusoe analogy can ever do justice to our understanding of their plight. This is why, on the other hand, any progress in technology is seen to materialize at an increasing rate, one progress not only making another possible but providing a short cut to it, as it were. Hence the famous analogy of the dwarf on the shoulders of the giant, the giant incarnating the achievements of ages past. "We are like dwarfs, sitting on the shoulders of giants, in order that we may see things more numerous and more distant than they could see, not, certainly, by reason of the sharpness of our own vision or the tallness of our bodies, but because we are lifted and raised on high by the greatness of the giants." [1] Or, in the words of Pascal, "All men together make continual progress as the universe ages, because the same thing happens in the succession of men that happens in the different stages of an individual. Thus in the course of so many centuries the whole succession of men must be regarded like a single individual who lives on and who is constantly learning." [2]

This accelerating rate in progress is witnessed when we contrast the dawn of history with the enormous span of time just surveyed. Immigrants from the Near East having brought the knowledge of agriculture to continental Europe, farming became a means of plenty. The permanent type of housing involved in this pastoral life also seems nowadays to have had its archetype in the Near East. The lake dwellers who raised cattle and crops in Switzerland about six thousand years ago may have been distant disciples of those dwellers whose site was recently discovered in northern Iraq. Permanent and safe housing in its turn ushered in an era of relative prosperity

[1] I owe this quotation to Professor Bruce Metzger's *Guide to the Preparation of a Thesis* (Princeton Pamphlets No. 4: Princeton Theological Seminary, 1950), p. 2. Dr. Metzger traces back the nucleus of this saying to the twelfth-century philosopher Bernard of Chartres. It reappears in various forms during succeeding centuries, being used in favor of both sides of the so-called "Battle of the Books" or "Quarrel of the Ancients and Moderns." Cf. F. E. Guyer, "The Dwarf on the Giant's Shoulders," *Modern Lauguage Notes*, XLV (1930), 398-402, and Gilbert Highet's chapter on "The Battle of the Books" in his monumental volume, *The Classical Tradition; Greek and Roman Influences on Western Literature* (Oxford: Clarendon Press, 1949), esp. p. 267.

[2] Emile Cailliet and J. C. Blankenagle, *Great Shorter Works of Pascal* (Philadelphia: The Westminster Press, 1948), "Fragment of a Preface to the Treatise on the Vacuum," p. 54.

and leisure favorable to the development of art and crafts. Henceforth culture progressed by leaps and bounds. Economic, social, and political life marked the beginnings of history proper, extending from today as far back as about four thousand years. The first civilizations were found widely scattered along the banks of rivers—Egypt beside the Nile, Mesopotamia between the Tigris and the Euphrates, India along the Indus and the Ganges, and China from the region of the Wei and Hwang Ho. Then crafts were truly flourishing; commerce expanded. Alphabets and calendars appeared, art and literature developed, and religion and magic inspired early forms of theosophy and philosophy, as the next chapter will show. Striking achievements in every realm of endeavor bear witness that civilization was well on its way.

The first conclusion, then, is that an elementary technology had to be devised before the progress of culture could become accelerated. Further, that insecurity and an utter lack of rudiments to start with, and subsequently of stored up knowledge to learn from, were at least partly responsible for a near stagnation extending over more than half a million years. In other words, there is here no evidence of darkness clouding the mind. Rather, there is from time immemorial evidence of an intellect comparable to ours, at the service of rational beings hunted as well as hunting on the insecure surface of the earth.

The disproportion sensed in our distant ancestors, then, cannot be traced primarily to their intellect. Quite the other way, the problem is raised by the very power of the intellect with which their rational nature was endowed. This appears increasingly to be the case, as we gain further insights into the experience of primitive man.

An Awe-inspiring View of Sensed Disproportion

A new awe-inspiring aspect of the problem comes within view as we witness during the Old Stone Age the Aurignatian hunter of some 45,000 years ago produce an amazing display of mural "paintings" whose perfection could be envied by our contemporary artists—

and this is hardly an overstatement for those who have been in a position to compare. The cycle under consideration would seem to begin with the hunter artist blowing powdered red ocher around the outstretched fingers of his left hand, thereby making an outline on the wall. A strong "participation" is suggested both in the hand that grasps and in the red color, that of blood. Outlines of the hunted animal appear here and there in the midst of the outstretched hands. Further artistic progress is noted with the increasing precision of the design, the accentuation of forms, and finally the polychrome quality which makes of the painting a masterpiece of magico-religious art. Such are, for instance, the bison and the reindeer of the Font-de-Gaume cave, so beautifully restored in the water colors of abbé Breuil.[3] Granting that the artistic means to an end became eventually an end in itself, the best interpretations suggested by comparative ethnology are unmistakable in most of these cases. *The painting is inseparable from the hunting.* Because the animal is there within reach represented in undertones of a bloodlike color, it is doomed. The rhinoceros of Marsoulas is not only stylized in sharp, red strokes, but strangely dotted all over its body with reddish black spots that leave no doubt as to "its" fate. The same interpretation holds for the Solutrean sculptures. The "hunter artists" who invaded Europe from Asia some 30,000 years ago had a most remarkable flint-flaking technique which they similarly used to make sure of the success of their hunting expeditions. In the Solutrean period the climate was cold. Horse and reindeer were the chief sources of food supply. And so the game was carved on limestone blocks[4] and thereby also doomed.

Among our contemporary primitives we find similar magico-religious practices involved in the daily occupations of the natives, more especially fishing and hunting. The fact that those operations

[3] See colored plates A and B in Georges Goury, *Origine et Evolution de l'Homme* (Paris: Picard, 1927), pp. 304-5.

[4] The reader who has the opportunity may want to see splendid restorations of this and similar Stone Age scenes in Hall C, Chicago Natural History Museum (formerly Field Museum of Natural History).

remain "mystic," [5] and that they are performed in nondifferentiated groups, itself implies a life bathed in a magico-religious atmosphere. We see an occasional chief officiate, the suggestion being that chiefs have been among the first magicians, and vice versa. In British New Guinea the preparation for catching the dugong begins with the designation of a chief, who thenceforth becomes *belaga* (sacred). But among the Ten'a (Denes) of the river Yukon it is a medicine man who, at the time when the fishing is to begin, is thought to go under the ice to the country where the salmon in great schools spend the winter—his purpose being to make sure of their favor. In Malaysia every boat which took to the sea had been carefully "medicined." Use has been made of many incantations and magic practices. After every catch the boat was swept with a tuft of leaves by a medicine man. The leaves had been made ready amid "mystic" ritual and placed on the prow. For hunting, then, as for fishing there is a *prefiguration* to insure the success of the operation. Among the Sioux one of the principal medicine men, covered with a whole bearskin, participated in the dance known as the bear dance. This took place on several successive days before setting out for the hunt. After the killing, normal relations again had to be established be-

[5] I use this term throughout this ethnological section according to the characterization of the "primitive" mentality by L. Lévy-Bruhl as ["prelogical" and] "mystic" in his epoch-making series on the subject. The following translations are available (the first three volumes at Allen & Unwin, London; the fourth one at Dutton, New York). The dates given are the original dates of publication in Paris: *How Natives Think* [abbr. *Fonct. Ment.*] (1910); *Primitive Mentality* [abbr. *Ment. Prim.*] (1922); *The Soul of the Primitive* [abbr. *Ame Prim.*] (1927); *Primitives and the Supernatural* [abbr. *Surn. et Nat.*] (1933).

To the above should be added the following: *La Mythologie primitive* [abbr. *Myth. Prim.*], Paris, 1935; *L'expérience mystique et les Symboles chez les Primitifs*, Paris, 1938. Attention should also be drawn to the Herbert Spencer Lecture delivered at Oxford, May 29, 1931, and published by the Clarendon Press under the title *La Mentalité primitive* (Oxford, 1931) in which the author explained his critique of the English school of ethnology (not to be confused with the book under the same title); also to the volume of selections chosen and arranged by Lévy-Bruhl himself under the title *Morceaux choisis*, Paris, 1936. The following references are to the original text according to abbr. indicated above.

On the actual data underlying the "mystic" experience of contemporary primitives, cf. *Fonct. Ment.*, pp. 58, 67, 74, 80, 271, 342, 344, 345, 350, 360, 367, 447-48; *Ment. Prim.*, pp. 93, 147-48, 183, 204, 221, 358-59, 421; *Ame Prim.*, pp. 54, 67, 69, 70; *Surn. et Nat.*, pp. 138, 149; *Myth. Prim.*, pp. xiv, xviii, 12, 54, 93, 108, 151, 199, 217, 222-23, etc.

89

tween the social group to which the hunter belonged and that of the slain animal. In equatorial Africa before the *manga* (a kind of lamantin) was cut to pieces, the magician performed certain rites, doubtless destined to nullify shed blood and ward off the vengeance of those animals belonging to the same species as the victim. In other words, *totemism* may be said to hold a large part of the secret of the hunting and fishing practices of primitive man.

I do not mean to equate our distant ancestors and our contemporary so-called primitives. L. Lévy-Bruhl, who was accused by representatives of the English School of Ethnology of having suggested an identification, pleaded not guilty in his 1931 Herbert Spencer Lecture delivered at Oxford. He freely admitted that to him also the term "primitive" remains an unhappy term, one which almost inevitably leads to confusion. It seems to imply that men so designated are still very close, or at least much closer than we are, to the original condition of human societies; that as such they represent what our most distant ancestors must have been. This is a view suggested by evolutionism, but one which we should be most embarrassed to confirm by actual facts. If, therefore, I persist in speaking of "primitives," it must be understood that I do so merely in a conventional way. I use the term, as the term "savages" was used formerly, to refer to men who are not more "primitive" than we are, but who belong to societies said to be "inferior" or "hardly civilized." [6]

I am satisfied in this part of the treatment to adopt the practical, noncommittal view underlying the comparative method now currently used in the interpretation of available data on physical anthropology, the study of fossil men, archeology, or prehistory, scientific linguistics, and cultural anthropology. Let us keep this in mind as we continue our consideration of the disproportion sensed in our most distant ancestors.

We have already come to the conclusion that there is no "darkened mind" involved in the matter, but rather a soul at grips with collective notions where magic seems strangely mixed with religion.

[6] See the Herbert Spencer Lecture, *op. cit.*, pp. 6-7.

We are confronted by a big-brained man, a hunter and an artist, who seeks most inaccessible recesses of a series of caves to paint or carve magico-religious prefigurations of his hunting. As one visits those remote recesses, half-den, half-sanctuary, he has the impression of somehow touching the naked souls of those men with his own naked soul.

What is of further special interest to us here is that a religious life may be directly inferred from available data. The middle-aged man of La Chapelle-aux-Saints especially, who has been particularly well studied, not only had an exceptionally large brain capacity, but was religiously cared for after his death. His grave had been specially dug. His head was surrounded by a protecting casing of stones. In similar cases the head is literally found to rest on a "pillow" of stones. Bodies are sometimes found buried in a special position (the "fetal attitude," as it is called). Bones may be anointed with red, indicating participation in the blood, that is, in life. Fragments of animal bones suggest food offerings and, maybe, sacrifices. An occasional stone ax completes the viatic for the journey beyond. The over-all picture, once more, is one of magico-religious collective notions.

Evolutionism in Cultural Anthropology

The Neanderthal-homo sapiens period is one during which early cultural groups are dominated by collective notions where magic is found to fuse and amalgamate with religion. Does this mean, then, that as Sir James G. Frazer affirms, an Age of Magic has everywhere preceded an Age of Religion,[7] and that this should be considered as a starting point in an evolutionary conception of culture? A Christian approach to culture must squarely face the situation created by this and similar evolutionary views, and first give a candid hearing to them. The further reason for doing this is that not only magic but religion itself will in the long run be similarly considered as a sort of vestigial concept in the mature mind. This view is in fact

[7] *The Golden Bough: A Study in Magic and Religion* (3rd ed.; London: Macmillan & Co., 1911), I, 237.

that formulated in a law in Comte's *Positive Philosophy* (1830-42). The first chapter of this monumental work states that "each of our leading conceptions—each branch of our knowledge—passes successively through different theoretical conditions: the Theological, or fictitious; the Metaphysical, or abstract; and the Scientific, or positive. In other words, the human mind . . . employs in its progress three methods of philosophizing": the theological method, which "supposes all phenomena to be produced by the immediate action of supernatural beings"; the metaphysical method, "which is only a modification of the first," and refers phenomena to abstract entities inherent in the activities of nature; finally, the positive method, according to which phenomena are merely considered in their law abiding relations of succession and resemblance. This view, an offshoot of the Enlightenment idcology of Progress, was in the long run combined with evolutionary views and became the approach of Evolution-Progress. As such it dominated the thinking of the late nineteenth and early twentieth centuries. William James took cognizance of the import of this theory in the conclusions of his 1901-2 Gifford Lectures on natural religion. "There is a notion in the air about us that religion is probably only an anachronism, a case of 'survival,' an atavistic relapse into a mode of thought which humanity in its most enlightened examples has outgrown; *and this notion our religious anthropologists at present do little to counteract.*" [8] Heeding this final, gentle hint, then, we should realize the importance of the issue at stake and face at this initial point the consideration of its relevance.

Frazer's view of the priority of magic proceeded upon the animistic theory defined by Sir Edward Tylor in his *Primitive Culture*. Tylor defined religion as the belief in spiritual beings, primitive religion consisting in man's efforts to establish a working relationship with these spirits of his animistic world and to obtain benefits from them. To Tylor, a spirit is "a thin unsubstantial human image, in its nature a sort of vapour, film, or shadow." [9] In 1909 an earnest student of

[8] *The Varieties of Religious Experience*, p. 480 (Modern Library ed.) Italics mine.
[9] London: John Murray, 1871. I, 429.

primitive religion, Robert Marett, went behind Tylor's animism to detect what he called a "preanimism" proceeding from a compound of awe, fear, and wonder, aroused by the supernatural. "I am ready to assert that before animism, regarded as an ideal system of religious beliefs, can have come into its kingdom, there must have been numberless dimly lighted impressions of the awful that owned no master in the shape of some one systematizing thought." [10] Rudolf Otto later expressed with great force the reality here hinted at. To him religion was among primitive people, and has remained among mankind generally, the consciousness of a *mysterium tremendum*, "the emotion of a creature, abashed and overwhelmed by its own nothingness in contrast to that which is supreme." [11]

The new element introduced at this point is a reference to "that which is supreme." I need not insist that until this reference is made there is hardly anything religious involved in the crude experience of animism or preanimism. The same can be said of the strange and mysterious experience of the power called *mana*, so ably studied by Codrington in the Malay Islands.[12] This term *mana* is simultaneously noun, adjective, and verb; it applies to attributes, actions, natures, and things. It is the strength of the arm, the quickness of the eye, the readiness of resource; generally speaking it is the reservoir of energy which makes for the efficacy of things as well as of beings. Thanks to *mana* the sailing boat proceeds faster, the weapon is more effective, the medicine more potent. This notion of *mana* is by no means peculiar to the Melanesian mind. It proves to be truly basic in the collective notions of "primitive" societies. It has been rightly identified with that of *Nkissie*, or *Moquissie* as it used to be called, among the Bantus, who constitute the largest of the African groups; again, it is identified with the *Dzo* of the Ewhe. The obvious fact is that the notion involved constitutes the adequate transcription of whatever reality was previously considered under the appellation of

[10] *The Threshold of Religion* (London: Methuen, 1909), p. x.

[11] *The Idea of the Holy*, tr. J. W. Harvey (New York: Oxford University Press, 1928), p. 10.

[12] R. H. Codrington, *The Melanesians, Studies in Their Anthropology and Folk-Lore* (Oxford: Clarendon Press, 1891).

fetishism, as far as the African continent is concerned. In America the same notion reappears in the *orenda* of the Iroquois, the *manitou* of the Algonquin, the *wakan* of the Sioux, the *naual* of central Mexico, as well as the *xube* of the Pueblo. There is further good reason to believe that the Vedic *Brahman* also is not without relation with the *mana* notion. What all these considerations mean is that in them we are confronted by realities which may at best constitute the raw material of religion, without the quality of being religious per se. In all of them we are dealing with an immanent power or efficacy constituting the *virtue* in which beings and things may participate. In other words, we are dealing not with religion, but with magic, magic proceeding essentially from a great dream of power.

It is at this juncture that Frazer's postulation of an Age of Magic having preceded an Age of Religion takes on full force. Although admitting that magic is found "to fuse and amalgamate with religion in many ages and in many lands," [13] he makes a clear-cut distinction between the humble man of God on his knees and the proud, ambitious, self-assertive magician craving for a control of available power. "Religion as a conciliation of the superhuman powers . . . implies that the being conciliated is a conscious or personal agent, that his conduct is in some measure uncertain, and that he can be prevailed on to vary it . . . by a judicious appeal to his interests, his appetites, or his emotions." [14] The self-confident magician, on the other hand, "does not doubt that the same causes will always produce the same effects, that the performance of the proper ceremony, accompanied by the appropriate spell, will inevitably be attended by the desired results, unless, indeed, his incantations should chance to be thwarted and foiled by the more potent charms of another sorcerer." [15] One of the implications of the magician's attitude, according to the magnificent characterization of Hubert and Mauss,[16] is that magic rites do not present themselves under the

[13] Frazer, *op. cit.*, p. 233.
[14] *Ibid.*, p. 224.
[15] *Ibid.*, p. 220.
[16] *Esquisse d'une Théorie Générale de la Magie*, Vol. VII *of Année Sociologique*.

aspect of an organized cult, susceptible as such of official recognition by society, of a kind of legalization by the group. Thus the essential character of magic would dwell in this aspect as a thing apart, secret, forbidden. The activity of the magician is bent upon an occult control of the efficacy identified as a kind of *mana,* of that "force par excellence," that "true efficacy of things which corroborated their mechanical action without annihilating it." [17]

Hence there is a still sharper contrast between religion and magic, inasmuch as religion proves inseparable from a resulting community, uniting its adherents. Durkheim notes in this connection "the marked repugnance of religion for magic, and on the other hand the hostility of magic towards religion." [18] He further points out the wicked pleasure that the magician takes in profaning sacred things and in using in his rites the counterpart of religious ceremonies. He proceeds to bring out the disfavor with which religious authorities have always regarded all magic rites, even when they did not go so far as to condemn or to prohibit them.[19] It appears to Durkheim that religion is essentially a group matter. It forms and expresses the unity of the collectivity, even in its individual forms of worship. Whence the following comprehensive definition: "Religion is a solidary system of beliefs and practices having to do with sacred things, i.e., things apart, forbidden—beliefs and practices which unite its adherents in one and the same moral community, called a church." [20] But, in Durkheim's view, magic possesses nothing of the sort. Such are not even its gatherings of the initiated, which in fact remain exceptional. They never present the characteristic of a moral community where priests and believers are associated in the same worship. "There is no such thing as a church of magic." [21]

---

[17] *Ibid.,* p. iii.

[18] *The Elementary Forms of the Religious Life,* tr. J. W. Swain (London: George Allen and Unwin, Ltd.; New York: The Macmillan Co., 1915), ch. 1, sec. 4.

My quotations are directly made and translated from the revised edition of the original French: *Les Formes Elémentaires de la Vie Religieuse* (2nd rev. ed.; Paris: Alcan, 1925).

[19] *Ibid.*

[20] *Ibid.*

[21] *Ibid.*

There are good reasons, then, for drawing a dividing line between religion and magic, and even for postulating a process according to which the magician will be progressively outlawed. Yet we want to look closer into this matter. The word "magic" has been used thus far in two distinct acceptations. There is a broad acceptation according to which the magician appears in many ways as the ancestor of the man of science. And there is, on the other hand, an acceptation according to which the magician becomes an occult power bent upon evil things—in other words, becomes a sorcerer.

Inasmuch and in so far, however, as any question of priority is concerned, even Frazer himself is forced to admit that magic and religious notions and practices are actually found together. So much so that once their undifferentiated manifestations are arbitrarily set asunder, excellent scholars find themselves building up a case of priority which amounts to a sheer reversal of Frazer's views. While Frazer holds that magic preceded religion, men like Andrew Lang[22] and Jevons, who follow his powerful argument, insist that religion as belief in the supernatural was prior to magic, magic appearing as a degenerate form of religion. Neither should we take the argument of this view to assert the priority of religion, for magic once more tends to be identified with sorcery, with black magic.

The record of actual facts has only one basic testimony to deliver, and it is this. All available data concerning primitive cultures refer to undifferentiated collective notions where religion and magic are hopelessly tangled up. No case of priority has ever succeeded in reaching anything approaching a consensus of opinion on the part of the science of man.

The preceding critique has further drawn attention to one aspect of the differentiation which comes to light here and there, as magic turns into evil-doing. The word "degenerate" has been used, pointing to a possible tendency to deterioriation involved in the magician's self-assertive attitude. A special reason for my attention being drawn in that direction, moreover, is that *the note is a familiar one even in our day.*

[22] *Magic and Religion* (London and New York: Longmans, Green, & Co., 1901).

Uneasiness in the Making

Whether secured through religious or magical practices, power can be thought of in only two ways: power to help, which is also power to harm. And whether we call it by name or use some sort of euphemism, witchcraft is as universal as religion and magic, the reason being plainly written in the human will.

From time immemorial certain seekers in the realm of mystery have repudiated any wish whatever to harm their neighbors, while others have deliberately aimed at harmful acts. Neither are we left to our own speculation as to the location of the stumbling block. In an article by the late orientalist G. Julien,[23] whose firsthand documentation was of unique value, precious statements are made as to the behavior of the Malagasy *ùmbiasa.* These *ùmbiasa* might well be regarded as the missing link by those who seek after a starting point in the separation between black magic and white magic. The *ùmbiasa* in question were first found to make charms and practice magic for defensive purposes. In this respect their acts have a priestlike character. "He who fulfills this function is honored and respected. He has a moral ascendancy in the tribe quite superior to that of the greatest political chiefs. The *ùmpanzaka*[24] always have one of these magicians by their side as confidential adviser." In answer to a personal inquiry Julien was kind enough to add the following elucidation:

The *ùmbiasa* of the little kings of the East and of the Southwest were merely official magicians. . . . There is no doubt that in the past, the magician was always a public official. This is clearly shown by what is said in the *Tantaran'ny Andriana* of Callet, in regard to the *mamono voalavo.* The custom in question consisted in punishing, by putting them out of the way, magicians who had been guilty of errors in their predictions, or who were under suspicion of having caused public calamities, epidemics, epizootics, cyclones, floods, locusts, etc.

The same letter mentions the quite typical case of such a magician whose right hand was cut off because he had erred in promising to the

[23] "Notes et Observations sur les tribus sud-occidentales de Madagascar" in *Revue Française d'Ethnographie et des Traditions Populaires* (1927).

[24] Literally, "one who rules."

king a return of good weather. Reverting to the special case of the *ùmbiasa*, henceforth characterized as magician-public-servants, we then witness the baleful deviation. The magician, doubtless to satisfy his clientèle, *falls out of his role of protector; he passes from defensive to offensive measures.* Julien writes further:

> Cupidity transforms many of them into vulgar casters of spells. It is at night, in such cases, that they give themselves over to practices which are no less mysterious than universally feared. Stark naked they prowl about, and coming near the place where the one to be bewitched is asleep, they execute an infernal dance, in imitation of what the natives call with terror "the sobbing of those who have gone." . . . With a thorn smeared with spell casting material, a spell may be cast upon anyone eating food offered by the hand in which the thorn is hidden. Thus—so claim the natives—numerous deaths and cruel diseases strike humanity without it being possible to cherish more than suspicion against their authors.

In a letter to Professor R. Allier, the author of *The Mind of the Savage,* Mr. Burnier, a good observer, explained to the same effect that a native whose field yields little, whereas that of his neighbor is more productive, hesitates between two alternatives. "He is under the urge of two feelings; the one springs from jealousy toward him who is more favored than he is, and the other from the desire of winning a like advantage. So he will try to procure one of the following medicines, or perhaps both at once: the first to make his own land prosper, the other to be hidden in his neighbor's field to bring about its ruin." He turns therefore to the maker of charms, not only for protection, but also with the thought of injuring. And here is a most important remark of Dean R. Allier, which is therefore italicized. *"Magic is beginning to be no longer an instrument of protection, but a weapon of evil. The charm maker is on the downward path which will lead to what is essentially witchcraft."* [25] The same downward path is found when we pass from the *urge* toward the act to the *means* to be employed. If charred flesh is to be used in the

[25] *Le Non-Civilisé et Nous* (Paris: Payot, 1927), p. 114. This book is available in English under the title *The Mind of the Savage,* tr. F. Rothwell (London: Bell & Sons, 1929). My own quotations here are directly made and translated from the original French.

making of a certain powder, at first the magician will obtain the flesh from the dead body of an enemy. His next step, if necessary, will be to murder, since he must conquer a power destined to satisfy unbridled passions. And these are not idle *a priori* speculations. Instances abound of horrors inspired by the urge in question. Here we find a murder for the purpose of obtaining fat, flesh, or skin, taken from a *living* man or woman. There he must obtain the heart and the skull of a woman, and so forth. And all these abominations for the occult satisfaction of unrestrained self-assertion. The sorcerer is henceforth caught at his own game. He comes to take delight in the worst disorders and sufferings which he himself has brought about. "Rejoicing in iniquity is the sorcerer's state of mind," as Dean Allier forcibly remarks.[26]

I need hardly point out that it would take little adaptation to translate this language into medieval, modern, *and* contemporary speech. For this is the *thing* that crouches at the door when man doest not well, and unto him is its desire, in the language of the book of Genesis (4:7). Where did we hear these words before? They were spoken to Eve, and this bold metaphoric transfer suggests a horrible parody of conjugal relations between man and his sin. Incidentally, since the detail was previously omitted, there are also amulets and charred bones found in the graves of our distant ancestors. Besides, the magic hands which appear on the walls of primitive caves have been evoked more than once by those contemporary ethnologists who have been in a position to restore the most unbelievable horrors performed in connection with the initiation of sorcerers. The hand of the human victim of the candidate is put up to dry and will be used in connection with his future practices of sorcery.[27] As such it may be compared with the frightful "hand of glory" of Middle Ages fame. Neither should it be taken for granted that the bloody allusions of some of the magico-religious paintings or totemic practices, pointed out in an earlier page, were limited to

[26] *Ibid.*, p. 119.

[27] Cf. Allier, *op. cit.*, pp.121-23, for unbelievable circumstances of a sorcerer's initiation studied by one of the best ethnologists of our day.

the candid hunting activities of our distant ancestors. Finally, while such practices as the red anointing of bones found in primitive graves suggests the notion of sacrifice, there seems to be no doubt that the sacrifices involved must have been for a large part human sacrifices. All we know of the substitutional character of animal sacrifice points in that direction.[28]

New Insights into Primitive Stagnation

Why are there "primitives" today? While Ellsworth Huntington would answer this question with his climatic hypothesis of civilization,[29] Wilhelm Schmidt would blame a faulty social system. Alexander Leroy,[30] who lived for half a century in the most "backward" parts of Africa before contacts with white man were made, concludes that retrogression has taken place. He has come again and again across evidence of a golden age now lost, when religion was much purer. Moral depravation and religious corruption among primitives are definitely ascribed by this great observer and scholar to what he calls "the tyranny of magic." [31] Dean Allier goes further still. According to him it is to magic that must be ascribed the moral and spiritual disintegration so deplorable among the noncivilized. What is said not only to have prevented the progress, but actually to have caused the retrogression of so many human groups and even races, is the unstable equilibrium brought about in their inner life by the excesses which are encouraged by the practices of magic.[32] Such unstable equilibrium continuing through hundreds and thousands of years has had its retribution in the life of retarded peoples. "The longer the vicious habits continue, the more powerful do they become. They eliminate everything which feeds their flame. They are

[28] Cf. Art. III, ch. xlvii, of the Salic Law.

[29] *Civilization and Climate* (New Haven: Yale University Press, 1915). See esp. ch. xviii.

[30] *The Religion of the Primitives,* tr. Newton Thompson (New York: The Macmillan Co., 1922).

[31] *Ibid.,* ch. 6.

[32] The reader may want to follow this up by consulting the Latin appendices of H. A. Junod's work on the Ba-Ronga.

incarnated in social effects which react upon them, and which in turn render them imperishable. These constraints become a veritable slavery. No longer is it second nature, it becomes nature itself, a nature falsified in its essence, which falsifies everything." [33]

Thus, the new and powerful suggestion of first-rate observers and interpreters is that far from offering us a survival of the primitive, *the present day noncivilized offers only a picture of degradation, decrepitude, and senility*. Moreover, if we bring together the monographs of contemporary ethnology for the purpose of reconstituting hypothetically the "progress" made by humanity, grave doubts arise as to an "evolution-progess" of cultures. Allier himself is "less and less disposed to accept a sociological romance founded upon observations classified and organized according to a preconceived plan." [34] Such an attitude, far from standing alone, is tending to become general. The striking experience of such a scholar as William Halse Rivers (1864-1922) is most illuminating in this connection, as the reader of the preface he wrote to his great *History of Melanesian Society* (1914) will realize. There the founder of the Cambridge School of Experimental Psychology, who turned explorer and became an outstanding ethnologist, explains how records of facts finally constrained him to abandon evolutionism as a working hypothesis in cultural anthropology. Graebner in his *Weltbild*, Wilhelm Schmidt in his *Culture Historical Method*, and the world of ethnology at large today have given up the stage sequences suggested by individual evolutionists. Lewis H. Morgan, one of the leading American evolutionists, himself seems to have been mostly concerned with *classifying* types of societies. The Eighth International Congress of Psychology held in Groeningen in 1926 may be said to have buried the issue. [35]

Applied to the immeasurably long age of our distant ancestors,

[33] Allier, *op. cit.*, pp. 266-67. See ch. 3 on "Magic and Moral Disintegration."
[34] *Ibid.*, p. 276.
[35] I refer especially to the memoir of Mayer Gross, *Zur Frage der psychologischen Eigenart der sogenannten Naturvölker*. Its conclusion was that we must discard the evolutionary approach in cultural anthropology. There are "primitive" traits in the modern and vice versa.

this would seem to mean that a great deal of what is found to be true of our minute bit of history must mave been true in their case also. While stagnation must be ascribed in part to an utter lack of tools and learning, we cannot avoid the evidence of a moral and spiritual regression, climactic and social deficiencies helping, but more especially a disintegration of the soul through a will under the spell of magic practices.

This chapter has impressed upon us the realities involved in general revelation. It has further led us to conclude that the strange disproportion which we sensed in our distant ancestors as they moved through the dim light of ancient days must finally be ascribed to a disproportion between a normally high degree of intelligence and a will in bondage. It is true, then, that in spite of their technological shortcomings these mortal men *already* had access to far more power than they could safely control.

CHAPTER SEVEN

A PREFACE to WESTERN PHILOSOPHY

THE biblical outlook of the Israel of God constitutes the clue to the understanding of human experience. It provides the student of philosophy in particular with a principle of interpretation which may be characterized in the words of Lewis Mumford as the "magnetic field at the center which will continuously polarize each fragment that enters the field." [1] In the measure that this principle is adhered to, moreover, the observer is in a position to be tolerant in his appraisal and appreciation of all genuine insights, however off the mark these may prove to be in actual practice.

It is a fact, however, that man's natural tendency is to view the landscape of reality from his own vantage point, according to his own standards, because the "heavenly directness seems oversimple to clouded human sight." [2] This natural bent has been responsible for arbitrary points of departure and false perspectives on the part of many a historian of philosophy. Thus, for instance, some remain under the impression that what Edwin A. Burtt calls "right thinking" [3] needs to go back only to sixth-century B.C. Ionian naturalism for its archetype. The presupposition involved is that to think as if philosophical views were at all conditioned by higher realities is a

---

[1] "The Unified Approach to Knowledge and Life" in *The University and Future of America*, p. 122, quoted by Frank E. Gaebelein, *Christian Education in a Democracy* (New York: Oxford University Press, 1951), p. 145.

[2] *Loc. cit.*

[3] *Right Thinking, A Study of Its Principles and Methods* (New York: Harper & Bros., 1946).

sign of intellectual indigence. And yet such a naturalistic persuasion is a faith also, the faith of men who will place a "ceiling" above their thinking—a faith, however, which has all the probabilities against it, if we may judge from all the data it induces its devotees to eliminate.

Writing in this vein on the pre-Socratic quest Professor Herschel Baker, of Harvard University, points out:

> The Ionians refused to enter the tantalizing area of the supernatural. It remained for their great contemporary Pythagoras, on the other, Italic, side of the Greek world, to develop philosophically the converse spiritual attitude toward the universe. . . . While Ionia was somehow producing a race of tough-minded materialists, southern Italy and Sicily were somehow nourishing a wide variety of Orphics, cultists, and mystical Pythagoreans who feared and derogated matter as instinctively as the Ionians celebrated it.[4]

Any student anxious to remain intellectually respectable will readily draw his own conclusions, and *the resulting naturalistic bias may well unconsciously affect his own thinking forever after*. Henceforth he will not go to "the other side of the Greek world" to learn from "cultists."

Before the Sixth-Century Cosmologists

When we deal with what our secular language likes to call the "origins" of culture, great names naturally become rare and far between. Our knowledge is restricted, many works have been lost, and selectivity always increases with remoteness in time.

With special reference to Greece, for instance, going further back than a few sixth-century cosmologists, further back than Thespis of Athens (*ca*. 535 B.C.), father of the drama, or beyond such early lyrics as the Spartan monodic poets, or the elegiac and iambic Solon of Athens (*ca*. 640-559 B.C.), Tyrtaeus of Sparta (*ca*. 650 B.C.), and Archilochus of Paros (*ca*. 650 B.C.), we reach the distant solitudes dominated by Homer (*ca*. 900-800 B.C.). But then, far from being "primitive" in any way, Homer henceforth appears as "an expurgator,

[4] *The Dignity of Man, Studies in the Persistence of an Idea* (Cambridge, Mass.: Harvard University Press, 1947), pp. 5-6.

a kind of eighteenth-century rationalizer of ancient myth, holding up an upper-class ideal of urbane enlightenment." [5] In other words, the distant solitudes which he dominates suggest a landscape of collective notions similar to those which ethnology studies among contemporary "primitives."

The same notion is forced upon us in a still more suggestive manner when our attention is drawn to the highly intellectual character of the pre-Socratic philosophers, as contrasted with the popular preoccupations of the common people of their day. The speculations of the cosmologists in particular point to an advanced degree of civilization which may be traced to the cultures of Egypt and Babylon.

Yet we should be cautious at this juncture. Thales, the first cosmologist (640-546 B.C.), did not write anything and is known to us only through a tradition which goes back to Aristotle.[6] The Stagirite is the one who tells us that according to Thales the soul is endowed with the power of motion, that the magnet may be said to have a soul because it moves iron,[7] and that the earth rests on water, floating on it, as it were, like a piece of wood.[8] It is again Aristotle who tells us that the elemental substance according to Thales was water, the unlimited (*apeiron*) according to Anaximander[9] (*ca.* 610-546 B.C.), and air according to Anaximenes.[10] These and similar statements,[11] however, reveal at closer scrutiny that they actually constitute answers to questions which were those of Aristotle himself. Precisely because we must go to him for our information concerning early Greek philosophy we are most naturally inspired to read his preoccupations back into the pre-Socratics, particularly into the cosmologists.

[5] Bertrand Russell, *A History of Western Philosophy* (New York: Simon and Schuster, 1945), p. 10.

[6] *Metaphysics* I. 3 (928b. 20).

[7] *De Anima* I. 2 (405a. 19); I. 5 (411a. 7).

[8] *De Caelo* II. 13 (294a. 28).

[9] *Physics* I. 4 (187a. 12).

[10] *Ibid.* III. 4 (203b. 7).

[11] *Metaphysics* I. 3 (983b. 6-11; 984a. 2-7).

A careful reading of such scholarly accounts of early Greek philosophy as those of Burnet,[12] Gomperz,[13] Zeller,[14] and more especially Robin,[15] in the light of our rapidly increasing knowledge of the origins of mathematics, astronomy, and, above all, technology, will help us toward a more pertinent formulation of the problems which preoccupied Thales, Anaximander, and Anaximenes. It will then appear that these problems were those of men immediately concerned about navigation, meteorology, and particularly the explanation of the storms which break so suddenly upon maritime populations.

Beyond these pressing problems the Milesians may be found to have played their part in the scientific activities of their day, particularly those going on in Egypt and Mesopotamia.

A New Dimension Added to Our Knowledge

The last hundred years have added a new dimension to our knowledge of the ancient world. We have become aware of a whole series of cultures developing along the Eastern end of the Mediterranean between the Hittite region of the north and the borders of Egypt on the south. The Phoenicians should probably be singled out in order of importance in the development of Mediterranean civilization. James H. Breasted pointed out in this connection that "important elements of Egyptian and Babylonian civilisation formed a substantial factor in the culture and life of the prosperous harbour cities, the commercial centers of the Phoenician coast." [16]

Behind these cultures recent scholarship in the light of the discoveries newly made at Ur in Mesopotamia has been led to consider the Tigris-Euphrates river valley as the cradle of civilization. Shinar

[12] John Burnet, *Greek Philosophy* (London: Macmillan & Co., 1914).

[13] Theodor Gomperz, *Greek Thinkers, A History of Ancient Philosophy* (London: J. Murray, 1901-12), Vol. I tr. L. Magnus; Vols. II-IV tr. G. G. Berry.

[14] Edward Zeller, *Outlines of the History of Greek Philosophy*, tr. Sarah F. Alleyne & Evelyn Abbott (London: Longmans, Green, and Co., 1886).

[15] Léon Robin, *Greek Thought and the Origins of the Scientific Spirit* (New York: Alfred A. Knopf, 1928).

[16] *The Dawn of Conscience* (New York and London: Charles Scribner's Sons, 1933), p. 346.

was the early name of that plain. There is at this point a precious coincidence between the results of the free inquiry of secular scholarship and the testimony of the Bible. It will be readily remembered that this land of Shinar is indicated in the book of Genesis as the center of the whole earth when the human race was of one language and of one speech. And it was there that the sons of Noah dreamed of building a city and a tower which turned out to be called Babel "because the Lord did there confound the language of all the earth: and from thence did the Lord scatter them abroad upon the face of all the earth" (Gen. 11:9). This would seem to be quite an interesting coincidence to bring to the attention of students in our day.

The Semites who throve in the rich plain of Shinar were overwhelmed some time before 4000 B.C. by the Sumerians who migrated there from the hilly country to the northeast. By 3500 B.C. they had achieved a high level of civilization, leaving the neolithic stage far behind. Their divisions, however, led to their doom. Almost one thousand years later they were conquered by the Semitic Akkadians. After various fortunes the old Sumero-Akkadian power fell victim to the Semitic Amorites from Syria, after the turn of the third millenium (seventeenth century B.C.). The king of these Amorites was Hammurabi, whose role in Sumerian history is likened by Toynbee to that of Constantine in the history of the Roman empire.[17] The *Cambridge Ancient History* had previously called the period of his rule "the Golden Age of Hammurabi." [18] Even if the *Pax Sumerica*, which ended with the death of Hammurabi (*ca.* 1686 B.C.) "turns out, on inspection, to be a thin shell encasing a wide welter of anarchy," [19] the ruler's mighty works of peace would seem to have been rightly exalted. He ruled wisely and collected taxes with care. It is true that the 282 articles codified in the collection of laws that bear his name, that is, the Code of Hammurabi, betray moral standards which we

[17] *A Study of History,* p. 484.
[18] *Cambridge Ancient History,* I, 487-503.
[19] Toynbee, *op. cit.,* p. 550. (Yet I follow the chronology of the Khorsabad List now confirmed.)

consider unfair and even low in our day. Yet we should remember that they reveal a striking superiority when compared with the customs prevailing at the time. Above all they reveal a Sumerian heritage of higher quality still. While Hammurabi recognized seventeen gods and goddesses, the Sumerians of 3500 B.C. originally believed in only one god. So also when Hammurabi is represented, on the six-foot-high stele of black diorite found at Susa, as receiving in prayer from the sun god (Shamash) the laws of the kingdom, we need not wonder at the comparisons made with Moses receiving the Decalogue from Yahweh on Mount Sinai. The alleged Sumerian origin of the creation and flood stories is of the same order. Here again we move in the light of general revelation, in a light that failed.

In the Beginning God . . .

It was in the dim light of ancient days that the crude creation myths took shape, myths according to which the creator-god fought and overcame the monster of chaos, cut it into halves, and made heaven of the one half and earth of the other. This and similar myths were current among the Babylonians when the Jews were deported in 597 and 586 B.C. to live in exile among them. Inspired by the famous letter recorded in Jer. 29:4-28, the exiles rested their faith on Yahweh. Instead of being assimilated by their conquerors, they gathered together as a believing and worshiping community. Among them arose the prophet Ezekiel, who developed Jeremiah's teaching about the "new covenant." His epic thirty-seventh chapter on the spiritual rebirth of a nation likened to a valley full of scattered, whitening bones inspired a new faith in his exiled countrymen. It was left to the great anonymous Prophet of the Exile, conveniently referred to as the "Second Isaiah," to reach a climax in the exaltation of the glory and power of the Living God of Israel (cf. Isa. 52: 7-12). This was the God whom they had encountered once more in the events of their life history. He who is the righteous and merciful Lord of history is truly the One who speaks and it is done. In this purely religious context the prophetic interpretation of history implied the prophetic interpretation of the universe. It was then, ac-

108

cording to the best available evidence, that the crude account of the making of a clay model of man of the second chapter of Genesis yielded priority to the majestic opening of the first chapter as we now have it. Even as this opening chapter is, however, it is better read in such a new version as that of James Moffatt, if one is to realize its profound relevance to the thinking of our day. "When God began to form the universe, the world was void and vacant, darkness lay over the abyss; but the spirit of God was hovering over the waters, God said, 'Let there be light,' and there was light."

When this first chapter of Genesis thus restored to its context is then compared with the passages of the Second Isaiah where the heathen gods are ridiculed as no gods, the inadequacy of the Babylonian story comes within full view.[20] While the Babylonian story was polytheistic, the presentation of Gen. 1 shows only the one true God. The contrast drawn by the Second Isaiah, then, exposes the unreality of the heathen divinities incapable of originating anything. There is defiance in Isa. 41:22-24, and a terrible finality in the conclusion, "Behold, ye are of nothing, and your work of nought: and abomination is he that chooseth you." A new climax is reached in 44:9-20 with the highly sarcastic evocation of a man "making an image of a god, using the waste parts of the wood to make a fire and cook his dinner, and fashioning the rest into a god, to which he bows down in worship." [21]

The True Perspective Restored

And so we come in the fifth century B.C. to the end of a long tradition traced back over thousands of years to a point where, the narrative of Genesis-to-Joshua being recast and rewritten on the basis of earlier traditions, the magnificent biblical view of the universe and of history has come to full expression. The last steps of this formulation are well nigh contemporary with the age when the Ionian cosmologists were in the midst of their elementary specula-

[20] On this see A. G. Hebert, *The Bible from Within* (London, New York, Toronto: Oxford University Press, 1950), pp. 12-18. The present paragraph follows Hebert's interpretation.

[21] *Ibid.*, p. 14.

tions as to the primal stuff of which nature is made. Neither should we lose sight of the fact that what came to a climax with the Second Isaiah was a prophetic tradition which began with Amos, Hosea, Micah, and Isaiah in the eighth century B.C. This means that two centuries before the cosmologists, the high moral and social notions involved in a vision of righteousness, already pointed out in these pages, had also come to a beautiful formulation and expression—as truth to be done. In other words, here was the imposing biblical world view of the universe and of history, permeated through and through with a moral philosophy in line with the will of God. As such it has remained the standard down to our day, renewed, of course, and transformed by the gospel. But we are looking at it here merely from the human, secular side. Seen in this context alone, which it admittedly transcends, the biblical view stands as the ultimate achievement recorded in the ancient world, dominating and determining its true perspective.

To leave out these developments, together with the ultimate reference which they uncover, and proceed from an arbitrarily set period of time, actually amounts to throwing out of balance the whole perspective of culture.

CHAPTER EIGHT

EARLY GREEK THOUGHT in PERSPECTIVE

A s THE observer proceeds to a consideration of early Greek thought through the poets, the dramatists, the philosophers, and the historians, he is impressed with its remarkable affinities for the independently developed Hebrew point of view. This awareness culminates in the consideration of the Socratic outlook as attempts are made to recover the "real Socrates" from available sources— admittedly a difficult task.

The Intimation of Righteousness

The reason Greek religion should not be dismissed lightly as mere paganism is that there was a profound religious insight at the core of the conception of Greek gods. They were said to be essentially *living* ones, *lording it over* the lives of men. This implied that these lives should somehow be in line with a divine will holding the secret of the deeper *why* of the human situation.

There is no hiding the fact that the Greek universe was not a *created* universe. Hesiod in his *Theogony* evokes the vision of the gods born of Earth and Sky in the midst of chaos, when the starry Heaven was loosened from its earthly embrace.[1] And so later Aristotle proclaimed the eternity of a world where everything comes about by the transformation of something else.[2] Greek gods, then, were integral parts of the universe—and the erroneous character of this conception

[1] 104.
[2] Cf. *Physics* VIII. 1; *On the Heavens* I. 10-12; III. 6; *Metaphysics* XII. 6; etc.

weakens and distorts an independently developed view of righteousness. It became a great temptation for man to blame the Immortals (they had no blood) for whatever evils came to mortals. Yet already in Homer we hear the Olympian Zeus state that human woes must be ascribed not to the gods, but to the blindness of the human heart.[3] Let it be noticed, incidentally, that this revelation of the gods came to men through the poets, who were the Greek equivalent for prophets and theologians.

As Homer appeared more and more obsolete to those who had sat at the feet of the Sophists, leaders of Greek thought paid more and more attention in their religious speculation[4] to the misleading character of what they exposed as anthropomorphism. The best illustration of this may be found in the passage of *Republic* where Adeimantus takes to task "the good old Hesiod" as well as Homer for promising an infinity of good things to the pious.[5] Grand are said to be the rewards promised in another life. Upon the authority of Hesiod and of Homer once more, we hear how sins may be easily expiated. But then, the poets who teach that the gods are ready to forgive and may easily be bribed are the only ones through whom the existence of the gods is known. The gist of the objection of Adeimantus is that justice per se is the greatest good, and injustice per se the greatest evil, whatever the consequences, and quite apart from "obsolete" religious conceptions.

So this case against anthropomorphism turns out to be a case against an old-fashioned conception of righteousness, according to which righteousness tends to life and happiness. Yet this "old-fashioned" notion was *also* that of the Hebrew prophets. It is noticeable that Matthew Arnold, studying the passage from sheer morality to righteousness, borrowed his examples not only from the Old Testament, but from Greek and Latin writers as well.[6] That "righteousness

[3] *Odyssey* I. 26.
[4] Especially Plato. An excellent guide on this may be found at the articles "God," "Gods, the," in the index to B. Jowett, *The Dialogues of Plato* (New York: Random House, 1937), II, 861-62.
[5] II. 362-67.
[6] *Literature and Dogma,* I, 2.

tendeth to life" might sound utilitarian, but the proposition in itself is not far from expressing the central message of the Hebrew prophets, just as we may find it expressing the gist of ancient Greek poets and dramatists. Seen in this light, the argument of Adeimantus is that of a "modernist" likely to shock a "fundamentalist" like Sophocles. And so, once more, Aristophanes may have to send Strepsiades to burn down the school of the Sophists, "because they have blasphemed the gods." [7] For truly Adeimantus in the *Republic* reasons in the same manner as Pheidippides in *The Clouds*, to the effect that there is no Zeus. Plato's *Republic*, then, constitutes a restatement of righteousness in terms of justice per se, in the context of a new world where the gods rendered obsolete by sophistry are abandoning the scene of the Ideas of Plato.

We ourselves are only too prone to dispose of genuine forms of ancient Greek religion in terms of the obsolescence of Greek mythology, the prestige and intellectual respectability of later Greek speculation helping. More objectively considered, the record will reveal in Greek literature and philosophy before Plato an impressive testimony to a notion of righteousness truly akin to that of the Hebrew prophets.

Homer does not tire of repeating that the omnipresent gods are constantly observing the ways of men and judging them.[8] They love justice.[9] Hesiod further stresses this teaching of righteousness and insists that the just shall prosper:

Famine waits not upon the righteous; neither does ruin; but in abundance do they go about the toil of their hands.
For them is the plentiful harvest, . . . and the fleeces of their sheep are heavy with wool.[10]

The whole passage may with due respect to differences in context, yet without irreverence, be placed in the margin of the first psalm:

[7] *The Clouds* (end of the play).
[8] Cf. for instance *Odyssey* XVII. 483.
[9] *Ibid.* XIV. 80.
[10] *The Works and the Days* 225. See also 230.

Blessed is the man that walketh not in the counsel of the ungodly. . . .

He shall be like a tree planted by the rivers of water, that bringeth forth his fruit in his season; his leaf also shall not wither; and whatsoever he doeth shall prosper.

The ungodly are not so: but are like the chaff which the wind driveth away.

Therefore the ungodly shall not stand in the judgment, nor sinners in the congregation of the righteous.

For the Lord knoweth the way of the righteous: but the way of the ungodly shall perish.

This is the kind of argumentation which Adeimantus would expose as utilitarian, superstitious, and ultimately immoral. Could it be that man likes to take the credit for everything good he may do, even in the name of an ethics without obligation or sanction? [11]

What then shall we say of the assurances of the Hebrew prophet to those whom the Lord will deliver and redeem? "Therefore they shall come and sing in the height of Zion, and shall flow together to the goodness of the Lord, for wheat, and for wine, and for oil, and for the young of the flock and of the herd: and their soul shall be as a watered garden; and they shall not sorrow any more at all" (Jer. 31:12).

Is this a mere appeal to utilitarianism?

Suppose we should turn to modern comments on this deep-seated Hebrew conviction that goodness and ultimate prosperity belong together.[12] We should find a critique of what is nowadays exposed as rude, outgrown notions, an aloof dismissal in many ways analogous to that of Adeimantus in Plato's *Republic*. As eschatological hopes fade away, there is abroad the same tendency to cast aside sanctions beyond the grave. The conclusion of a recent book on Christian doctrine puts it tersely: "The Faith is not a fire-escape." [13] In the same vein the New Testament scholar C. H. Dodd leaves the

[11] Cf. Guyau, *Esquisse d'une Morale sans Obligation ni Sanction* (Paris, 1884).

[12] For example H. E. Fosdick, *A Guide to Understanding the Bible*, ch. 3, "The Idea of Right and Wrong," and esp. ch. 4, "The Idea of Suffering."

[13] J. S. Whale, *Christian Doctrine*, p. 186.

reader of *The Bible Today* with the remark that what happens next "lies between a man and his maker." [14] Once more, as in the days of Plato, representative men of our age are talking as if man's achievements were best appraised "within the limits of reason alone," apart from any consideration of divine sanction. Admittedly such views pertain to a status developed under the sign of Protagoras for the sake of intellectual respectability.

Yet this kind of approach will prove to be wrong, however tempting, if God *is* the measure of man's being and behavior, and ordains man's destiny accordingly—that is, in utter disregard of what our "higher," "nobler" conceptions of justice may be. Are we sure, moreover, that the older view of Greek poets and dramatists, more fully disclosed in the Hebrew prophets, is not ultimately *the deeper view?* Let us again turn to Matthew Arnold, whose masterful treatment of the subject, to my knowledge, has not been equaled:

Look a little deeper, and you will see that one strain runs through it all: nations and men, whoever is shipwrecked, is shipwrecked on *conduct*. It is the God of Israel steadily and irresistibly asserting himself; *the Eternal that loveth righteousness.*

In this sense we should read the Hebrew prophets. They did not foresee and foretell curious coincidences, but they foresaw and foretold this inevitable triumph of righteousness.[15]

I may even go further and remark that this universal relevance of righteousness has been, and continues to be, vindicated in the actual life of men and nations, while whole sections of the metaphysics of Plato and Aristotle, in spite of their grandeur, belong to the museum of obsolete cosmologies.

Instead of following our contemporaries in taking for granted the superiority of Plato's and Aristotle's views over the religious thought of ancient Greece, let us dwell further on the latter.

[14] New York: The Macmillan Co., 1947. P. 163.

[15] *Literature and Dogma*, XI, 4. This eleventh chapter on "The True Greatness of the Old Testament" should be read in its entirety by anyone who aims at formulating a correct judgment on this all-important issue.

The Problem of Job in a Greek Context

What has been said thus far calls for an important correction. There is undeniably a strain of "primitive" [16] mentality in the view that suffering implies some form of curse, as in the Latin dictum *Res est sacra miser*, which may be literally translated, "The miserable one is untouchable." It is this strain which is heard from the friends of Job: "Remember, I pray thee, who ever perished, being innocent? or where were the righteous cut off?" (Job 4:7.)

A genuine, religious overtone cannot be missed in the harshness of this logic, however. There is first implied a new insight into the personal way in which God deals with men, whereas the primitive views of those days were those of *collective* reward or punishment— a "primitive" society being a totalitarian society. This same new insight comes forth in Ezekiel's oft misunderstood disclosure: "The soul that sinneth, it shall die: the son shall not bear the iniquity of the father, neither shall the father bear the iniquity of the son; the righteousness of the righteous shall be upon him, and the wickedness of the wicked shall be upon him" (Ezek. 18:20).

What is implied in this statement is that individual sanctions henceforth replace collective sanctions. There is present above all the everlasting strain of righteousness so wonderfully expressed in Micah. "He hath shewed thee, O man, what is good; and what doth the Lord require of thee, but to do justly, and to love mercy, and to walk humbly with thy God?" (Mic. 6:8.)

The tragedy of Job pertained to the whole mystery of the suffering of the righteous man who does that which the Lord requires of him. What makes this tragedy more acute is that simpler souls look for the immediately tangible. It is at this point that they need a further quest and disclosure. The godly are afflicted that they may be brought to self-knowledge and self-judgment as a prelude to a greater commitment and fruitfulness, above all to a higher knowledge of "the Eternal not ourselves who makes for righteousness."

[16] See ch. 6, the section "New Insights into Primitive Stagnation," for use of this term as already explained.

116

Jehovah had to warn Job out of the whirlwind, "Wilt thou condemn me, that thou mayest be righteous?" (Job 40:8.) That is, will you change the divine rule *and make your own rule, to your own measure so as to justify your ways?* And it was only then that Job saw the light and exclaimed, "I have heard of thee by the hearing of the ear: but now mine eye seeth thee. Wherefore I abhor myself, and repent in dust and ashes" (Job 42:5-6).

And at the end "the Lord gave Job twice as much as he had before" (Job 42:10).

The problem that confronted Job came within view of ancient Greece. Recall the awareness on the part of Homer and Hesiod that the omnipresent, all-seeing, justice-loving gods observe the ways of men; they cause the just to prosper and the wicked to suffer. This awareness was shared by dramatists and philosophers alike. Aeschylus, for instance, knew that righteousness inclines to the upright heart, and that while misery follows upon sin, the house of the righteous is blessed.[17] As for the philosopher Pythagoras (*ca.* 572-497 B.C.) we learn from Iamblichus that he conceived the rule of the gods as most efficacious for the establishment of righteousness, and that observance of that divine rule in all matters became the higher principle of his life and thought.[18]

And yet, why should the wicked prosper? This made Theognis wonder at Zeus, for was he not king of all?[19] And the "fundamentalist" Sophocles himself echoed the same preoccupation. How strange that "impious men issued from wicked parenthood, should prosper, while good men sprung of generous breed should know reverses of fortune"[20] The various answers to this problem as we know them today were formulated of old by ancient Greece. First, there is always the fact of human limitations. Who are we that we should hasten with judgments on such deep mysteries?

"My son, the end of all things is in the hand of Zeus the Thunderer,

[17] *Agamemnon* 759.
[18] *On the Pythagorean Life* 174.
[19] *Elegies* 373.
[20] *Aletes*, fr. 107.

117

and he disposes as he will. Wisdom is not within man's scope." So taught Semonides of Amorgos in the seventh century B.C.[21]

Aeschylus came forth with the classical explanation that suffering is the hard but sure way to wisdom. We should therefore praise Zeus for suffering, for it is he who guides the feet of men in the way of wisdom. The rule of his instruction is the firmly established rule of suffering.[22]

There was, above all, the calm assurance of Sophocles, so beautifully expressed by the chorus of *Oedipus King:*

> Ah! Zeus knows, and Apollo, what is dark to mortal eyes;
> They are gods.[23]

> Toward God's great mysteries, oh, let me move
>   unstained till I die
> In speech or doing; for the laws thereof
> Are holy.[24]

Admittedly such personal views supersede corporate views. Yet it should further be pointed out that both Aeschylus[25] and Herodotus[26] echoed collective feelings of righteousness when they read a divine judgment upon Greek presumption into the defeats of Marathon and Salamis. And so the twilight of Greek cities was in the likeness of their dawn, a divine light. The fulfillment of the oracles had come swiftly indeed, at the hand of Zeus.[27]

It is readily admitted that the preceding presentation has been one-sided. The reason for this is that in this consideration there was a perspective to restore from the outset. All contrary arguments which could be drawn from Euripides' *Trojan Women,* and from Thucydides' account of Athenian depravity have not been overlooked. But then, such arguments would mostly constitute a counter

[21] Fr. 1.
[22] *Agamemnon* 170.
[23] 490-91.
[24] *Ibid.* 862-65.
[25] *Persians* 799.
[26] VII. 10.
[27] *Persians* 739.

proof of the religious truths disclosed through the poets, the dramatists, the philosophers, and the historians of ancient Greece.

Socrates at the Apex of Restored Perspective

The remarkable affinity of early Greek thought for the independently developed Hebrew point of view comes to the observer's awareness more forcefully still as it reaches full expression in Socrates. The reason this point is currently missed by theologians is that a basic incompatibility between Hebrew "religion" and Greek "thought" has long attained to the status of a dogma. The reason this same point is currently missed by candid students of Greek culture is that the real Socrates is deeply embedded in various sources of a hopelessly biased nature.

We meet Socrates for the first time in *The Clouds* of Aristophanes. This was in 423 B.C. and Socrates (470-399 B.C.) was then forty-seven. The portrait is a satire bordering on the farcical. It is just that Aristophanes needed a native Athenian universally known who might lend himself readily to personifying the sophistry the comedy set out to challenge.

After Socrates' death, we have the Socratic dialogues of his disciple Plato, written in an indignant and apologetic vein, the *Apology* and the *Crito*. Idealized portraits then follow in a calmer, reverent mood, *Phaedo,* the *Symposium, Theaetetus,* and *Parmenides*. Finally there are the works where Socrates becomes a natural and convenient mouthpiece for the teaching of the Academy, Plato's school of philosophy in the suburbs of Athens. Xenophon's *Memorabilia,* written later, probably as late as 370 B.C., adds little to our knowledge of Socrates, being mostly an adaptation of conversations previously related. Finally, and apart from a few allusions, some of them by Aristotle, there is a tradition mostly hostile to Socrates which persists throughout the Hellenistic age with Porphyry (A.D. 232-304), Libanius (fourth century A.D.), and the Epicureans.

It would seem that Socrates is rarely seen on his own, but rather being dragged into causes he would most probably have shunned. More widely known to us through Plato, as seen through Plato's

119

eyes, he is as a rule found in the role of introducing the student to his illustrious disciple. We would consider here a Socrates on his own, as far at least as is found feasible.

What makes this reconsideration important to our subject is that, as we see it, a new turn taken by Greek thought with Plato and Aristotle must be ascribed mostly to a speculative approach to the religious truth which came to expression through Socrates.

The Temptation of Socrates

Socrates is usually hailed as the man who broke the deadlock which the contrasting views of Heracleitus and Parmenides had brought about. Heracleitus saw the nature of reality in change, and expressed this forcefully by saying that one cannot step twice into the same river, for fresh waters are always flowing in upon him.[28] To which Cratylus, of whom Plato in his youth was a disciple, added that it could not be the same river anyway.[29] That is, it could not be known as such because there can be knowledge only of the permanent, of that which *is*. It was precisely while arguing from language on this that Parmenides (sixth-fifth century B.C.) identified reality with the permanence of a "being" without differentiation, homogeneous, unchangeable, filling all space. In so doing he actually formulated our notion of "substance." One cannot know that which is not—that is impossible—nor utter it, he insisted, for it is one and the same thing that can be thought and that can be.[30] Trying to think "being," then, Parmenides was led to postulate one continuous material block. This is the type of thing which happens when one argues from language on the most elusive aspects of truth, and on that basis one could almost excuse Protagoras' jibe, "Concerning the gods I cannot know assuredly whether or not they exist, nor what they look like. Many things there are which hinder assurance —the matter is obscure and life is short."[31] The skepticism of

[28] Fr. 81. "In the same river we step and do not step; we are and we are not."
[29] Aristotle *Metaphysics* 1010a.
[30] *Concerning Truth* 35-40.
[31] Fr. 4.

120

Protagoras extended much further, however, in fact to everything. He was the first to maintain that there are two sides to every question, for "man is the measure of all things, of things that are that they are, and of things that are not that they are not." [32] Here, then, a perfect deadlock was reached which led to sophistry. It is this deadlock which Socrates is credited with having broken by showing that the only accessible object of knowledge to the individual man is man himself. Hence the sum of all wisdom is "Know thyself."

We have, however, a more direct access to Socrates' early experiences in philosophy, namely, the record in Plato's *Phaedo* of a conversation said to have taken place on the day of his master's death. This is important because we are truly dealing here with what the Germans call a *Grenzbegriff*, a "Limit Concept" at a time when Socrates would bring out the very essentials of his own thought. What he recalls, then, at the hour of death, is that at a crucial moment of his quest for truth, he was led to have great expectations from the doctrine of Anaxagoras that all was *mind*.[33]

Note that Socrates was elated at the prospect of finding, as it were, the secret of the gods through speculation:

Then I heard some one reading, as he said, from a book of Anaxagoras, that mind was the disposer and cause of all, and I was delighted at this notion, which appeared quite admirable, and I said to myself: If mind is the disposer, mind will dispose all for the best, and put each particular in the best place; and I argued that if any one desired to find out the cause of the generation or destruction or existence of anything, he must find out what state of being or doing or suffering was best for that thing, and therefore a man had only to consider the best for himself and others, and then he would also know the worse, since the same experience comprehended both. And I rejoiced to think that I had found in Anaxagoras a teacher of the causes of existence such as I desired, and I imagined that

[32] Diogenes Laertius, from the Hick's translation (Loeb Classical Library series), II, 463 sq. Quoted from T. V. Smith, *Philosophers Speak for Themselves* (University of Chicago Press, 1934), p. 61.
On Protagoras see also Plato's *Protagoras* and *Theaetetus*, 152 sq.
[33] The *nous:* Reason, "Thought-stuff," characterizing the force-substance which disposes movements according to ends and rules them. The interesting point about this is that we uncover here for the first time a *teleological* explanation of nature.

121

he would tell me first whether the earth is flat or round; and whichever was true, he would proceed to explain the cause and the necessity of this being so, and then he would teach me the nature of the best and show that this was best; and if he said that the earth was in the centre, he would further explain that this position was the best, and I should be satisfied with the explanation given, and not want any other sort of cause. And I thought that I would then go on and ask him about the sun and moon and stars, and that he would explain to me their comparative swiftness, and their returnings and various states, active and passive, and how all of them were for the best. . . . These hopes I would not have sold for a large sum of money, and I seized the books and read them as fast as I could in my eagerness to know the better and the worse.[34]

But great was the disappointment of young Socrates who had experienced "a prodigious desire to know that department of philosophy which is called the investigation of nature." [35] As he proceeded to read Anaxagoras, he found his philosopher altogether forsaking mind or any other principle, but having recourse to air, and ether, and water, and other eccentricities:

I might compare him to a person who began by maintaining generally that mind is the cause of the actions of Socrates, but who, when he endeavoured to explain the causes of my several actions in detail, went on to show that I sit here because my body is made up of bones and muscles; and the bones, as he would say, are hard and have joints which divide them.[36]

Having then failed either to discover himself, or to learn of anyone else, the nature of the best, he realized that he had "failed in the contemplation of true existence." Then he thought that he ought to be careful that he did not lose *the eye of his soul*, "as people may injure their bodily eye by observing and gazing on the sun during an eclipse." [37]

It was this "converted Socrates" who exclaimed in the *Republic*:

[34] *Phaedo* 97-98. I follow here Jowett's translation taken from *The Dialogues of Plato* (New York, 1892, 1920, 1937), I, 482.

[35] *Phaedo* 96.

[36] *Ibid.* 98.

[37] *Ibid.* 99.

I may be a simpleton: but, in my opinion . . . whether a man gapes at the heavens or blinks on the ground, seeking to learn some particular of sense, I would deny that he can learn, for nothing of that sort is matter of science.[38]

True knowledge is here opposed to opinion based on mere appearance; but clearly we are not dealing in this with a serene view of Parmenidean inspiration, but with the passionate protest of a disillusioned student. Socrates never forgot the burning deception that the reading of Anaxagoras had brought to him. He no longer went out into the country because neither trees nor flowers could "teach" him anything. He turned his back on the mysteries of astronomy, as well as on that type of land-measuring they call geometry, because such things led nobody anywhere.

Yet the radicalism of Socrates went beyond the realm of the natural sciences. Even Plato could not make him take part in legislative innovations. He had no political doctrine. Nay, he was not interested in defending philosophy when Callicles attacked it in the third part of *Gorgias*. And yet, with all this, when Callicles advised him to be the servant of the state and not run the risk of popular enmity, Socrates agreed that this latter danger existed and that he was aware of it. Yet he considered himself to be the only or almost the only Athenian living who practiced the true art of politics. Said he, "I am the only politician of my time"—by which he meant that he was not interested in gaining favor. "I look to what is best and not to what is most pleasant." [39]

His aim had not changed. He was interested only in the best. To his passionate soul all the rest was mere matter of opinion and could be ignored.

The Divine Mission of Socrates

Socrates' exclusiveness cannot be explained solely by the lasting impression left on his passionate soul by a disappointment of youth,

[38] *Republic* VII. 529.
[39] *Gorgias* 521.

however keen. There was in it the buoyancy of supreme assurance, the finality of a deeper call.

At this juncture we have the testimony of a Socrates put on his mettle, facing his accusers, as "reported" by Plato in the *Apology*. The hour was a solemn hour and the testimony a sacred testimony. Socrates begged permission from the judges to speak in his accustomed manner. He had been slandered as an evildoer teaching false doctrines, as a Sophist taking money, all accusations arising, in fact, from a sort of wisdom which he seemed to possess. But then, the word which he *must* speak was not his own word:

> And here, O men of Athens, I must beg you not to interrupt me, even if I seem to say something extravagant. For the word which I will speak is not mine. I will refer you to a witness who is worthy of credit; that witness shall be the God of Delphi—he will tell you about my wisdom, if I have any, and of what sort it is. You must have known Chaerephon; he was early a friend of mine, and also a friend of yours, for he shared in the recent exile of the people, and returned with you. Well, Chaerephon, as you know, was very impetuous in all his doings, and he went to Delphi and boldly asked the oracle to tell him whether . . . any one was wiser than I was and the Pythian prophetess answered, that there was no man wiser. Chaerephon is dead himself; but his brother, who is in court, will confirm the truth of what I am saying.[40]

This revelation made the philosopher uneasy. So he proceeded to stop the wisest of his contemporaries wherever he met them in order to clarify his own situation. For it is true that, in the words of the poet,[41] the one who finds himself singled out by Divinity at once becomes "powerful and solitary"; it would still be more pertinent to say "uneasy." Why should he be singled out? What could the divine design be on his life?

[40] *Apology* 20-21.

[41] A. de Vigny, in *Moïse* (1822). Moses, having been chosen by the Lord to lead his people, is weary of a tremendous weight of responsibility and begs to be allowed to sleep the sleep of the earth. The refrain is heard four times in slightly modified form:

> *Je vivrai donc toujours puissant et solitaire?*
> *Laissez-moi m'endormir du sommeil de la terre.*

Henceforth, Socrates was bent on finding what "truth for him" [42] was; that is, he no longer speculated in a detached manner on truth in the abstract—if it may be said that he had ever done so. We are reminded at this point of the strangely pungent Hebrew phrase "doing the truth" as embedded in the Gospel according to John, "he that *doeth truth* cometh to the light" (John 3:21). This was precisely the Socratic concern. And, lo and behold, the age-old tension between Hebrew and Greek is now increasingly relaxed.

The Kingdom Within

The light in Socrates was that of his *daemon* attending him and guiding his destiny.[43] "The divinity," said Socrates, "gives me a sign." [44] His prayer was simple enough, "Give me what is best for me;" [45] and the reader of this present chapter will remember that this same concern has been found all through the treatment of Socrates thus far.

The reason for what we previously called the "radicalism" of Socrates comes to light by the same token. Socrates was in actual practice extolling the infinite worth of "the kingdom within." To him also it was in a real way the pearl of great price, for which the wise man gladly exchanges all his other possessions; it was the hidden treasure, whose vision makes a man forget that he ever wanted anything else. To lose it would be losing everything. "Athenians, I hold you in great esteem and affection; but I shall obey God rather than you." This was in fact the gist of Socrates' statement in court in the face of death, and with Pascal we believe those "witnesses" who are willing to die for the sake of their testimony. Socrates was such a "witness," and the idea of witnessing is also a thoroughly Hebraic

[42] A striking expression of Kierkegaard, who at the age of twenty-two wanted clarity with respect to what he ought to do. He wanted to find the idea for which he could live and die. The author of *Concluding Unscientific Postcript* realized that "existence constitutes the highest interest of the existing individual," and that "his interest in his existence constitutes his reality." (1846, tr. Swenson and Lowrie [Princeton University Press, 1941], p. 279.)

[43] Cf. Plato *Euthyphro* 3b; *Alcibiades* 103-5e; Xenophon *Memorabilia* I. 1. 2-4.
[44] *Memorabilia* I. 1. Also Plato *Apology* 31.
[45] *Ibid.* I. 3.

view. Like Jesus, then, Socrates in his own way made the "kingdom" the text of all his teaching. Like Jesus also, he gave his life for the sake of his testimony.

Kierkegaard, who traced his own approach back to Socrates, may have learned from him that "Purity of heart is to will one thing." [46] The most exacting Christian of modern times went as far as stating, also when close to the hour of death, "The only analogy I have before me is Socrates. My task is a Socratic task, to revise the definition of what it is to be a Christian. For my part I do not call myself a 'Christian' (thus keeping the ideal free), but I am able to make it evident that the others are that still less than I." [47] Like Socrates also, Kierkegaard found himself facing an abyss of sophistry. [48]

Attention has already been drawn to the fact that the Hellenistic methods of sophistry had penetrated even the exclusive schools of the Pharisees and Sadducees, as may be realized in the cunning ways of their pupils in their formalistic arguments with Jesus. The reader of Plato's *Euthyphro* will find a striking parallel to such false conceptions of piety as theirs in the ways of the pompous legalist who was about to prosecute his father on the highest religious grounds.

The Socratic View of Knowledge

True knowledge to Socrates, then, consists essentially in the clarification of a life situation in the light of his call from the religious *reality* within, and not in metaphysical speculation in remote realms of intelligibility, far from what Professor Montague in our day calls "the shores of fact." [49]

Strongly established at the metaphorical apex of existence where his human nature is in contact with a divine actuality, he becomes

[46] *Purity of Heart Is to Will One Thing* (1846), tr. Steere (New York and London: Harper & Bros., 1938).

[47] *Kierkegaard's Attack upon "Christendom,"* "The Instant No. 10," Fr. dated Sept. 1, 1855, p. 283.

[48] *Ibid.* "It is in an abyss of sophistry Christianity is lying—far, far worse than when the Sophists flourished in Greece."

[49] William P. Montague, *Great Visions of Philosophy* (LaSalle: Open Court, 1950), p. 14.

aware of a great variety of personal calls and of personal circumstances. His ethicoreligious method can only be an enlightened *art*, and this is still the situation in our day. Pascal himself realized this in his fragment on the *art* of persuasion.[50]

It would seem that Plato and, further, Aristotle read back their own speculative designs into Socrates, to the point of ascribing to him a metaphysical approach to religious "truth," which henceforth appears to us foreign to his genius. This would indeed suggest a new emphasis in the development of Greek thought and, as a result, a mistaken attribution of resulting tensions to a basic incompatibility between Hebrew "religion" and Greek "thought"—a theme only too familiar to students in theology.

[50] In Cailliet and Blankenagel, *Great Shorter Works of Pascal*, pp. 202-11.

PART THREE

The Ontological Deviation

CHAPTER NINE

The RISE of ONTOLOGY

A s we proceed from Socrates to Plato, an important change of emphasis is increasingly impressed upon us. Yet this fact has not attracted sufficient attention because Socrates is known chiefly through Plato, and because both Plato and Aristotle read their own preoccupations back into Socrates, thus hiding the real Socrates. When we become aware of this and recover the "real Socrates" as was attempted in the preceding chapter, the change in emphasis from Socrates to Plato comes to our awareness more and more.

The emphasis of Socrates was on a clarification of reality in the light of his faith. The emphasis of Plato was on postulations born of intelligibility. Plato was both a mathematician and a disciple of Socrates. He wanted to find out what the cosmic realm must be like for both mathematics and the teachings of Socrates to be grounded in reality. The way he did it, in the main, was to postulate archetytpes for justice, truth, beauty and, above these, for the good, in terms of "realities" similar to those involved in numbers. Pythagoras (*ca.* 572-497 B.C.) was the direct source of inspiration in this, for it was he who originally caught the tremendous insight that *number* must constitute the basic pattern of reality. This Pythagorean aspect of Plato's emphasis proved in many ways to have been one of the most fruitful insights ever reached by science. As such it will be singled out for consideration later in these pages.[1] At this

---

[1] See chap. 11, the section "The Reformation and the New Science."

point we are mostly concerned with Plato's tendency to transmute the human mind, whose essential function is that of a knower, into a "pseudo-maker." By this expression is meant the type of thing Plato did in granting independent reality to his Ideas.

The fallacy involved in this procedure is twofold; it is not only that the Platonic man colonizes reality with abstractions, but that these abstractions in turn have a way of standing between him and the actual reality. Thus the thinker involved runs the risk of becoming a prisoner of his own mind. He is so engrossed in his artifacts, that is, in things that are not there, that he no longer sees the things that actually are there.

On the Danger of Arguing from Language

The ontological emphasis which came into its own with Plato was initiated by Parmenides (sixth-fifth century B.C.) as the latter developed the conception of "Being" in opposition to that of the "Becoming" of Heracleitus. The gist of the Parmenidean critique of Heracleitus was what we characterize today as "argument from language."

Parmenides, we remember, had been impressed by the fact that there can be no true knowledge of transitory things. Such changing appearances as constitute what we like to call a "passing show" cannot even be *named*. Cratylus of Athens, a Heracleitean and early teacher of Plato, had carried the irreconcilability of "Being" and "Becoming" to such an extreme as to renounce the use of spoken language. While Plato himself later criticized the theory in this extreme form,[2] the fact remains that to him as to Parmenides, what is constantly becoming cannot truly be said to be, hence it cannot truly be known. Let us illustrate this with the famous dictum of Heracleitus, to the effect that we never step into the same river, for lo and behold, new waters always flow in upon us. Cratylus improved upon the dictum by saying that it could not be the *same* river anyway. Why, we could not even *name* such a river. An overstated point, admittedly, but one whose relevance could

[2] Cf. his dialogue under the same name, *Cratylus,* esp. end 427 and 428 sq.

hardly be missed. And so it was that Parmenides laid down the principle that we can know only that which actually *is*. What is constantly becoming something else cannot truly be said to be. In other words, to be known and to be are one and the same thing.

Let us now direct our attention to the very core of the Parmenidean proposition as he further developed it in his poem *On Truth*. Since thinking implies being, being must be *absolutely*, that is, as he put it, without beginning, indestructible, universal, existing alone, immovable, and without end. This proposition proved epoch-making. It originated the philosophical notion of *substance* and also the notion of *ab-solute* being, which was to be applied later to the living God of Scripture. Last but not least, as already pointed out, this statement of Parmenides was the first characteristic manifestation of *arguing from language*. Since to be known and to be are one and the same thing, the fact that a concept imposes itself upon the mind implies that there is a reality that corresponds to that concept. In this particular case Parmenides ended by "establishing" the "existence" of reality as being like the mass of a rounded sphere, equally distant from the center at any point.

Should anyone pronounce this inference "absurd," he would merely be saying that the Parmenidean approach involved a "paradox." The plain fact is that Parmenides paved the way for the greatest paradox known to ancient philosophy, namely, the Platonic paradox of the reality of the intelligible. It is because Socrates was interpreted in terms of that paradox that the reality of the God, which was his immediate concern, yielded priority to a pseudo-reality seen to have been postulated by the concepts underlying his commitment.

A Basic Distinction to Keep in Mind

Before coming to a closer consideration of the Platonic paradox, it is necessary to attempt a further clarification of its terms. In doing so, it is hoped that there will be brought out a distinction which dominates not only this part of the development, but the development as a whole. This basic distinction, which should be kept in

133

mind, concerns the meaning of the words "reality" and "intelligibility."

A convenient way of going about this subject is to begin its consideration as the Greeks themselves did, with the plain data of everyday experience. You and I could name a number of particular oak trees which we know and love. Each time we see a new oak tree, we pronounce it to be an oak tree because we identify its "oakness." We identify it so well, in fact, that leaving out of consideration each and every particular oak tree we have known thus far, we find ourselves in a position to give quite a good characterization of *the* oak tree in general. Yet, as soon as we engage in that dissertation on the oak tree, we have already abandoned the domain of actual oaks in order to use the *concept* of "oakness" as a convenient shorthand. In other words, we have passed from reality to intelligibility.

Intelligibility proceeds from reality in order to provide a better understanding of reality. Yet intelligibility is no longer reality. To familiarize oneself with the difference between the two is the best way to shun error and confusion in the realm of metaphysics. Oakness per se has no reality. Of itself, it does not exist. We may say that it exists in the "mind" of God the Creator, and that it existed there, in fact, before there was any oak tree in existence. It existed in this manner, that is, *before* the thing ever was—*ante rem,* as the scholastics finally put it. Or we may say that the "oakness" is in the oak tree as the Creator made it, that is, *in* the thing—*in re,* or *parte rei* (part of the thing). And because it is in every particular oak tree that we observe, we may derive the concept of "oakness" from this observation. And so, in this case, the concept comes *after* the thing—*post rem.* As far as we are concerned, then, "oakness" does not exist by itself; it is a concept; it pertains, not to reality, but to intelligibility.

Hence the abstract concepts thus devised by ontology do not designate existing entities. Each one is but *flatus vocis,* the breath of voice, at best a convenient shorthand concept. To the critics of ontological realism the so-called "essences" are the definitions not of given realities, but of their names. They are but nouns. Hence the appellation of "nominalists" is applied to those who take this opposite view.

The necessary order which is seen to preside over reality, nay, the order of which reality is always an incomplete realization, is not reality itself, but it belongs to the realm of the *possible*. It is not a *substance*. It is truth. It refers to intelligibility. The mind either progresses towards the intelligible or regresses towards intuition, according as to whether it aims at the truth *or* at the real. What must be freely admitted, however, is that our grasp upon reality is bound to remain feeble if it is attempted without the help of intelligibility. The more I understand, the more I become able to penetrate reality so as to order it according to my need or intention. The higher the flight into the intelligible, the deeper the subsequent dent into the real. This is what Bacon meant when he said that one can lord it over nature only by obeying nature. When a man like Bergson advocates intuition above intelligence, he does not mean to deprive us, and certainly not to deprive himself, of all the means of analytical interpretation provided by science. Otherwise the Bergsonian intuition would become an empty gesture. The fact is that it has been dismissed as an empty gesture by those critics who do not understand that what made Bergson's case against intellectualism so potent was Bergson's exceptionally high degree of intelligence. A similar form of misunderstanding may yet prove to have been partly responsible for the tension postulated by theologians between the Hebrew-Christian and the Greek approaches to the religious problem. The Hebrew-Christian concern is mostly with reality; the Greek concern is mostly with intelligibility. Supposing an ontological *notion* of God should appear at the apex of a mental process of Platonic inspiration, the result may temporarily satisfy the thinker. Yet the religious man would become aware of the deep frustration of one who had been cut off from the reality of his deep experience and biblical knowledge.

Professor Erwin R. Goodenough, of Yale University, puts the paradox this way. "If the only realities are qualities, abstract qualities like

135

form, the forms of mathematics, as well as of justice, beauty, equality, or being, then the God who produced them must be a quality more abstract than they in order to be more ultimate and real than they." [3] Hence there is the strange phrase "reality of the intelligible" currently used to characterize the paradox of Platonic realism.

The Paradox of Platonic Realism

We said of Plato that he wanted to find out what the cosmic realm must be like for both mathematics and the teachings of Socrates to be grounded in reality. The immediate implication of this intention is that Plato's ontological speculation was of an essentially scientific nature. The Platonic Ideas were patterns of clues destined to penetrate the nature of the universe.

Once approached in this light, Plato's intention must be pronounced legitimate. The gist of the matter is that his first move was a perfectly normal scientific procedure. The notion that the Ideas may well prove to constitute the core of reality did not essentially differ from the working hypothesis of modern science—that is, provided this status of the Ideas as a working hypothesis was kept in mind. Had this been the case, the analogy between Plato and the modern scientist would be fully justified. The "Ideas hypothesis" would then be acknowledged as an early version of the type of clues devised by a physicist. Following upon a coherent set of mathematical speculations, our scientist becomes aware of the *possibility* of certain phenomena. Yet he will never assert anything beyond this possibility until a crucial experiment has vindicated his position. In other words, the laws "invented" by the scientist must constantly take account of the witness of observation and experimentation. A negative answer emanating from the realm of reality, on the other hand, may well set the pace for new speculations, for new patterns of clues. This is what happened when the crucial Michelson-Morley experiment of 1881 failed to prove the existence of "the ether." Einstein was then led to venture his revolutionary theory of relativity. Yet Einstein himself is always the first to admit that nothing

[3] *Religious Tradition and Myth,* p. 43.

is established in the realm of intelligibility until a crucial confirmation has finally come from the realm of reality. And so the conversation between the scientist and nature goes on by means of constantly restated working hypotheses.

Keeping the above principles in mind, let us see what actually happens as we proceed from a consideration of Socrates to that of Plato.

It is noticeable, in the first place, that Socrates failed to define courage in *Laches,* piety in *Euthyphro,* or temperance in *Charmides.* What we have in these early Socratic dialogues is a series of attempts at a clarification of experience, mere attempts at definitions—and unsuccessful attempts at that. Obviously, then, when Aristotle ascribed to Socrates a concern for the "essence" of universals,[4] he was once more reading his own preoccupations back into Socrates' humble attempts, just as we have already seen him read his own preoccupations into the work of the cosmologists. Admittedly Aristotle made it clear that Socrates himself did not make the universals or definitions exist apart. It was *they*—according to the context, the Pythagoreans—who took the ultimate step. Almost by the same syllogistic argument ascribed to Socrates by Aristotle, they concluded that there must be Ideas of all things. And so it came about, still according to the same text of Aristotle,[5] that the actual existence of Forms was postulated. Thus the humble and guarded Socrates, who was satisfied to come short of a definition of courage, piety, or temperance, was henceforth credited with a syllogistic bent and a concern for ontology which led to the postulation of eternal Forms of reality. Of these, our human notions of courage, piety, and temperance were but the shadowy expression.

The paradox of Platonic realism is further aggravated by the fact that Plato had no word to translate "reality." He spoke in terms of the "existence" of the intelligible, as the mathematician in him referred to the "existence" of a number. This is well illustrated in the *Meno,* also an early dialogue, where analytical analysis is substituted

[4] *Metaphysics* XIII. 4 (1078*b*. 17). Cf. Xenophon *Memorabilia* IV. 6.
[5] *Metaphysics* XIII. 4 (1079*a*).

for the purely Socratic type of discussion—a most interesting transition. To Plato, then, ideas precede and outlive the particular instances in which they are actualized. The existence of Ideas manifests itself in their independence from both single notions derived from experience, and the mind through which these notions are thought out as individual instances.

No further difficulties need have appeared had the postulation of the Ideas amounted to nothing more than a working hypothesis on the nature of reality. It was at this juncture that trouble developed. The relevance of what should have remained a mere pattern of clues, calling for proving or disproving, was tested only by means of dialectical reasoning until the matter-of-fact Aristotle challenged it in the light of his science. This, however, did not prevent the followers of Plato from proceeding upon the alleged existence of the "realities" postulated by their mental processes.

The Aristotelian Critique of Platonism

Aristotle (384-322 B.C.), the Macedonian, the son of Nicomachus the physician of King Amyntas of Macedon, the matter-of-fact classifier and scientist with his feet planted solidly on the ground, first strikes us as a sort of counterpart of his master Plato. But this is a wrong impression, at least partly so. We should not lose sight of the fact that he was Plato's disciple, studying at Plato's Academy for nearly twenty years. There is no doubt that his critique of Platonism began at the Academy, *in co-operation with Plato himself*, who is seen to have been his own critic in such dialogues as *Parmenides* and the *Laws*. Plato was dead when Aristotle proceeded with the critique of the Ideas in his *Metaphysics*,[6] and his approach to the same subject in the *Nicomachean Ethics* reveals toward a beloved master a gentleness which our own day might do well to emulate:

We had perhaps better consider the universal good and discuss thoroughly what is meant by it, although such an inquiry is made an uphill one by the fact that the Forms have been introduced by friends of our own. Yet it would perhaps be thought to be better, indeed to be our

[6] *Metaphysics* I. 9.

138

duty, for the sake of maintaining the truth even to destroy what touches us closely, especially as we are philosophers or lovers of wisdom; for while both are dear, piety requires us to honour truth above our friends.[7]

Aristotle's critique of the Ideas is actually directed at those representatives of Platonism alive in his day, who are more in the nature of rivals than of disciples. Their teaching is remote from that of Plato, whose flexible and penetrating insights have by now given way to a hardened dogmatism. Their attitude reveals a striking example of the way in which a Hellenistic tendency to define changed the liberal *dokei moi*, "It seems (good) to me," into a decree-like form of doctrine, a hard-set *dogma*. But more, the matter-of-fact scientist who mapped out the whole field of human knowledge[8] approached his momentous task as one who had studied with discrimination.

From Plato, Aristotle remembered that first philosophy is the science of being, as distinguished from passing relations that *appear* to be. Plato's essential message to Aristotle, and even to us, may be seen in this connection in a vindication of the eternally significant *possible*, regardless of the actual vicissitudes of the existence in place, time, and custom. In the words of Professor Montague, "The rain on Monday night as an idea in my mind is created on Tuesday morning by the visual perception of puddles. But the puddles are themselves the consequence of the rain the night before." While it is true that the conceptual world is constructed out of our percepts, it is undeniable that this same conceptual world is *presupposed* by those percepts. "I create, or seem to create, the very world which contains and creates me."[9]

The eminently practical man from the north further showed discrimination in refusing to lend any kind of independent reality to

[7] *Ethica Nicomachea* I. 6. (1096a), as translated by W. D. Ross (London: Humphrey Milford, Oxford University Press, 1925).

[8] Cf. *Organon* (the collection of Aristotle's logical treatises), *Physics, On the Heavens, On Generation and Corruption, On the Soul, On Memory and Reminiscence, On Dreams, The History of Animals, On the Parts of Animals, On the Generation of Animals, Metaphysics, Nicomachean Ethics, Politics, Rhetoric, Poetics.*

[9] *Great Visions of Philosophy* (La Salle, Ill.: Open Court, 1950), p. 464.

the ideas inherent or immanent in the particulars. It is just that reality is a world of concrete things which are never found without *form*. As there is no matter without form, there is no form without a substratum of matter. Thus we are left with matter and form, these two—matter, *hyle*, that of which a thing is made, and the idea or form, *eidos*. Form is far more than mere shape. It is the sum total of the characters which constitute an intelligible structure. As such it causes things by being the goal at which they aim. Matter will strive for this goal which implies its completion, *entelecheia*. Hence there is the basic Aristotelian notion of causality as actualization of a form in matter. The bird is the actuality, *energeia*, of the egg. The whole Aristotelian universe thus appears as a hierarchy of potentialities, where the heretofore puzzling fact of change is explained in terms of matter and form, of potentiality and actuality.

Thought, then, according to Aristotle, proceeds from the reception, through sense experience, of the sensible form of the particulars, reason finally apprehending the universals and first principles, that is, the intelligible. Does this mean that everything in reality is material? How could a passive intellect secure this higher power of active intelligibility which is actualized in the intelligence of man as well as in the hierarchy of beings and things? But more, since every movement or change is due to an operative goal, and since intelligibility has just been seen to imply a supreme form, there must be one principle of process and unity.

In postulating this matterless form or pure actuality, this first mover unmoved, whose activity consists in pure thought, Aristotle seems to contradict his own contradiction of Plato's *separate* Ideas. Hence a final stage of development, an ideal apex at which the last matter subsidizes in the form of Pure Act.[10] This culmination is reached in matterless form, every pantheistic conception of the absolute being therein excluded.[11] A thin concept, admittedly, even if its "purity" seems to increase its intensity, as theologians of Thomistic inspiration like to point out. *Yet it remains a concept.* Even at this

[10] *Metaphysics* VIII. 6. (1045b), XII. 3, 9.
[11] *Ibid.*, XII. 6-7.

point we may not come to terms with a last residue of the Platonic paradox of the reality of the intelligible. In the eternal first mover unmoved, whose existence is postulated in the *Metaphysics* of Aristotle, we may at best identify the ultimate shadow of the fancies of popular religion, shunned by a Socrates in line with the best tradition of the poets, dramatists, and historians of ancient Greece. There is deep meaning in Etienne Gilson's statement that "with Aristotle, the Greeks had gained an indisputably rational theology, but they had lost their religion." [12]

What the Greeks had actually lost at the school of Plato and Aristotle was not only their mythological fancies, but their genuine sense of religious relationship with reality.

[12] *God and Philosophy* (New Haven: Yale University Press, 1941), p. 34.

CHAPTER TEN

AUGUSTINIANS and THOMISTS

THE Aristotelian critique of Platonism was revived in the thirteenth century when Thomas Aquinas directed at Augustine the same constructive objections which Aristotle had made to Plato. The parallel becomes still more relevant when the reverent attitude of Aquinas toward Augustine is likened to Aristotle's gentle reluctance to disagree with his master. This lends to the whole subject an atmosphere of gentlemanlike, mellowed scholarship.

Before we proceed with the subject at hand, let us make sure that we remain at all times aware of the immense debt of gratitude the Western civilization owes to this giant Augustine. He was raised of God at the time when the dying empire in the West was passing on to the barbarians. To these new rulers our ancient tradition of culture meant nothing. The new rule implied moreover that the Western world was cut off from the great theological thinking which had been at work chiefly in the East. It was Augustine who shifted the center of gravity and set our Christian Western culture on its God-given course. In and through Augustine the best of a classical culture, recast in the framework of Christian thinking, was transmitted to the educators of the new Europe. Not only did Augustine thus give priority to Christian thinking, but he stated and developed all the great Christian truths concerning God, namely, the doctrine of grace and, above all, the doctrine of the Trinity. It was Augustine's vision that gave meaning and orientation to the new social order. *The City of God* laid the foundations of a Christian sociology.

Like all great pioneers, however, Augustine had first of all to solve the problems at hand for himself. He came to Christianity through a nerve-racking, passionate experience. Bent from the outset upon self-gratification and self-assertion, the young rhetorician had to learn through trial and error. Under the sway of a sexual tyranny finally identified as evil, he naturally turned for light to the Manicheans who dramatized for him the problem of evil. After nine long years, however, it appeared to him that while this notion of a separate creator of evil against God the Creator may have been convenient in his own case, removing his own guilt, it was not intellectually consistent. Could it be, then, that evil was primarily nonbeing as opposed to being, an absence of good, as it were? Obviously the tyranny came from the realm of the material. Platonism taught that man is a soul using a body and, in more than one way, prisoner of that body. Nay, the soul is divine and truth is divine; it belongs to the realm of the immaterial. The One of Plotinus (205-70) must be God the Father. Yet, if matter is an element of degradation, how could one think of God incarnate in Jesus Christ? The Gospel according to John seemed to provide the clue to that which Neoplatonism left unexplained. The prologue to this Fourth Gospel made it clear that the Second Person of the Trinity is the Word, and through his ill-forgotten Neoplatonism Augustine transcribed the same as the *nous,* the Intellect. The fact of the Second Person, then, was to be understood in terms of the primacy of the immaterial over the material. And so, to the diligent student of both the *Enneads* of Plotinus and of the prologue to John's Gospel, there was God the Father, and God the Word—and there was the creation.

What we have here is the postulation of a would-be Christian reality remade in the image of a mind still very much under the sway of Neoplatonism. As a result we witness a never-ending tension between the Neoplatonist and the Christian within the soul of Augustine. In the long run the Christian gets the upper hand. Yet deep-seated contradictions exact their toll of confusion. The ultimate confusion is found at the point where Augustine, having found the

143

true God of Scripture, still strives to explain him and relate himself to him in terms of an ontology of Platonic inspiration. In other words Augustine the *knower* of God in his glorious reality cannot help thinking of him and his creation as postulated by his mind— a mind which cannot be persuaded to remain a mere knower, but attempts again and again to make its own landscape of reality.

Hence Augustine's is a wisdom wont to neglect the reality of sense experience, to seek gratification and comfort in visions born of its own strivings.

A Cloistered Wisdom and Its Aftermath

The *Confessions* of Augustine, written some eleven years after his conversion (which took place in 386), constitute a somewhat misleading version of his intellectual and religious development, from the standpoint of the more developed orthodoxy of a strenuously busy man. The reader will remember the great garden scene when Augustine, having prayed to God, poured forth a shower of tears. Then, admonished by a voice (*Tolle, lege*), he opened the "volume of the apostles" and came upon the words in Rom. 13:13. Changed in his whole soul, he disclosed the divine favor to his friend Alypius and to his mother, Monnica.[1] It will be further recalled that, having decided to abandon his profession, he went into retirement in a villa at Cassiciacum, just outside Milan, so as to prepare for baptism. During his fall and winter sojourn there he wrote four dialogues. These are actually based on the transcripts made by a stenographer who attended the meetings of Augustine with his companions. The works here under consideration are *Contra Academicos, De beata vita, De ordine,* and the curious *Soliloquia,* or dialogues between Augustine and his own reason. Strangely enough they contain no reference to the great garden scene. Not only are they all genuinely Neoplatonic in character, but the name of Jesus Christ is absent from the *Soliloquia,* a profoundly religious inquiry into the knowledge of God. Four letters, also composed at that time, confirm an

[1] Augustine *Confessions* VIII. 12.

144

evident discrepancy between their enthusiastic, pronounced Neo-platonic author and the Augustine of the *Confessions*.[2]

Since the four above-mentioned dialogues, together with the contemporary letters, give a far more authentic view of the true Augustine immediately following his conversion, it appears that this same "conversion" was *not* immediately to Christianity. As the context further indicates, the reference is to Augustine's decision to abandon his profession, to devote himself exclusively to a quest for God through philosophy. Finally, the inspiration which henceforth dominated his moral reformation as well as his intellectual and religious development was Neoplatonism, and not Christianity. Therefore, the version presented in the *Confessions* must be ascribed to a Christian fruition read back into the events as related ten years hence. To transpose this whole situation in terms of "two psychologically possible Augustines," as suggested by a wide controversial literature on the subject, amounts only to adding interesting commentaries on human nature in general.

The fact remains that the thought of Augustine had to contend with the tension resulting from a Christian orthodoxy growing in the face of a deep-seated Neoplatonism.[3] Of no author more than of Augustine is it true to say that his treatises must be read in the context of the man's life. And this life remained under the vital inspiration of a piety born of an ontological view of God, phrased in a Neoplatonic grammar of concepts. Hence there are constant relapses into an inconsistency which amounts at times to juxtaposition. To illustrate, I humbly confess to great difficulties in following the line of thought in many a section of even such a short essay as the one *On the Immortality of the Soul*.

Seen in its true light, the tension is one within a created mind wont to be both a pseudo-maker and a grateful receiver at the same time. Augustine's language testifies to this. It constitutes an eloquent

---

[2] This discrepancy was first pointed out by Gaston Boissier in "La Conversion de Saint Augustin," *Revue des deux Mondes*, 85 (1888), 43; and Adolph Harnack, *Augustins Confessionen* (Giessen, 1888).

[3] *Soliloquia* II. 4; *Conf.* VII. 9. 13. VII. 10. 16; VII. 19. 25. *De genesi ad litt.* XII. 16; XII. 24; *De Trinitate.* X. 5; *Lib.* 83 *Quaest.*, Q. 46.

vehicle for penetrating thought as well as tenderness of heart, with figures of repetition and sound running through devout and reflective passages. The Christian in Augustine craves for communion with God as a Person existing in the three ways of memory, understanding, and will or love.[4] The philosopher in him cleaves to the Neoplatonic idea of an absolute being apart from which there is neither good nor reality.[5]

The dominant theme, the true vein of an Augustine at ease with both his piety and his thought, remains that of his first love as expressed in the beautiful apostrophe of the *Soliloquia.*[6] "God, from whom to turn away is to fall; to whom to turn back is to rise again; in whom to abide is to stand fast. God, from whom to part is to die; to whom to return is to live again; in whom to dwell is to live."

This, in fact, is the way the Middle Ages understood Augustine. They saw in him the Christian Neoplatonist inspirer of a pious cloistered wisdom, blissfully absorbed in the intellect's picture of reality identified with reality, however colonized with abstractions. This pious wisdom found its ideal in the purging of the soul from the evil unreality of this world's fetters, with a view to contemplation in the unity of a Church of the elect upheld by God. As a result these cloistered contemplatives were satisfied to meet current intellectual needs by devising fancy cosmologies, all the more comfortable as they were made after the likeness of their mind. Such were those of Gilbert de la Porrée (1076-1154), bishop of Poitiers and chancellor of the school of Chartres,[7] who followed Plato's *Timaeus* in his elaboration of an allegorical world view.

What characterized this basically Platonist-Augustinian approach, then, was that it considered the human intellect not so much a knower as a pseudo-maker.

On the other hand, the main characteristic of the Aristotelian ap-

[4] Cf. Augustine *De Trinitate* V. 9. 10; IX. 2. 2; X. 12. 19; XIV. 8. 11; XV. 6. 10.
[5] *De Trinitate* V. 2. 3.
[6] *Soliloquia* I. 1. 3.
[7] The School of Chartres was otherwise distinguished for its classical culture. This led to a revival of interest in the natural sciences through the study of the works of Hippocrates, Galen, and the medical treatises of the Arabs.

146

proach was that it considered the human intellect essentially as the knower of a phenomenal world. This world is the immediate reality in which we actually live, and move, and have our being. The Aristotelian approach, however, implied many features which were inconsistent with the biblical understanding of this same landscape. These features were further aggravated by the Arab interpreters of Aristotle, more especially by Averroes (1126-98), and it was this aggravated Aristotelianism which forced itself upon a cloistered wisdom during the twelfth century. The fact is, the materialistic and pantheistic theses of the Arabs were condemned by Rome, while an indiscriminate reading of Aristotle was similarly censured by the Pope in 1210, 1215, and 1231.

It should be understood at this point that materialistic, humanistic, and mystical tendencies had contended for primacy in the heart and mind of man from time immemorial. The wisdom of the Chaldeans was already an astrology dominated by deterministic tendencies. Aristotle, then, was true to a historical pattern of long standing when he argued for the eternity of the world, for the eternity of time and of motion,[8] and for circular movement as the primary kind of locomotion.[9] Hence there was an implied belief in alchemy and astrology which remained alive in our Western world down to the eighteenth century—to take an optimistic view of the subject. The naturalist Pliny the Elder (23-79) expressed a perennial view of the universe in his proposition, "Man is a relative of the stars and our soul a part of the heavens." [10] A point by point opposition could be drawn between such views and the biblical view. The eternity of the world contradicts the biblical truth of creation, just as the law of eternal recurrence is opposed to the biblical notion of time so beautifully developed by Augustine into a Christian philosophy of history.

We may now understand the gravity of the emergency which confronted the Church when such "scientific" views burst upon

[8] Cf. the whole argument of his *Physics* culminating in the final Book VIII; *On the Heavens* I. 10-12; III. 6; *Metaphysics* XII. 3; XII. 6.; etc.

[9] *Physics* VIII. 9; *On the Heavens* I. 4.

[10] *Historia naturalis* II. 95.

the twelfth-century scene. For the first time the problem now known to us as that of "science and religion" came within full view. What did our pious Augustinians know about the new science; nay, how could they understand the grammar of the new concepts? It was then that the college appeared, first in the chapel in the form of a cathedral school, then next to the chapel as a more independent institution. Not so much that the chapel proved benevolent in all this; the plain truth is that the chapel needed the college.

Soon, however, the new views took the faculties of art by storm. All the known treatises of Aristotle were publicly taught in Paris, then in Oxford. A man like Siger of Brabant (ca. 1235-81/84), the leading representative figure of Latin Averroism, canon of St. Martin's at Liège, became master of arts in Paris. There arose endless conflicts between this Averroistic modernism and an ultraconservative Augustinianism, while the academic freedom of the university was challenged by a secular clergy whose income began to decrease.

In the main the problem of "science and religion" took the specific form of a conflict between the science of Aristotle on the one hand, and cloistered Christian forms of Platonism and Augustinianism on the other.

It was in the heat of this conflict, and in order to meet the resulting crisis, that Thomas Aquinas (1225-74) intervened, reverently using against his beloved master Augustine the same basic argument that a reverent Aristotle had reluctantly raised against Plato, more especially against his would-be disciples.[11]

Aquinas' master stroke was to size up the gist of the whole difficulty. This he diagnosed as an innate tendency on the part of the Platonic-Augustinian tradition to substitute for the genuine world of things the imprint obtained by forcing the intellect upon it. As opposed to this method of approach he advocated a submission of the knowing intellect to the existing world.

The perennial value of this intervention may be seen in the fact that the Platonic-Augustinian man and the Aristotelian man we

[11] The gist of this Thomistic critique may be found in Summa Theologica I. Q. 84 (in eight articles).

have always with us. Only in safeguarding the primary concern of the Aristotelian man for a *sine qua non* study of our genuine world of reality may we safeguard a genuine culture, not to say anything of a genuine Christian culture.

The crux of this is well brought out in the introduction Anton C. Pegis wrote to the *Basic Writings of St. Thomas Aquinas,* especially in the following passage:

It is not extreme to suggest that when St. Thomas succeeded in disengaging Aristotle from Platonism and in seeing the full power of the Aristotelian critique of Platonism, he had in his hands the solution of the major issue of the thirteenth century. An Aristotle so disengaged was able to expose the basic errors of Platonism. An Anti-Platonic Aristotle— an Aristotle who saves the reality of sensible things, who defends the unity of man, and who refuses to make reality to the image and likeness of the human intellect on the pretext of giving knowledge a basis in reality— was a veritable defender of Christian thought at the point of its greatest vulnerability, the age-old Platonism of St. Augustine and Boethius.[12]

The Primacy of Existence

We may now return to the Aristotelian apex reached at the end of the preceding chapter, the apex at which the last matter fades away as it were, in the form of Pure Act. Whatever the "intensity" of such a "pure" concept, it had to be acknowledged as a mere concept.

An objection to the above conclusion may be drawn from that enigmatic passage in Aristotle's treatise *On the Soul* (III. 5. 430a), in which an ambiguous meaning invites various interpretations. The matter involved is the distinction between passive intellect and active intellect, to which a rapid allusion was already made. This distinction is one between a mere receptive power and a creative power. What is at stake is the nature of this creative power of original thought—"for always the active is superior to the passive factor, the originating force to the matter which it forms." Now the intellect as passive is destructible, according to Aristotle; only the active intellect set free from its present conditions is said by him

[12] New York: Random House, 1945. I, xliii. Used by permission.

to be immortal and eternal. Does this separation, however, imply mere separability, that is, some form of individual immortality? Or does it imply a separate essence, that of a pure intelligence identifiable with God? Admittedly there is here an ambiguity of which Thomas Aquinas did not fail to take advantage in his elaboration of a Christian view. While to him, as to Aristotle, the soul is the form of the body (*anima est forma corporis*), the ways in which it comes to dominate the body as an immaterial principle can only pertain to the creativity of God within the order of nature.[13] This, however, is at best a more indirect way of joining the real issue at hand, which remains that which is involved in the paradox of the reality of the intelligible. And this paradox Aristotle himself did not solve.

A bridge across the genuinely religious views followed in these pages up to Socrates, and Christian philosophy, comes within view with the Thomistic conception of being, on which Aristotle himself had surprisingly little to say. As for Platonism, it only made use of the notion of being in terms of being *as it is thought,* thus becoming responsible for the grievous paradox with which we are still at grips. It is noteworthy that this ambiguity is the specific matter on which Aquinas himself again and again contends with Platonism.[14] The gist of his conclusions is summed up as follows by Anton C. Pegis:

(1) that Plato was depriving being of the constitutive causes of its actual existence; (2) that he was limiting the human intellect to knowing only that sort of being which, in fact, exists in the intellect and of which the intellect is the author; (3) that he was eliminating the world of sense from existence to the extent that he was incapable of deriving it from the abstract Forms of Ideas which are supposed to be its causes; (4) that he was building between thought and the world of sense an insuperable barrier of essences, a barrier that the human intellect would never be able to cross.[15]

The way Aquinas finally disposes of the vexing paradox of the

[13] On this see *Summa Theologica* I, Qq. 75-76.
[14] See for example *Summa Theologica* I. 6. 4; I. 65. 4; I. 76. 3; I. 79. 3; I. 84. 1, 2, 4, 5; I. 85. 3; I. 110. 1; I. 115. 1; etc. *Summa Contra Gentiles* I. 44. 2; III. 24. 69; etc.
[15] *Op. cit.*, p. xlvii. Used by permission of Random House, Inc., publisher.

reality of the intelligible is to show that Being, in the biblical context of Exod. 3:14,[16] is prior to our ideas about it. The profound originality of Thomas consists in showing that our thinking must begin with existence, not with definitions in conceptual terms (essences). The task of the Christian philosopher, as he sees it, is that of expressing the essence of existence in conceptual terms. Henceforth the Aristotelian grammar of concepts may, with a minimum of straightening up, be used to say things Christian, of which the Stagirite never thought. And this is truly a master stroke. By the same token the Platonic-Augustinian approach stands challenged in its essentials.

The ontological argument for the existence of God as stated by Anselm of Canterbury (1033-1109) is a good case to the point. First remember that it is an Augustinian argument originally suggested in the *Confessions*.[17] Anselm is the first to take pride in the fact that there is nothing in his works which is not inwardly related to the writings of Augustine.[18] In true Augustinian manner Anselm strives within toward God, and he stumbles but on himself. How then could he measure his own thought against that altitude? Summing up his own faith in this despair, he exclaims, "I wish to understand that thou exist . . . as that which we believe thee to be. Now we believe that thou art something than which a greater cannot be conceived (*aliquid quo majus nihil cogitari potest*)." [19] But may we truly proceed from the mere *notion* of infinite being to its actual and necessary *existence*? In rejecting the ontological argument in its Anselmian form, Aquinas had in mind the fact that the course ordinarily followed by our natural knowledge is just the reverse of the supernatural order according to which, in his own words, *dicitur esse ipse*

[16] Quoting again, for the sake of convenience: "And God said unto Moses, I AM THAT I AM."

[17] *Confessions* VII. 4.

[18] *Monologium*, Preface in Migne, *Patrologia*, CLVIII, 143.

[19] *Proslogium*, ch. 1. Cf. the classical but debatable objection of Kant in his *Critique of Pure Reason*, tr. Norman Kemp Smith (London: Macmillan & Co., 1929), pp. 500 sq. Also the valuable interpretation of Karl Barth, *Fides quaerens intellectum, Anselm's Beweis der Existenz Gottes im Zusammenhang seines theologischen Programms* (Munich: Chr. Kaiser Verlag, 1931).

actus essentiae—"to be" is the very act whereby an essence is.[20] Proceeding from the existence of a necessary being, we may safely argue that such a necessary pure being must be infinite. Yet, since only one such infinite being is possible, it must be the one and only God. I report this argument as an illustration of the sharp reversal between two approaches, the Platonic-Augustinian and the Thomistic.

The contrast is further seen in the fact that the Thomist argument *par excellence* for the existence of God is the argument from contingency, which proceeds from empirically given existence in true Aristotelian manner. All such existing contingent beings point to some noncontingent existence upon which they are existentially dependent. And here, once more, we immediately detect the first premise of Thomism, that actual existence is prior, while mere possibilities never gave birth to anything.

Henceforth the Platonic paradox of the "reality of the intelligible" would seem to resolve itself. Metaphysical thinking must proceed from existence, not from essence. We ourselves proceed from empirical existence, whether we act or are acted upon. Then we formulate the character and conditions of all such processes in conceptual terms. In so doing we proceed from an existing reality in order to raise ourselves to the conceptual intelligible.

Ideas or universals, so-called, exist within the experienced reality of particulars, *in re*. Then, once abstracted from the reality of such particulars, they become concepts *post rem* in the mind. Only in Him Who Is may the universals be said to have real existence as creative causation *ante rem*. But no distinction is possible at this point, either between God's attributes and God, or between one of God's attributes and another, for God is what he has.

And so, just as we thought we saw religion end where speculation began, we now see metaphysics culminate in a supreme Act of existing and thus come to an end where religion begins. Not that we

[20] Cf. E. Gilson, *Réalisme Thomiste et Critique de la Connaissance* (Paris, 1939), pp. 220-22; J. Maritain, *Existence and the Existent* (New York: Pantheon Books, 1948), pp. 22-35, with special attention to notes 13 and 14.

should separate religion from philosophy, or renounce one for the other, but rather we should keep truth, and keep it whole. Yet the whole burden of the Scholastic formulation is that "only those can do it who realize that he who is the God of the philosophers is HE WHO IS, the God of Abraham, of Isaac, and of Jacob." [21]

A Lofty Ontological Construction

Henceforth it would seem, a Christian culture may run a smooth course. Supreme wisdom is found in the understanding of the end of creation, which also is the first truth, the measure of all truth. More deeply understood, both human wisdom and divine wisdom have the same object and the same origin, since we come from God and our true destiny is to return to God. If the object and the origin are the same, however, the method differs.

Reason proceeds from the things of sense, the most remote from God in the hierarchy of creation. These are effects inadequate to the first cause. They can never allow the creature to attain perfectly unto the Creator. Hence there is the necessity of a form of knowledge superior to that of reason. Not only is the rational method inadequate, but it is difficult and beyond the capabilities of most men. Besides, it needs the stimulation of a desire commensurate with the laborious nature of such an ascension. Nothing short of a glowing vision of the divine goal will suffice.

Hence there is the method of faith, proceeding directly from tradition and Scripture as mediated by the Church. Through this method of faith, eternal life, which consists in a true knowledge of God, has already begun in man. This method is adequate to its object. It guarantees to simple souls the light which they need. In illuminating the goal, moreover, it guards the pilgrim against the faltering of his reason.

A deep agreement between reason and faith is ultimately realized through a supreme reference to God, Principle and End of his creation. Henceforth a strengthened intellect strives to understand what

[21] Gilson, *God and Philosophy*, p. 144.

it already believes. At this apex we come to a truer appraisal of the life of the mind in an almost liturgical atmosphere, for such a dedicated life is already a form of worship.

We live as it were on the borderline between the spiritual world and the world of sense experience—spiritual beings, and yet engaged in matter; God-inspired, yet restricted by the limitations of matter. In the words of Thomas, "we see and judge of all things in the light of the first truth, in so far as the light itself of our intellect . . . is nothing else than an impression of the first truth upon it." [22] "If there existed in our souls a perfect image of God, as the Son is the perfect image of the Father, our mind would know God at once. But the image in our mind is imperfect." [23]

The hierarchy of creation thus reflected in the *Summa Theologica* rises in the domain of thought like the spire of a cathedral piercing the blue mist of a glorious morning. The great Bible of stone, as Emile Mâle called the medieval cathedral, suggests in turn a rich sense of participation with God. It speaks in type in the manner of the Old Testament preparing the way before the gospel. Because the synagogue could not read the harmony therein, it was represented as blindfolded in the art of the thirteenth century. The ultimate rapture of Thomas Aquinas in the chapel of St. Nicholas, as that of Dante at the end of *Paradiso*, is in a real way suggestive of a great vision of the universe caught by them that were born after the Spirit.

And so it would seem that an equilibrium has now been reached between Christianity and culture under God's high heaven. There are sacred places where a man wishes he could make an abiding tabernacle, hallowed moments when he prays it were in his power to suspend time, in the awareness that it is good for him to be where he is. As we reach the end of this chapter, one is tempted to say that such a place must have been the Paris of the thirteenth century where Thomas Aquinas, "the silent ox," as he had been affectionately

[22] *Summa Theologica* I. Q. 88. 3. Reply Obj. i.
[23] *Ibid.*, Reply Obj. 3.

154

nicknamed, dreamed his great theological sum within view of the rising towers of Notre Dame.

Yet a plain fact stares us in the face as we look at the record. Hardly had Thomas been summoned from the earthly scene than the breakdown came to pass. What, then, was the source of all this strain that broke down the lofty ontological construction to which his name remains associated and which only his genius could hold together?

CHAPTER ELEVEN

The AFTERMATH of the ONTOLOGICAL DEVIATION

However great his genius, especially as it led him to realize that our thinking must proceed not from essence but from existence, Thomas Aquinas did not succeed in overcoming the ultimate impact of the ontological deviation which came to our awareness after the consideration of Socrates. However pertinent his reminder to an Augustinian Platonism that the mind is essentially a knower, not a pseudo-maker, he himself paved the way for the Vatican's assertion of the self-sufficiency of the philosopher.[1] To a Roman Catholic, philosophy is emphatically not to be governed by theology, nor does it need theology to defend its premises. It is merely "subject to the external control and negative regulation of theology." [2] The dividing line thus drawn between natural and revealed theology invited from the outset a disruption in the field of created knowledge which Augustine kept whole in his insistence upon "the utility of believing," in his unswerving persuasion that the believing Christian is the only genuine rationalist. The very dividing line Aquinas drew up was the one along which disruptive tensions actually took effect. It was along this line that the "razor" of William of Ockham (1270?- 1349?) proceeded to cut between a full-fledged science henceforth

---

[1] In the year 1870 the Vatican Council defined the point that the existence of God can be established by the human reason without the aid of revelation and made this point binding to Roman Catholic faith (*de fide*).

[2] Jacques Maritain, *An Introduction to Philosophy* (New York: Sheed & Ward, 1937), p. 127.

disengaged from Aristotelian metaphysics, and a biblical Christianity similarly freed from scholastic entanglement. To exalt the powers of "unaided reason" is to invite the self-assertion of a faithless reason, and by the same token, the subsequent revolt of an evangelical conscience. To the consideration of the aftermath of this situation we now turn.

The Reformation and the New Science

The Thomistic supreme Act of Existing, elaborated on this side of natural philosophy as a static, Self-contemplative, Self-contained, ab-solute Entity, bears witness to the fact that the ontological deviation that appeared after Socrates was never fully atoned for. The identification of the living God of Exod. 3:14 with the supreme Act of Existing came as the belated culmination of a laborious ontological development. Hence there arose an ambitious substructure of human concepts partly involved in obsolete scientific notions. It has been insisted that Plato's postulation of the Ideas was essentially a scientific attempt at explaining the ultimate nature of reality. By the same token the Aristotelian-Thomistic synthesis and the new science were in some ways disputing the same ground.

We readily acknowledge that Thomas and his followers came to an increasing awareness of the advisability of disentangling scholasticism from whatever remained of its original scientific scaffolding. It may be argued [3] in this connection that the notions implied in the Thomistic grammar of concepts are so general as to constitute a system of propositions similar to those of formal logic or pure mathematics; that, as a result, no "science" is involved in them; finally, that their naturalness, as well as their resulting universality, creates a common ground between philosophers and men of culture. To this we also agree.

What comes to our awareness at this point, however, is that in the measure as Thomism thus succeeded in its expurgation, the re-

[3] Cf. Richard McKeon, *Selections from Medieval Philosophers* (New York: Charles Scribner's Sons, 1930), II, 422-23 n. 1; also Jacques Maritain, *op. cit.* Part Two, ch. vii, "Ontology; Act and Potentiality," esp. n. 1, pp. 253-54.

sulting notions are actually seen to be so general as to amount to nothing more than tautologies.[4] They are open to what Theodore M. Greene likes to expose as "empty, meaningless verbiage." Jean Wahl concludes a laborious survey of them with such discouraging comments as: "The effort to give significance to the term 'Being' seems bound to fail." [5] "If, finally, we had to choose between the acceptance and the rejection of the idea of substance, we should even have to go so far as to reject it; it has brought so much mischief to philosophy—as much perhaps as the ideas of Being and of cause." [6] Similarly Dorothy Emmet, considering the Thomistic analogy of Being, summarizes some of her conclusions as follows:

If we try to abstract the general, univocal character of structure of Being as such, pure Being, considered as a universal, becomes, as Hegel saw, the lowest and emptiest, and not the highest category. But this is the very opposite of what Thomist writers intend. . . .

The "Transcendentals," unity, distinction, good, truth, which purport to say something about the universal character of Being, in effect tell us no more than that "It is what it is." And since we do not know how the divine attributes are realized in the divine existence, the Analogy of Proportionality in effect tells us no more." [7]

Finally, even those Thomistic concepts which have been purified of any "scientific" connotation, to the point of becoming tautologies bordering on verbiage, remain mostly ignored as a universal means of communication between philosophy and science. A Roman Catholic philosopher like Etienne Gilson in our day is thus left to deplore "the hostility exhibited by a wholly mathematized science toward the irreducible act of existence." [8] He is further chagrined by Sir Arthur Eddington's way of exposing the ambiguity of this and similar terms, "There *is* an overdraft at the bank. Is an 'overdraft at a bank' something that exists?" [9]

[4] Charles W. Morris, *Signs, Language, and Behaviour* (New York: Prentice Hall, 1946), pp. 175 sq.

[5] *The Philosopher's Way* (New York: Oxford University Press, 1948), p. 53.

[6] *Ibid.*, p. 27.

[7] *The Nature of Metaphysical Thinking*, p. 187.

[8] *God and Philosophy*, p. 138.

[9] *Ibid.*, p. 139.

158

By the same token, and in the measure as the Thomistic ontology claimed the prerogatives of natural theology, it was bound to claim the ground strongly held by an evangelical Christianity of Paulinian and Augustinian inspiration. From both Paul and Augustine the Reformers have learned that the field of created knowledge should be kept whole. They also insist upon "the utility of believing" in an unswerving persuasion that the believing Christian is the only genuine rationalist. The consideration of God's agency actually belongs to the warp and woof of thousands of years of human awareness. As such, surely, it is no intruder in human thought. Yet it is this solution which stands condemned in the very nature of Thomism as already stated. It must be avoided at all costs in order to safeguard the autonomy of even a Christian philosophy.

But then, again, how great the cost! The Protestant Reformation was part of that cost.

The Reformers were in line with such men as Tertullian and Bernard of Clairvaux in their opposition to the speculative method in natural theology, and more especially to a philosophic approach of Aristotelian inspiration. The best way the Reformers found to avoid what they considered unprofitable and perverse contentions as to the First Cause was to point to the living God of Scripture. Thus Calvin's main concern was always with the honor of God. He appealed to the fact of God, as against unbridled speculation on the first principle of philosophical intelligibility which might not be God at all.

But more, the lay scientist himself has learned to practice in his own way that same *credo quia absurdum* of Tertullian, and in strikingly similar circumstances. For this is what Galileo actually did when he appealed to "irreducible and stubborn facts" as against the inflexible rationality of Aristotelian logic. Seen in this light, both the Reformation and the advent of modern science prove to have been aspects of the same historical revolt against Scholasticism, as Whitehead has shown. Neither should this essential feature of our modern times be blamed on the Cartesian departure from the Scholastic analogy of Being, as is done by the Neo-Thomists today. Such reasonings amount to mistaking the symptoms for the malady. The

159

THE CHRISTIAN APPROACH TO CULTURE

feature here under consideration must be ascribed on the one hand to what Whitehead would call the "remorseless inevitableness" that "pervades scientific thought," and on the other to the set purpose of isolating natural philosophy from a theology of biblical inspiration.

The gist of the scientific method at its best is that a pattern of clues on a given situation has to be experimentally and critically worked out to a point where it may be expressed in mathematical terms. Henceforth it will rule over the realm of available facts concerned, to the exclusion of other theories, until, fresh information having been brought forward, a reconsideration takes place. Thus the relativity theory brought us to a closer estimation of known facts than did the Newtonian view of the universe.

The Pythagorean doctrine emphasized that mathematical aspect of scientific knowledge. The same was further refined by Plato. But the method was lost sight of by Aristotle who was essentially a biologist emphasizing classification. Whitehead points out that, as a result, the popularity of Aristotle's logic "retarded the advance of physical science throughout the Middle Ages," and he concludes with this telling exclamation, "If only the schoolmen had measured instead of classifying, how much they might have learnt!" [10]

This Aristotelian stagnation came to an end the day Galileo rediscovered the method inaugurated by Pythagoras and perfected by Plato, in other words, the mathematical emphasis inseparable from any fruitful quest. Thus, for example, Galileo's discovery of the principle of inertia put an end to the rationalizations of Aristotle on his first movers, and it paved the way for the Newtonian view of the universe and ultimately for the views of relativity and quantum.

In the context of such developments our notion of causality, according to *The Philosophy of Physics* of Max Planck, the father of the quantum theory, has become in our day a mere heuristic principle, a way of asking questions, as a child does. In other words, that principle of causality allows us to find a path through the confusion of events, in order to know in what direction the investigation "must

[10] A. N. Whitehead, *Science and the Modern World* (New York: The Macmillan Co., 1925), p. 43.

proceed so that it shall reach useful results." What quantum physics revealed to one of the greatest physicists of our day and age in this matter of causation is that, however relevant and useful our so-called first principles may be, they will prove to be beyond verification. To quote again from Max Planck: "It is true that the law of causality cannot be demonstrated any more than it can be logically refuted: it is neither correct nor incorrect." [11]

What has actually happened in modern times now becomes clear. A great deal of damage has been done to the Aristotelian notion of causality, both in systematic theology and in science, through that "remorseless inevitableness that pervades human thought at its best." Jean Wahl puts it this way: the history of the philosophical—and chiefly Aristotelian—theory of causality "is the history of the diminishing number of causes, and finally even of the vanishing of the idea of cause." [12] No wonder Thomists find it hard to reconvert either Protestant theologians or contemporary physicists to Aristotle.

Thus attention is drawn once more upon a deep solidarity between the Reformation and the new science. It appears from the record that by birth and by right the Reformed tradition was destined to clarify and apply a good neighbor policy with the growing catholicity of science through which the thinking of the world of men and affairs was to be framed increasingly. There is, as has been pointed out,[13] a Christian view of nature and of human nature; there is more especially a Christian outlook on history, including our own life history; there is a Christian approach to psychology and human relations; there is a Christian epistemology preparing the way for constructive Christian metaphysics. It has been further insisted that such views were destined to appeal to the scientist as a person, if carefully defined. The scientist may pause even in his scientific capacity, as his new friend the Christian proceeds to suggest deeper interpretations of available uncolored data in such fields as history, psychology, and ethics, or to submit further propositions on points where science had

[11] *Op. cit.*, pp. 82-83. Used by permission of W. W. Norton & Co., publisher.
[12] *Op. cit.*, p. 111.
[13] Chap. 5.

nothing to say because it never paused to consider the deeper, religious "why" issue—for example that ours is a *created* universe, utterly dependent upon God for its existence. Thus, it was concluded, the Christian scholar would render unto Caesar the things that are Caesar's only to secure a firm hold upon the things that are God's.

Yet the record shows that the Reformed tradition did not take advantage of its solidarity with the new science for assuming its God-given responsibility of providing a genuine leadership for culture. Whitehead states unhesitatingly that "the Reformation, for all its importance, may be considered as a domestic affair of the European races. . . . When we project this great revolution upon the whole history of the Christian Church, we cannot look upon it as introducing a new principle into human life." [14] What actually happened is that a relapse into scholastic ways of thought, followed by the reaction of a growing liberalism, brought about in the long run a partial assimilation of Protestant Christianity to culture by surrender to an increasingly secularized culture. The reason culture became increasingly secularized, on the other hand, is that having belatedly realized the hollowness of its ontological premises of old, it yielded more and more to the scientific and moral conditioning of modern thought. These points will retain our attention in the following sections.

The Secularization of Culture

We cannot understand the climate of modern thought if we fail to realize that it labored for a long time under the false premises of ontology—and of a decadent ontology at that. It is a fact that Descartes, the "father" of modern philosophy, himself proceeded from scholasticism and remained profoundly under the sway of ontological thinking. His language is permeated through and through with scholastic terms. The cartesian "revolution," as a result, comes short of having been the "break" it is currently supposed to have been. What actually happened is that Descartes and his followers, whenever they were concerned about God, would seek his reality in the ontological realm where it admittedly was not to be found. This

[14] *Op. cit.,* p. 2.

162

explains in large measure why modern thought lost its way in the wilderness of this world amidst the dry bones of scholastic concepts. Hence there developed an increasingly debilitating climate, a dreary landscape where there was not left so much as a statue to the unknown God of Scripture.

As the living God thus recedes from man's consciousness, human existence tends to become the primary fact. Descartes devised a new method which proceeds from methodical doubt, while his own existence becomes the starting point of his *Meditations*. Henceforth moderns live, and move, and have their being in a world of self-assertion. They do so to such an extent that they become acclimatized. They are no longer aware that agnosticism is in the air they breathe, in their very flesh and blood. The basic truth which has been acknowledged at the beginning of the present book as the charter for all sound thinking would now seem out of place in such a climate: "In the beginning God . . ." And yet, because it faded away, everything *ipso facto* was found beyond verification. Should the modern then at some point actually make contact with the deeper reality, he would no longer have the means of convincing himself or others that it was so. Such conviction constitutes the undeniable privilege of those who constantly proceed from the acknowledgment of the Christian landscape of reality as the *norm* it actually is. The fact that the *other*, faithless norm henceforth becomes the premise of all sound thinking gives the measure of the falling away of modern man.

When Descartes made up his mind never to accept a thing as truth which he did not "clearly and distinctly" know to be such, he established his own reason as the supreme judge of what is true or false. His rule of evidence set up a new deal in human thinking. Although Descartes made careful reservations in setting apart the truths of religion and the sphere of conduct, the implications of the rule of evidence are so radical that men like Bacon, Hobbes, and Leibnitz appear to be conservative in their thinking, as compared with the author of the *Discourse on Method*.

Man, the individual, is now on his way to supreme sovereignty. He is becoming the center and the measure of all things, proceeding on the assumption that reality can be compassed by his own understanding of it, that it is no greater or richer than his own individual conception of it, and again that truth is purely a matter of cold rationality. And this conception condemns man to ignore that which in the universe may be impervious to thought. It may even be that this world of rationality which Descartes constructed in his mind on the model of geometry is precisely the one which matters least to man! So extreme a rationalism amounts to a virtual expulsion of man from true reality. So truth is one and the same with clarity? Are our deeper convictions always concerned with clear ideas? Isn't it fair to claim, on the other hand, that certain notions may be clear without being true?

If there is a God, this so-called "method" is bound to pass him by, for it eliminates at the outset all that in man infinitely surpasses man. That such an attitude of mind eliminates the supernatural, that is, the divine, need not surprise us any longer, because the conclusion is implied in its very method. Some will again remark that Descartes did not mean to apply this method to "revealed religion," but his disciples would ignore such a limitation.

Such a consequence, however, will make itself felt rather slowly because of the fact that philosophers of following generations, especially in England and America, will retain religious beliefs which will act as a check on too wild a radicalism. A study of John Locke would well illustrate this point. Indeed, the author of the *Treatises of Government* owed much to a moderate disposition, to scientific interests, to a rich political experience, and to a splendid training in toleration, in which John Owen, the liberal vice-chancellor of Oxford, had played a large part. But if John Locke seems to be one of the pioneers of modern liberalism, it is chiefly because his Puritan ancestry destined him to steer a middle course between traditionalism and empiricism. He avoided the extremes to which his unrestrained followers were to go. In fact he would have been horrified to see what the Deists or the Sensationalists made out of his *Essay Concerning Human Understanding*.

In search for "the limits and extent of human knowledge" Locke had been led to the formulation of a new psychology. Awakened by the lucidity of Descartes, he had followed the meditations of this teacher and discovered a new path of investigation. Descartes was interested in clear and distinct ideas as a criterion of truth; Locke's attention was drawn to the value of the instrument we use in our quest for truth, namely the human mind. How does it work? How deep can it go? Capital questions these, for a man who was then formulating his program of enlightenment. The fact is that the two *Treatises of Government* and the *Essay Concerning Human Understanding* were in the making as early as 1671, although completed only years later. Denying innate ideas, Locke was to state that we are born with a mind which may be likened to a piece of white paper, and that any marking made upon it will be derived from our own sense experience. Our own, let us insist. This is why each one of us is entitled to his ideas, for "nothing is in the intellect that has not been first in the sense." Since his individual mind starts without any prejudices, man is free. And since each one of us enjoys the same privilege, toleration is in order. The *Essay* leads naturally to the *Letters on Toleration.*

We may recognize the shadow of Cleopatra's nose in the fact that the spreading of Locke's ideas should be helped by Marlborough and the British Fleet, and we may therefore discard here that aspect of the question. The best messenger of Locke on the Continent was Voltaire. In his *Lettres philosophiques sur les Anglais*—in the thirteenth letter, to be more specific—he could hardly contain his admiration for "Mr. Locke." The whole French eighteenth century was ready to welcome a doctrine that could prove to be extremely useful in coping with the excesses of a divine rights monarchy which called for immediate reform. In a new environment the *via media* philosophy of Locke was destined to be formulated in terms of an extreme radicalism.

To begin with, Condillac arbitrarily reduces Locke's psychological analysis to a sensationalism pure and simple, in which the very personality of the individual often vanishes. Or rather, the mind is subordinated to things. Its main function is merely to reflect back the

165

order existing in the universe. To use an expression of Bacon—and it is not by mere chance that Bacon should be quoted at this point, since the eighteenth century is on the whole a continuation of the sixteenth—the function of the mind is to be that of a "perfect mirror." Indeed, it is originally like a piece of white paper. Progressively the outside world marks upon the mind its immutable order. The outer world penetrates man through the medium of sensations. These sensations in turn develop into more elaborate forms, finally into ideas, at the same time shaping the mind in the image of the universe, after its likeness. What we call reason, then, is nothing but the residue of the various impressions left us. So *philosophes* and *encyclopédistes* will argue, truth comes from nature alone. So does virtue. Let us therefore in all our activities return to nature as to the source of all good. Through the language of pain and pleasure it will tell us what to do; it will free us from the struggles born of obsolete moral notions. Churchmen who pretend to have claims on our behavior are liars trying to exploit the people.

Such conceptions direct society to the study of nature with a view to its utilization for human happiness; they call for an industrial revolution; they are to shape a matter-of-fact spirit of positivism chiefly concerned with direct observation and experimentation, within the limits of a horizon without poetry or mystery. This gives to liberated man a tremendous confidence in himself and in his own achievements.

Meanwhile, a considerable increase in experimental knowledge confirms an optimistic view of man and his power, and, at the same time, upsets a view of the universe to which Christianity had long been attached. A Newtonian universe is taking the place of the Aristotelian universe. In this new framework of human thinking everything seems to be determined by the mechanical play of natural law.

The laughter of Voltaire ushers in the new outlook. For example, to Voltaire a metaphysician is a great man with whom one learns little, metaphysics being made of two parts, the first stating that which everybody knows, the second that about which no one will ever know anything. Kant indirectly justifies this position when he shows that the *noumena*—we may say, the realm of things divine—is definitely beyond our reach. Kant believed himself called upon to effect in philosophy a revolution comparable to that of Copernicus and Newton in physics. Just as the motions of the heavenly bodies were explained by Copernicus as appearances due to our position on the moving earth, so, according to Kant, the particulars extended in time and space were only *phenomena* or appearances due to the peculiar make-up of the human mind. What things are in themselves, *an sich* (*noumena*), we have no way of knowing ultimately. There can be no final knowledge of the deeper reality of the things that are, as they really *are* in themselves. Thus the real reality must remain unknown. There can be no transcendental metaphysics. All this notwithstanding, the laws which govern the workings of nature remain valid when we interpret them as grounds of the possibility of experience, but then, they only apply within the bounds of experience. And this takes in the whole classical physics *ipso facto* justified. In other words, the position which entails the rejection of metaphysics by the same token implies the validity of a Newtonian conception of nature seen to be in conformity with the structure of the mind impressed upon it. Henceforth, natural philosophy is absorbed by Newtonian physics as the natural philosopher once more becomes a prisoner of his own intellect.

History has it that at this point, when the great German philosopher had completed his *Critique of Pure Reason,* he heard sobbing behind him and, turning to his valet, found him crying, "You have taken my God away!" To console him, Kant thereupon wrote the *Critique of Practical Reason.* Since the *a priori* categories of the understanding once drawn out of their strict empirical use produce at best a transcendental illusion,[15] the only escape from the resulting agnosticism was that offered by Rousseau, whom Kant admired as much as he did Newton. There remained in man the categorical

---

[15] *Critique of Pure Reason,* tr. Max Müller (Rev. ed.; New York: The Macmillan Co., 1927), pp. 238 sq. I hardly need to remind the reader that the Transcendental Dialectic as a whole constitutes the crux of the Kantian critique.

exigencies of duty, the divine voice of conscience. "Duty! Thou sublime and mighty name." [16] Here, at least, was the whole realm of human will firmly oriented, nay, unconditionally swayed by a moral obligation which could be apprehended by reason.

The last two paragraphs thus direct attention to two essential aspects of the conditioning of modern thought, namely, the scientific and the moral aspects. Undeniably, human thought has always been thus conditioned. It is of special interest here to see what forms this conditioning would take in the modern climate.

The Scientific Conditioning of Modern Thought

Whatever is stated in the following pages of this section should admittedly be appraised in the context of the more general fact of a cosmological conditioning of culture. It appears in this larger context that Western man has been thinking thus far within two great cosmological frames of reference, namely, the Aristotelian and the Newtonian. Further, it would seem that from the second one he is now slowly proceeding into a third, that is, the framework of relativity and quanta. It should also be pointed out that each transition involved a cultural crisis. The passage from the Aristotelian to the Newtonian frame of reference was reflected in the crises known as the Renaissance and the Reformation, just as the present period of transition from the Newtonian framework to that of Einstein and Max Planck calls forth on every side the outcry of "crisis" too. Not that these changes in cosmological conditioning of themselves suffice to account for the crises involved, or even that they constitute the essential set of circumstances. All that is meant is that there is some relation between man's thinking and the dominating cosmological conception of the time.

With this in mind, then, let us turn our attention more especially to the ways in which the unprecedented progress of scientific thinking since Galileo has precipitated the drama of Christian metaphysics, whose aftermath we are only beginning to realize.

[16] J. J. Rousseau, "Profession of Faith of a Vicar of Savoy," *Emil, or On Education,* Book IV.

168

In his book *Science and Common Sense,* James B. Conant charac- terizes science as an interconnected series of conceptual schemes which have arisen out of successful experimentation and observa- tion.[17] This being the case, scientific activity remains fruitful only in the measure as it is productive of *further* experimentation and observation. In the same vein Richard Kroner insists that each and every cultural pattern constitutes a living answer to the essential contradictions of experience.[18] Let us now bring this criterion to bear upon the case of Aristotelian physics. It actually ceased to be pro- ductive of further development and became stagnant due to Aris- totle's relative neglect of the mathematical approach to natural science. It has already been pointed out that the Stagirite favored a rationalizing and classifying approach. It must be granted, moreover, that he was further restrained by the limitations of technology in his day.

Albert Einstein and Leopold Infeld help us locate the point where a fault developed and a break came. Just as is the case in the reading of fiction, a false clue confuses the story and postpones the solution.[19] For our purpose the wrong clue was Aristotle's law of motion as stated in the *Mechanics,* and according to which a moving body comes to a standstill when the force which propels it no longer acts upon it.

The "break" occurred when Galileo found the clue which led Newton to the formulation of the law of *inertia.* Suppose someone pushing a cart along a level road suddenly stops pushing. Although the cart will come to a halt, it will not immediately do so. It will move on a short distance, gradually decelerating through the retard- ing action of friction and whatever small obstacles it may strike. Hence there comes the new formulation: "Every body perseveres in a state of rest, or of uniform motion in a straight line, unless it is compelled to change that state by forces acting thereon." What mat-

[17] New Haven: Yale University Press, 1951.

[18] *Culture and Faith* (Chicago: University of Chicago Press, 1951).

[19] *The Evolution of Physics. The Growth of Ideas from Early Concepts to Rela- tivity and Quanta* (New York: Simon & Schuster, 1938), p. 6.

ters, then, in the idealized experiment is change, either in motion or direction. It is not velocity itself, but *change* in velocity or direction, which has to be taken into consideration. In classical mechanics, therefore, the immediate data are force and change in velocity or direction. But what is force? It is a push or a pull which tends to produce in motion a change in either velocity or direction, or both.

The initial clue to the laws of motion was thus found when it appeared that force is that which produces a change in motion, both force and change of velocity vector having the same direction. At this point a quantitative formulation was called for to express the magnitude or the change involved. A consideration of this further aspect of the problem led Newton to complete his first law of motion with a second, and ultimately to formulate his general law of gravitation. Mass particles in the universe attract each other by a force directly proportional to the product of their masses, and inversely proportional to the squares of their distance apart. This is known as the inverse square law.

A scientific problem having been patiently and critically worked out to a point where its solution may be expressed with mathematical precision, the resulting formula will henceforth "rule" over a corresponding realm of reality to the exclusion of all others. The limitations and imperfections of this solution, as universally acknowledged in the world of science, give the status of its actual scope. This would be the case for Newton's square law as he presented it in manuscript form to the Royal Society in 1686: *"Two particles of masses m_1 and m_2 which are at a distance r apart at a definite instant of time, are at that instant attracted to each other by a force of magnitude $\beta m_1 m_2 / r^2$, where β is a universal constant."*

Both the law of inertia and the law of gravitation originated in physical hypotheses which had to be checked at every point by observation. As they were confirmed, they enabled the physicist to describe and *predict* in a convenient way an ever-increasing group of observable phenomena. Once again, therefore, the criterion of a genuine science is found in the element of *continuity* in the success of the scientific enterprise.

Once justified by observations on the motion of the moon, the Newtonian laws[20] allowed a calculation of the masses of the earth, the sun, and other astronomical bodies to a high degree of precision.

Further generalized, the Newtonian concept was extended to other fields and culminated in what is now called classical physics. A line of thought developed in one branch of physics was applied to another. From the notion of temperature, for example, classical physics passed to notions of heat, heat capacity, or specific heat. Heat could not be a substance. It was an energy of motion, a "kinetic," that is, motion-producing energy, as opposed to "potential" energy. This kinetic energy was further found to obey the conservation laws. Henceforth the world was conceived of as made up of matter and energy. Heat being energy, every problem concerned with it became a mechanical problem. According to this type of generalized mechanical view, all phenomena could further be explained by the interaction of forces representing either attraction or repulsion. These, in turn, depended only upon distance as they acted between unchangeable particles. In the case of the kinetic theory of matter, this mechanical view arising from mechanical problems finally encompassed all heat phenomena and led to a successful structural picture. And so the universe of Newton, from the Brownian particles[21] to the most distant planets known, truly became a clocklike machine whose mechanism could be transcribed with mathematical precision.

And yet we know that even this seemingly perfect picture of

[20] Completed with Kepler's laws of planetary motion:
  1. The planets move in ellipses which are nearly circular, with the sun as one focus.
  2. The radius vector from the sun to a planet sweeps out equal areas in equal time.
  3. The squares of the period of revolution of the planets are proportional to the cubes of their greatest distances from the sun.

[21] This reference is to Brownian movement, that is, to the rapid oscillatory movement of small particles suspended in liquids, discovered by Dr. Brown around 1827. For the sake of convenience, let us recall the dates of Kepler (1571-1630), Galileo (1564-1642), Newton (1642-1727).

reality broke down in the fullness of time. This happened when, fresh information having become available, it became impossible to explain *all* phenomena by assuming the action of simple forces between unchangeable particles. Curiously enough, at least for the layman, the breakdown did not come about from progress in astrophysics, but it occurred in the realm of electric and optical phenomena. For instance, in the case of a moving charge acting upon a magnetic needle, there was neither attraction nor repulsion, but evidence of a force acting perpendicularly to the line connecting the needle and the charge. This force, moreover, instead of depending solely upon distance, varied also according to the velocity of the charge. In optics, meanwhile, it proved ultimately impossible to reduce phenomena to mechanical terms.

The mechanical interpretation, then, broke down because the time came when it proved inadequate to cope with the data resulting from fresh information. An answer had to be sought in the two fields in which inadequacy had been revealed, namely, those of electricity and optics. Neither should this brief account postulate a perfectly methodical continuity in the research involved. The plain truth is that physical theories are for a large part the product of "free" imagination, as pointed out by the French mathematician Hadamard.[22] Imagination, on the other hand, is inspired and oriented by the necessity of resolving discrepancies. The scientist is perforce engaged in a form of detective work. He is a sort of Sherlock Holmes, aiming at a transcription likely to fit the facts. His task in the presence of nature, according to a parable of Einstein, is very much like that of a man who had been given a closed watch which he could not open. His business would then amount to figuring out the workings of that watch. The link which provides an element of continuity between previous findings and newly discovered discrepancies in the process of invention is obviously the mystery of the closed watch.

James Clerk Maxwell (1831-79) was evidently looking at this mystery from the angle of either electricity or optics, or both, when

[22] Cf. *An Essay on the Psychology of Invention in the Mathematical Field* (Princeton University Press, 1945).

he proceeded to measure the strength of a current electrostatically, then electromagnetically. It was startling to him to discover that the resulting ratio agreed numerically with the speed of light. This must mean that electromagnetic waves are of the same nature as light waves. For the Newtonian view of widely separated events in terms of mass or substance, distance, time, and space, he substituted the notion of a *field* where electric and magnetic phenomena could be described in accordance with the laws of conservation of energy. Having substituted the field-view of nature for the attraction-repulsion view, Maxwell proceeded to formulate the equation representing the structure of the field, thus preparing the way for Max Planck and Einstein, for quanta and relativity.

Since Maxwell's discovery, energy has tended to replace substance more and more. By far the greatest part of energy is indeed concentrated in matter, but the field representing the particle *also* represents matter, though in incomparably smaller quantity. The contemporary physicist is tempted to speak in terms of matter where there is a great concentration of energy, and in terms of field where the concentration of energy is limited. As a result, the distinction between matter and field is more and more felt to be an artificial one. Could it be that the very concept of matter could be given up and a pure field physics set up? This has been found impossible so far because the Maxwell laws and the gravitational laws break down in the case of great concentrations of energy. Thus the physicist still needs matter—at least for a while.

Cosmological views have a strange destiny indeed. At first they have to struggle for recognition. Once firmly established, they in turn fight for survival and become reactionary. Both the law of inertia and the law of gravitation resulted from a consideration of the difficulties inherent in an obsolete concept. Hence there arose a conflict between this concept and the new solution offered. Galileo appealed to "irresistible and stubborn facts" as against the inflexible rationality of Aristotle's *Mechanics*. The resulting laws of classical physics were justified because they actually worked. They enabled the physicist to describe and *predict* an ever-widening portion of observable

173

phenomena in more convenient ways. It is noteworthy that this way of looking at the situation was taken for granted in the middle of the nineteenth century. By then the laws of classical physics had become part and parcel of a set view of the universe, so well set, in fact, that from Kant down to Spencer there was no doubt but that it was possible to establish it by way of demonstration. It was taken for granted that the universal relevance of Euclidean geometry and Newtonian physics had been established forever, and further, that the Kantian critique as a whole implied the perennial character of classical physics. It would seem, then, that a philosophical world view remains open to the danger of involving to a certain degree the crystallization of the science that used to prevail. In the words of Philip Frank, "Each philosophical creed petrified the state of physics that prevailed at the time." [23] And so, in a way, comprehensive philosophical views prove to be in part abandoned rationalizations of an obsolete science.

Do these conclusions apply to the Kantian critique? There seems to be no doubt that they do. Etienne Gilson states the case as follows:

The *Critique of Pure Reason* is a masterly description of what the structure of the human mind should be, in order to account for the existence of a Newtonian conception of nature, and assuming that conception to be true to reality. Nothing can show more clearly the essential weakness of physicism as a philosophical method. The pure reason described by Kant could last no longer than the Newtonian physics, which it was its proper function to justify.[24]

This is admittedly the extreme view of a Thomist who is aware of the truth that "what makes it difficult for us to go back to Thomas Aquinas is Kant." [25] It is a fact that all modern, anti-Thomistic tendencies come to a head in the Kantian critique, that the metaphysics therein condemned have found their most adequate expression in the Thomistic synthesis. It is mostly at the ontological realism of Aquinas that the Kantian critique is aimed. But more, behind this

[23] *Modern Science and Its Philosophy* (Cambridge, Mass.: Harvard University Press, 1949), p. 23.

[24] *The Unity of Philosophical Experience* (New York: Charles Scribner's Sons, 1937), pp. 229-30.

[25] Gilson, *God and Philosophy,* p. 114.

ontological realism of Thomas, it is the whole edifice of Roman Catholic thought which is threatened by the Kantian critique. Ever since the epoch-making encyclical *Aeterni Patris* (August 4, 1879) in which Pope Leo XIII advocated a return to the *perennis philosophia,* Rome has urged a return to the teaching of Aquinas. The formula of Leo XIII was "*vetera novis augere,*" that is, "enrich the old with the new." The *augmentum* element was meant to "nourish" a venerable teaching called upon to meet the needs of a changing world of culture. What is at stake, then, for a Roman Catholic philosopher in the face of the Kantian critique is his whole way of thinking. The implication is that deep feelings are involved on his part in the issue under consideration.

It has been made clear in the opening part of this chapter that it would be inadvisable to return to the ontological realism of Aquinas. Neither is it necessary to espouse the extreme view above expressed by Gilson with reference to the Kantian critique. Besides, it would be wrong to subscribe to the radicalism which leads the Thomist philosopher to state that "the pure reason described by Kant could last no longer than the Newtonian physics." It would seem from the outset that there is more in the pure reason described by Kant than a mere justification of the Newtonian physics.

With this in mind, let us now turn to the further problem previously pointed out, that of the *moral* conditioning of modern thought. This one also will be found to culminate in the Kantian critique as already hinted.

The Moral Conditioning of Modern Thought

As the Age of Enlightenment came into its own, a Christian view of ontological persuasion had disintegrated to such a degree that religion at its best had already become what Matthew Arnold was to call later "morality touched with emotion." Even at that, the emotional factor was sadly lacking in many instances. It was this moralism which increasingly conditioned the thinking of modern man.

The most memorable episode of the undermining of a supernatural religion of grace had been David Hume's treatment of beliefs in miracles.[26] By the time Wesley appeared on the scene, a frigid deism had gripped even the Presbyterian Kirk of Scotland. "The deists held such a diversity of beliefs," writes Professor Torrey, "that the term 'deism' has come to be descriptive . . . of a purely philosophical attitude. We may define it, however, as consisting in the acceptance of a natural religion based on common ideas of morality and including the worship of an impersonal deity, whose laws are plain and engraved in the hearts of all men, as opposed to revealed religions with their supernatural doctrines and specific religious duties." [27] It is a fact that Enlightenment itself testifies to the rebirth of a naturalism at least as old as Epicurus, which had come into its own with the humanism of the Renaissance. In such an age, the voice of conscience seemed to provide the only reliable witness.

The plight of Christianity notwithstanding, the morality prevalent in many a noble soul testified to a biblical legacy. This was the case for Rousseau's faith in the divine character of the voice of conscience, of the sublime and mighty name of Duty—obviously a residue of scriptural teaching in the heart of Geneva's prodigal son. As such it found a responsive chord in whatever was left in Kant of a long tradition of pietism.[28] In other words, the sublime and mighty character of the resulting Kantian imperative may be identified from the outset as Christian by birth and right.

What actually happened is that while Kant saw in the sublimity of duty a revelation of the categorical imperative in man's conscience, he could not fail to realize at the same time and by the same token that the *experience* involved pertained to the empirical realm. Yet the practical rules derived from actual practice were seemingly independent of scientific knowledge. It was only later that the relevance of an empirical approach to "moral science" became a familiar

[26] Contained in Section 10 of his *Enquiry Concerning Human Understanding* (1748).

[27] N. L. Torrey, *The Spirit of Voltaire* (New York: Columbia University Press, 1938), p. 228.

[28] On this see Theodore M. Greene's introduction to his translation (together with H. H. Hudson) of *Religion Within the Limits of Reason Alone* (Chicago: The Open Court Pub. Co., 1934), pp. xii-xxii.

notion, as the human sciences (*Geisteswissenschaften*) defined their methods. They are still at work on this complex task. Kant then was still very much in the same position Plato had been when the time came to account for the inspired morality of Socrates. His solution, in fact, was in many ways similar to that of Plato. Philosophers are impatient by nature, forgetting that time may be likened to an old gentleman who respects only that which is done in his company. And so, in their anxiety to solve even the highest problems, they close the debate before the fullness of time is reached. Their greatest temptation, then, is to fill in the unknown ahead of them by spinning out of their mind some ontological entity. In the case of Plato the Ideas came into "existence." In the case of Kant the artifact was derived from the "categorical imperative."

An impressive imperative given empirically was found by Kant to be scientifically unaccountable. So Kant concluded that there must be a reason for such a unique situation. It occurred to him that the rules of moral practice were not to be derived from a scientific and objective empirical study of reality simply because they did not need to be. The reason for this was there for every thinking man to see. The "absolute" character of the categorical imperative carried within itself its own justification. Clearly the "fact" therein involved was a unique fact. Kant, therefore, devised a unique name for it; he called it "a fact of the reason"—that is, in a way "an intelligible-reality" (the hyphen is important). Thus the Platonic paradox reappeared at this end of the by-pass designated as the ontological deviation. Only this time the paradox revealed in the thinking of Kant a boldness unknown even to Plato. What came into being in the Kantian categorical imperative was a hybrid artifact where intelligibility and reality were wrought out in one act of existence. Nay, the critic of Thomistic ontological realism outdid Thomas himself by that feat. Neither do we need to insist that the Kantian artifact was much farther away from the living God than Aquinas' Supreme Act of Existing had ever been. There was essentially this difference, that from the latter a man could emerge to lay hold upon higher realities pointing the way to their Creator. Kant's "fact of the reason," on the other hand, sealed

177

off the way to a supernatural God of grace. In the name of what amounted to a materializing concept of reason, access was closed to the very source of inspiration from which Kant had originally derived the best of his moral certainty. His radicalism in the matter is betrayed by the title of his later work, *Religion Within the Limits of Reason Alone*.

While the moral service to God so strongly emphasized in this work suggests a righteousness originally learned from the Bible, a supernatural Christianity of grace is systematically ruled out therein. Kant does not tire of exposing a false piety which goes beyond a "disposition of obedience to all true duties as divine commands" and is "directed exclusively to God." [29] He goes as far as transposing the current religious practices of private prayer, churchgoing, baptism, and communion into a purely moral context. "Religion within the bounds of reason alone," writes Alfred Weber in this connection, "consists in morality, nothing more nor less. The essence of Christianity is eternal morality; the goal of the church is the triumph of right in humanity. When the church aims at a different goal, it loses its raison d'être." [30] Or, as Kant himself puts it, the professed faith becomes a mere "fetish faith." [31] According to him, this type of "religious illusion" is bound to appear wherever and whenever religious practices are considered as *"means of grace."* The distortion exposed at this point is ascribed by Kant to a *clericalism* taking advantage of a natural bent in man, which he characterizes as follows: "It is tedious to be a good *servant* [32] (here one is forever hearing about one's duties); man would therefore rather be a *favorite*, where much is overlooked or else, when duty has been too grossly violated, everything is atoned for through the agency of some one or other favored in the highest degree—man, meanwhile, remaining the servile knave he ever was." [33]

[29] *Ibid.*, p. 180.

[30] *History of Philosophy*, tr. F. Thilly (New York: Charles Scribner's Sons, 1896, 1925), pp. 379-80.

[31] *Religion Within the Limits of Reason Alone*, p. 181.

[32] All these are Kant's own italics.

[33] *Ibid.*, p. 188.

178

The burden of Kant's conclusions is that the religion thus identi-fied with active morality is best apprehended in opposition to grace and the so-called means of grace. Who cannot see for himself, he ar-gues, that the so-called elects fail to surpass the naturally honest man, who can be relied upon in social intercourse, in business, or in trou-ble?[34] Nay, the plain fact is that those "favorites" of grace can hardly abide comparison with that honest, reliable man. This being the case, then, it should become clear that "we cannot know anything at all about supernatural aid."[35] Prayer is at best a heartfelt wish through which man works upon *himself*. For how could the praying man presume to affirm the certainty of the existence of God? Kant does not hesitate to ignore the total impact of the teaching of Jesus within the gospel context of the abiding presence of the Father who is in heaven. The "Teacher of the Gospel," as he calls Jesus, actually characterized prayer as nothing other than "the resolution to good-life conduct" in an awareness "of what *nature* in us demands."[36]

The extent to which man has been excluded by Kant from that person-to-Person relationship with God, which is so essential to biblical Christianity, has by now come within full view. Not only is such a reliance upon grace exposed as confidence "of a fancied occult *intercourse* with God,"[37] but the very notion of the person-ality of God also is exposed as the anthropomorphic transfer of the concept of man (including his faults) to the Godhead. Therefore, any idea of personality wherein God is to be thought of by way of analogy loses all relevance.[38] What this means, in the last analysis, is that far from relieving the strain brought about in the name of pure reason, practical reason intensified it. Kant's valet rejoiced prematurely when he thought that his learned master was about to restore to him the God he had taken away from him.

Religion Within the Limits of Reason Alone therefore provides a precious clue to the Kantian critique. It allows the observer to

[34] *Ibid.*, pp. 189-90.
[35] *Ibid.*, p. 179.
[36] *Ibid.*, pp. 183-84.
[37] *Ibid.*, p. 189.
[38] *Ibid.*, pp. 188-89.

realize the meticulous care with which Kant worked out a well-nigh perfect parallelism between his *Critique of Pure Reason* and his *Critique of Practical Reason*. This concern, in turn, betrays in the philosopher of Königsberg that same natural tendency we have seen at work ever since Plato, namely, a tendency to transmute the human mind into a pseudo-maker whenever its capacity as a knower comes short of meeting a crisis situation. Then recourse is taken to a seemingly inexhaustible faculty of that same mind to spin out of its own substance what turns out to be an ontological artifact in a new guise. The result is always the same at the end; man once more becomes a prisoner of his own mind for having devised new ontological means of ending all ontology.

This is what happened in the case of Kant under the impact of the essential manifestations of the conditioning of modern thought. In him the resulting influences reach their culmination and become "petrified," as Philip Frank would say. Only a superficial interpretation can lead one to assume that the *Critique of Practical Reason* actually wrought out a liberation from the materializing constructions of the *Critique of Pure Reason*. Neither do Kant's posthumous works published in 1920 by Erich Adickes affect this conclusion. Such is the symmetry of the Kantian end product, in fact, that it does suggest the crystallization of the already abandoned rationalizations of an obsolete science and of an obsolete moralism.

CHAPTER TWELVE

The POST-KANTIAN "LIBERATION"

A KANTIAN in our day may be characterized as a repentant Newtonian taking advanced work at the Princeton Institute for
Advanced Study while wondering whether he should keep up his
membership in the Felix Adler Ethical Society. He rightly insists
that the true legacy of the patriarch of Königsberg is an epistemology[1] henceforth enjoying full privileges of citizenship in the
curriculum—a status made all the more important by academic philosophers today because the advance of science is otherwise forcing
them out of business. Scientists are developing their own critical
methods, moreover. They even declare to their colleagues of the
department of philosophy whom they meet at the Faculty Club that
the realm marked out by forbidding Kantian signs has by now become their playground. Physicists have broken loose from the con-
finement to which they had been restricted by the Kantian charter
of Newtonian physics. Our previous chapter has already hinted that
moral science is coming of age as one of the human sciences
(*Geisteswissenschaften*).

Yet everything is not for the best in the best of the worlds for a
post-Kantian science. While physicists are rapidly eliminating the
misleading and terribly inadequate human recording set from their
laboratories, they find themselves unable to derive from a mathe-

[1] It is noteworthy that the word "epistemology" itself was used for the first time
in the middle of the nineteenth century by J. F. Ferrier. On this, see R. Eisler,
Wörterbuch der Philosophischen Begriffe (Berlin: E. S. Mittler & Sohn, 1927-30),
I, 356.

matical formula a description out of which they can make a mental picture for the layman's understanding and guidance. This, for instance, is the case for the knowledge of the atom. All the enigmatic representations that are made of it are admittedly phantasmagorical. An atom can be expressed mathematically, but it cannot be pictured. Neither need we insist that the difficulties of moral science are worse than those of physics. While physics is increasingly eliminating the human recording set, moral science finds this impossible to do. Rather, this very impossibility proves to be one of the main characteristics of the data of moral science. In other words, the need for a faith principle is more keenly felt in moral science than in physics. Yet whatever the degree of need, the need remains there, and it is a crying need.

To a more detailed consideration of these all-important facts let us now turn.

The "Liberation" of Physics

We have had occasion to say that until late in the nineteenth century Kantians were agreed that the universal relevance of Euclidean geometry had been established forever, and further, that the Kantian critique implied the perennial character of classical physics. As a result, Einstein brought a near catastrophe upon Kantianism when he demonstrated the possibility, and even the plausibility, that Euclidean geometry might have its shortcomings in a non-Euclidean world—admittedly an understatement. *Ipso facto* a strict Kantian formulation lost its basis in classical physics. In a way, the developments of relativity and quanta may be said to have given the lie to the type of intelligibility strictly codified by Kant as the only permissible one in the context of Newton. Hence there arose the efforts of the Neo-Kantians to recast Kantianism in such ways as to make it amenable to the views of the new physics. A fine illustration of this is provided by the work of Ernest Cassirer. Others may be found in the various reformulations of Neo-Criticism as attempted by Paulsen and Vaihinger in Germany, Cournot, Renouvier, and more especially Brunschvicg, in France. The clearest outcome of these reformulations is to bring to a head the epistemological formulation implied in the Kantian critique.

The physical sciences have been further liberated from the Kantian tutelage by an increasing emphasis upon depersonalization on the part of the individual scientist. What is mostly found to be responsible for phenomena is the scale of observation. It is for such reasons that the human recording set is now being rapidly replaced by mechanical devices. For instance, the astronomer looking through his telescope has now become a legendary character. The two-hundred-inch telescope is a reflector with a mirror weighing two hundred tons and made of pyrex glass. Most of the work of this giant instrument is done by photography. Special studies call for special instruments. Motion pictures of the prominences of the sun are taken daily from the towers of the McMath-Hulbert Observatory, Lake Angelus, Michigan. In the Climax, Colorado, station of the Harvard Observatory, there is installed a coronagraph with which the solar corona may be seen without waiting for a total eclipse of the sun. The instrument's limitations, moreover, are subject to correction. Thus the Schmidt cameras, which can photograph large areas of the sky with excellent results, now have a correcting plate of thin glass placed at the front of the telescope. Prolonged exposure will reveal amazing details in nebulae which are practically invisible in even the largest telescopes. Such is the case for the famous Horsehead nebula, located just below the "lowest" star in Orion belt. A three-hour exposure reveals in that best dark nebula in the sky edges illuminated from behind by a star we cannot see. Similarly, in the constellation of Sagittarius the telescope reveals another galactic nebula, the Trifid, with dark matter dividing it into three main parts, this diffuse nebula being composed of cosmic dust and gas "excited" into shining by hot stars near them.

All this notwithstanding, the best the contemporary physicist can do in the face of this mysterious universe is to become aware of a world underlying, but not identical with, that which he observes, as Dirac has shown in *The Principles of Quantum Mechanics*.[2] Of this

[2] P. A. M. Dirac (Oxford University Press, 1935).

substratum he cannot form *a mental picture* without introducing irrelevancies, for the substratum itself is controlled by fundamental laws which do not actually control the world as it appears in our mental picture. Our mental picture is not the true picture, for the true picture is not picturable. The best that can be achieved by the most careful reformulations, taking account of the data revealed by an ever-perfected technology, is the elaboration of such *concepts* as that of Vaihinger's "useful fiction."[3] Fundamental equations, however, need not be picturable. What matters in their case is to know whether picturable conclusions can be *derived* from them, which conclusions can be tested by means of gross mechanical experiment. This was brought out in a beautiful way when Heinrich Herz "invented" the method coping with the problem posed by Maxwell's theory, identifying the same with Maxwell's equations. Hence we are led to Duhem's well-taken conclusion that the *experimentum crucis* is impossible in physics. It is the theory *as a whole* which is verified by the whole body of experimental facts. And so "the experimental verifications are not the basis of the theory but its culmination."[4]

The Physicist's Inability to Provide a Reference

The physicist's invention of an economical solution thus becomes a mere heuristic principle which he introduces at any point of his investigation until a working theory can be formulated, namely, one which may allow for a minimum of *prediction*. Once the resulting script begins to make sense, everyone concerned is given a chance to discuss it and to criticize it. Fresh information having been

[3] Cf. Hans Vaihinger, *The Philosophy of "As If": A System of the Theoretical, Practical, and Religious Fictions of Mankind* (New York: Harcourt, Brace & Co., 1924), p. 219.

[4] Quoted by Philip Frank, *op. cit.*, pp. 15-16. See further Sir Edmund Whittaker, *From Euclid to Eddington, A Study of Conceptions of the External World* (Cambridge, Engl.: University Press, 1949), Part II, Sect. 34: "The Aether, before Maxwell"; Sect. 35, "The Electromagnetic Theory of Light"; Sect. 36, "The Aether, after Maxwell." A most illuminating section is II, 32, "Unification in Physics," as illustrated further by Maxwell's unification of theory of currents, pp. 83 sq.

brought forward, a reconsideration takes place until nobody can any longer find fault with the outcome, at least for the time being.

Scientific truth, then, is what remains at the end of the last cross-examination. Very much in the manner of the battle of Corneille's hero against the Moors, the battle ends because there are no warriors left on the battlefield—shall we say, until the next "last war"? Accordingly, such truth amounts to a depersonalization through socialization of thought. As such it may have little to do with the deep reality of the things that *are*. What a post-Kantian science calls scientific knowledge now turns out to be a sort of temporary script, a series of clues about that which is, and the manner of its being what it is. Such knowledge is best expressed in mathematical language, as already noted. Nay, it is an invention born of a mathematical speculation that turned out to be successful.

But then, to expect from such scientific scripts any decisive axiology, and, still more, to expect affirmations or negations as to the existence of a supernatural being, nay, reasons why there should be any supernatural form of existence at all, is to expect from the scientist the very things he cannot produce. It is only in legends that a good fairy will emerge from a dusty scientific treatise and proceed to dance on the printed page!

It will readily appear to the candid observer that whenever a scientist in general or a physicist in particular submits a religious proposition as the odd by-product of his speculation, such a proposition is actually one which forced itself upon him from the outside as providing a clue to his problems.

This can be illustrated with a consideration of Whitehead's postulation of a "pre-established" harmony.[5] What is to be said, however, does not begin to invalidate, among many other contributions, the rich grammar of concepts which the eminent philosopher provides for those concerned with the problem of communication today. The fact is, the writer is one of those so concerned, and it is his intention to avail himself in these pages of many a feature of Whitehead's

[5] Cf. A. N. Whitehead, *Essays in Philosophy* (New York: The Macmillan Co., 1947), p. 79.

185

philosophy of organism. Based as it is upon the patterned process of events, it is beautifully fitted for a statement of views taking cognizance of the ways in which the new physics affects our thinking. Instead of remaining satisfied with a static consideration of qualities based on the simply located bodies of Newtonian physics and the "pure sensations" of Hume, Whitehead attempts to formulate the concepts involved in relativity and quanta. It is while doing this that he is led to postulate the reference that seems to him to give meaning to his view of Process.[6] A recent critique of this, his solution, comes to a head in a final chapter which deals with Whitehead's conception of God.[7] The progress of this notion in Whitehead's thought is carefully followed until it appears that the author of *Religion in the Making* runs into an unresolvable dualism. On the one hand there is Process or creativity, and on the other there is some permanence. Whitehead cannot avoid coping with a problem which has dominated the human scene ever since the days of Parmenides and Heracleitus—that of permanence versus change, the problem of the one and the many. Whitehead, then, postulates an ideal realm of forms of which Process or creativity must be the realization. In other words, the realization in the actual world of what is already conceptually realized in the ideal world is what Whitehead calls Process or creativity.[8] Once more the mind of man tends to become a pseudo-maker. Whitehead's view implies even a double postulation. In the first place there is the postulation of an eternal, prior realm of ideal entities; in the second place there is the postulation of a completed ideal harmony destined to bring together the two aspects of the universe thus determined. And it is this completed ideal harmony which Whitehead calls God. Hence Whitehead's "God" has as his function "not the saving of the world from 'wreckage,' but rather the salvaging of Whitehead's philosophic system from its pervasive and unresolvable bifurcation or dualism." [9]

[6] *Process and Reality* (New York: The Macmillan Co., 1929).
[7] Harry K. Wells, *Process and Unreality* (New York: King's Crown Press, 1950).
[8] *Religion in the Making* (New York: The Macmillan Co., 1926), p. 154.
[9] Wells, *op. cit.*, p. 174.

We should not be as severe as Harry K. Wells on Whitehead's first postulation, however. We have had occasion to say that the contemporary physicist has become aware of a world underlying, but not identical with, that which he observes. Of this substratum let us remember that we cannot form a mental picture without introducing irrelevancies, for the substratum itself is controlled by fundamental laws which do not actually control the world as it appears in our mental picture. Our mental picture is not the true picture, for the true picture is not picturable.

This is the background which must be kept in mind if we are to do justice to Whitehead's view of the Divine. It is at this apex of human effort and achievement, where a unique cultural endeavor is at stake, that Whitehead *introduces* his crucial working hypothesis. This "unpicturable" which science cannot postulate, this ultimate irrationality, which is also the antecedent and ultimate limitation, is God—a "pre-established harmony" further requiring fluency for "His" completion in a consequent temporal nature. But then, the question is how does an "it" become "His"?

In the company of one of the greatest scholars of our time, who was also a noble soul and reminds one of Spinoza, we reach the very point where a faith-principle becomes a working hypothesis, and *vice versa.* Or rather a religious explanation remembered from Sunday school days forces itself upon a mental landscape heretofore bereft of genuine significance. The conclusions just reached from a consideration of Whitehead's religious postulations may also be reached from a consideration of William P. Montague's conception of a God whose will is the creative force of an all-inclusive life, or from E. W. Lyman's idea of him as a Cosmic Creative Spirit.

Surely there is something misleading about such ways of presenting religious views as would-be conclusions at the end of a learned inquiry.[10] Etienne Gilson made this point with much gusto with reference to Sir James Jeans. Said the author of *The Mysterious*

---

[10] Cf. Edward L. Long, *Religious Beliefs of American Scientists* (Philadelphia: The Westminster Press, 1952): "Such agreement as comes in religion comes from outside man's own search." (p. 147)

Universe, "Modern scientific theory compels us to think of the creator as working outside time and space, which are part of his creation, just as the artist is outside his canvas." [11] Upon which Gilson comments, "Why should modern theory compel us to say what has already been said, not only by Saint Augustine, whom our scientist quotes, but by any and every one of countless Christian theologians who knew no other world than that of Ptolemy?" [12]

While the contemporary physicist may provide the Christian philosopher with precious means of transcription and communication in a world of change,[13] the higher realities he postulates can never be substituted for biblical realities, still less become the measure of things Christian.

The Rise of Moral Science

We have had occasion to say[14] that while Kant saw in the sublimity of duty a revelation of the categorical imperative in man's conscience, he could not fail to realize at the same time and by the same token that the *experience* involved pertained to the empirical realm—the very realm to which his *Critique of Pure Reason* granted relevance and validity. Yet the practical rules derived from actual practice seemed to Kant to be independent of scientific knowledge. In other words, an impressive imperative given empirically was found by Kant to be scientifically unaccountable. So it occurred to him that the reason the rules of moral practice were not to be derived from a scientific and objective empirical study of reality was simply that they did not need to be. The "absolute" character of the categorical imperative carried within itself its own justification. To

[11] London: Pelican Books, 1937. P. 183. Quoted in Gilson, *God and Philosophy,* p. 125.

[12] Gilson, *God and Philosophy,* pp. 125-26.

[13] I refer to such categories as Whitehead's notions of "physical feeling," "low-grade organism," "conceptual feeling," "mental pole," "prehending activity," etc., as compared to a scholastic grammar of concepts. The alternative to such forward steps for Christian thought would seem to be more theological stagnation, increasing alienation from secular thinking with all accompanying woes. As Whitehead himself beautifully puts it, "The death of religion comes with the repression of the high hope of adventure" (*Science and the Modern World,* p. 276).

[14] Cf. previous chapter, section "The Moral Conditioning of Modern Thought."

THE POST-KANTIAN "LIBERATION"

further account for this unique situation, Kant developed a theory of his own which has already been critically examined in these pages.

The point which retains our attention here is that Kant's ethical views developed into *a theory,* thus adding to the long series of philosophical ethical systems formulated through the ages. Meanwhile the Kantian critique had granted to a scientific, empirical investigation a scientific status which would be extended from physics to ever-widening realms of investigation, *including the investigation of moral nature.* Hence we are led to consider another and a most important aspect of the post-Kantian "liberation."

One of the first things which impressed the critical minds tutored by Kant was precisely an aspect of moral nature which had also impressed Kant from the outset, namely, that morality is given— given, that is, in actual experience. Whereupon the critics wondered why the data of moral experience could not be explored like other empirical data. Instead of proceeding with such a scientific investigation, however, philosophical ethics had been satisfied thus far with inventing one ethical "theory" after another, each being devised as a necessary foundation for actual practice.

Now the strange thing about all such theories was that while they contradicted one another sometimes to the point of cancellation, they actually ended in advocating the same practice at a given time, in a given society. Another surprising feature was seen in the fact that, as a rule, the authors of such "theories," who walked together although disagreeing even in their silence, hardly ever admitted to difficulties or limitations in their ready-made solutions. For, as a rule, each one provided from the outset answers to all problems involved, a fact which should immediately put the wary on their guard. As Archibald MacLeish would say today, they knew all the answers, but they had not as yet asked the questions.

Is it not evident that in all such cases the so-called "theory" is but a mere afterthought, a rationalization of actual practice, at best a dialectical feat? Even the public at large, as well as its leaders, are aware of this, the moral scientist further argues; they will allow theorists to speculate to their heart's content, in the awareness that

189

the clever opponents will fall in line, like everyone else, when the time comes to do so. What we have in mind for the present, the scientific outlook, is the kind of practice which may be observed in what Bunyan called the "village morality." This village remains quite typical of the world at large.

Each and every society at a given time actually *has* a moral code, or better, a pattern of moral codes which may direct its individual members to strange forms of behavior. The senseless taboos you and I are unable to sweep aside in the realm of fashion thus are seen to give the measure of our slavery. It must have been in this connection that George Eliot once remarked, "We are all born in moral stupidity."

Now such patterns of collective behavior are observable facts. It is therefore the contention of the moral scientist that they are subject to scientific investigation. In this vein we should welcome, for instance, the concern of the research worker bent on the solution of problems such as those related to production and distribution, the function of labor leaders, the technique of relief and charity, and others. As soon as a solution is attempted, however, the "brain-trust" so-called realize that they have hardly begun a formulation of the same. They find themselves unable to provide, and, or so the scientists think, the result is that the "grapes of wrath" reach maturity. To the research worker, an inability to provide appears once more to be a symptom of an inability to foresee, of a lack of adequate knowledge. Therefore it is that wild theories, unheard-of utopias, solve nothing. The science of tomorrow will have to go into such problems, our scholars conclude.

Moral Science Also Proves Unable to Provide a Reference

An important remark is called for at this point. Human motivation has thus far been taken for granted as perfectly normal and legitimate. The reason for this is obvious. Such motivation referred solely to basic concerns we may be said to share with frogs in a pond. Intelligence then was applied to the mere safeguarding of life and health, and beyond that, merely to the satisfying of urges and motives natural to man as a tool-using, food-preparing, weeping or laughing animal.

Yet, pausing too long on such elementary aspects with reference to our animal nature may prove unfair even to animals, for there is seen to be in man what Professor C. H. Dodd has called that "ingrained wrongness," an almost uncanny propensity to wickedness, which is unknown to animals.

How much of a guide, then, can moral science be in these circumstances? This, we readily discern, is not a mere academic sort of issue. We are dealing with stark realities and hard facts. When argument is taken, for example, from George Eliot's contention that "we are all born in moral stupidity" to prove that what we need is more research and statistics, it becomes obvious that this is at best a small portion of the truth. There are, as a matter of fact, whole areas of human behavior which have been thoroughly investigated and where, as a result, the "how" is fully known. Yet could it be said that, *ipso facto*, human behavior is being straightened out in such areas? To begin with trivial illustrations, is it true that we men dress intelligently? Is it true that doctors do not smoke? That a tremendous advance in our scientific knowledge of human adjustment prevents divorce? That the most enlightened and statistically supported methods of progressive education *ipso facto* produce moral fiber?

The moral truth about this whole matter, if it be the truth we want, is written in letters of fire and blood all over the pages of history. Let us be positive about this also. Can anyone study the annals of our civilization without being driven back upon human nature, back to what the Bible calls a "lost" humanity in need of redemption? True enough, Calvin considered politics as an earthly discipline. As such, he added, however, they have little to do with the intelligence of things divine—namely, "the rule and reason of true justice, and the mysteries of the heavenly Kingdom." And so the best this great humanist of the Renaissance could say about political science was that in such a realm as that of the government of men, human understanding does not labor entirely in vain.

In the words of our late friend Hartley Burr Alexander, "Truth is of faith fulfilled, faith is in truth anticipated, and of both our intelligible life is the expression." Such is the divine order. Allow truth and the faith to be divorced and see our best patterns of humanism become the motives of an infernal sabbath, not unlike *Dies Irae* in the last movement of the *Fantastic Symphony* by Berlioz. In Italy during the Renaissance, in England during the Restoration, in France under Robespierre, in Germany under Hitler and his Gestapo, nay, in the midst of a sinister caricature of medical research at Buchenwald, cold-blooded calculation, brutal selfishness, that untranslatable *thing* called *Schadenfreude*, will come and crouch at the door, as it had already done in the days of Tiberius. And unto thee, O man, shall be its desire, in a kind of parody of conjugal relations, dreadfully suggested in the book of Genesis.

Let a merely academic knowledge ignore such roots and such depths and miss the mark. If lack of power be the test of truth in theories, as our scientists proclaim, then let us ponder, as enlightened humanists stare at this present-day world of ours, aghast and powerless. Neither can they explain its worst features in terms of glandular deficiency. The practitioners of scientifically secularized psychology, ethics, history, government, or economics, by being unaware of their heritage, living and thinking in ungrateful ignorance of it, are most likely to play into the hands of their worst enemies.

The Christian philosopher, then, would be careful to draw a counterpart to the picture just given of a life and knowledge divorced from the Faith. Thus we see great battles for liberty won by men whose motivation is grounded in Holy Writ. William Wilberforce leads the crusade to emancipate Negro slaves in the British empire; his successor, Lord Shaftesbury, in Parliament successfuly champions the cause of factory workers in industrial England. The tradition of the American philosophy of government goes back to the Pilgrims of Plymouth, Connecticut, and Rhode Island. Roger Williams it was who asserted the necessity of liberty of conscience and the equality of opinions before the law. Men to whom "God alone is Lord of conscience" were well prepared to become stanch supporters of a free church and of a free state. In Pennsylvania, especially, they were among the foremost to advocate American independence. If indeed we mean to understand documents such as the Declaration of Independence, the Constitution, and the Bill of Rights, we must realize that while they reveal strong rationalistic trends, they are essentially Christian documents. The very psychology of the American founders is derived from deep-seated religious convictions. Even men like Franklin and Jefferson, who particularly liked to assume a rationalistic attitude, will fight oppression in the name of the Lord. To them "rebellion against tyrants is obedience to God." To them the Creator of heaven and earth was the Giver—and remains the Guarantor—of the rights of man.

Once more, however, in the realm of ethics as in that of physics, only in an infinitely more meaningful sense, the Reference which lends relevance and significance to the scientific investigation must come from outside.

But let the Reference be ignored or allusions to it cease to make sense, and physics *ipso facto* loses itself in physicism, morals in moralism, and an aimless, endless, empirical quest, in empiricism and scientism. A culture born of the post-Kantian "liberation" remains increasingly open to the dangers invited by a vacuum. Frustration within the secular order will then seek or welcome the most unwholesome means of relief and gratification. Of this the situation we face provides ample proof.

193

PART FOUR

The Situation We Face

CHAPTER THIRTEEN

The TRUE NATURE of MODERN FRUSTRATION

I N the measure as modern man has lost his religious relationship
with reality, together with the ability to "think" his faith, he has
become a frustrated man.

The late G. Campbell Morgan has given us a profound interpretation of the temptation of our Lord which points to the true nature
of the frustration of modern man. After a chapter introducing the
temptation, his book *The Crises of the Christ* proceeds with three
chapters devoted to the first, the second, and the third temptations
respectively. Then the whole argument is brought to a head in a
"final" chapter which constitutes the clearest elucidation of the
great mystery this writer has seen as yet.

The replies of Jesus reveal to Campbell Morgan the order of the
attacks: first the enemy offered *bread* to the hungry Man Jesus;
then, insinuating himself behind the satisfaction of material appe-
tite, the enemy endeavored to break this Man's *trust* in God; finally
he tried to divert His worship and allegiance from the true to the
false. This, then, may be said to be the order of the devil: first
bread, then trust, then worship. Consider now the answers of the
Man Jesus, as taken from Deuteronomy, in their order of succession,
references being to Deut. 8:3, 6:16, and 6:13, respectively. It will be
immediately noticed that as such our Lord's replies provide an entirely reversed order, namely: *worship, trust, bread*. This, then, is the
order of God. It calls man to worship, first of all, as a recognition of
his spiritual nature. In the words of G. Campbell Morgan:

197

The Divine plan is ever that of recognizing the Divinity in man, the magnificence of his spiritual being, ruined magnificence today, and yet truly magnificent in the ruin, because capable of communion with God. The Word of God is ever, "Seek ye first His Kingdom"; and then He appeals to the trust in man, and promises him bread and all things necessary. Satan called this Man to feed His physical life, and endeavoured to break down His trust in God, and to divert His worship from the true to the false, and so change His allegiance and His service to bondage and slavery.[1]

Having thus restored a scriptural perspective as indicated by our Lord himself, we should by now be much closer to a right interpretation of the data at hand. That we needed nothing short of this help may be surmised from the revolutionary view here implied. Anyone who was asked what the primordial need of man is would naturally name bread in the first place. The Lord's Prayer's insistence on our daily bread suffices to indicate that this, our essential need, was very much on His mind. His whole ministry, in fact, illustrated in such an occurrence as the miracle of the loaves and fishes, in His own assuming the Name "the Bread of Life," amply reveals to what extent our need for bread looms large in the Divine Providence. Yet, all this notwithstanding, Scripture as interpreted by our Lord teaches that in the order of God worship, not bread, is the first and foremost need of man. This author will never forget the occasion when a friend of his, the wife of an officer of the Salvation Army, was much delayed after a meeting. She had been assisting a poor lost soul at the Mercy Seat. When asked by her husband for further details, she broke down in tears—incidentally, this gift of tears, so much frowned upon in our day, used to be regarded as a sign of high calling in God's people.

"Why," the good lady exclaimed, "this man did not even know how to kneel down and pray!"

These were the words of a Salvation Army officer. And who, in our day, knows more than a Salvationist about man's need for bread?

[1] *The Crises of the Christ* (New York: Fleming H. Revell Co., 1903, 1936), pp. 201-2.

Yet she also, in the manner of her Lord and Master, named worship as the most elementary need of man.

Could it be, then, that once everything has been said and done with relation to the intellectual, political, and social plight that came to expression under the heading of Enlightenment, the root of that plight was basically a heartache born of the most basic frustration of all—namely, a growing incapacity to worship the true God?

A Frustration Affecting Man's Need to Worship

How profoundly suggestive, when we come to think of it, is the fact that the much exalted Age of Enlightenment should now appear indissolubly associated with the *Weltschmerz,* or *mal du siècle,* which characterized Romanticism! The vagueness of romantic moods can no longer mislead us at this state of our inquiry because we are already familiar with the sequel of the story. Not that Romanticism itself is to be identified with vagueness, as such scholars as Seillière, Babbitt, or Lasserre would have us believe. It was characterized by vagueness at the outset because it had not come as yet to a glaring awareness of its true natue, had not as yet been clearly diagnosed with increased clarity as the deeper heartache it always was.

When Thackeray portrays the clergy of the days of George II as corrupt and indifferent amidst the indifference and corruption of the court life, he omits a third dimension in his picture. Admittedly, in the presence of the *immediate* reality thus depicted, a Whitefield could only cry out in the wilderness, and a Wesley leave the insulted temple to pray on the hillside. The Christian historian has nonetheless the duty to remember that the clergy had not always been indifferent and corrupt. There had been backsliding because spiritual power had leaked out as age-old assurances had for some time been on the wane. The same was also true of the Kirk of Scotland. The same was true again of the eighteenth century clergy of France.

It is noteworthy, moreover, that wherever the bishops of the Church of England continued to show ability and initiative, their high-mindedness was rooted in a truly enlightened will to rethink their faith. Such was the case with Atterbury, Warburton, and more especially Berkeley and Butler. This we say in the awareness that the courtly, easygoing type of clergy was a by-product of a decadent secular order, in England as well as on the Continent. Yet, behind such a decadent secularism was a deeper crisis of faith which must, at least in part, be ascribed to what Paul Hazard has characterized as "the crisis of the European conscience from 1680 to 1715." [2] No impartial reader having studied the three-volume series the late scholar devoted to the subject will henceforth be tempted to oversimplify the problem or be provincial about it. The sordid story of eighteenth century primates or lesser prelates, during the reigns of the first two Georges, and during the early years of George III, has too often confused the symptoms with the malady. And the malady lay in the fact that it had become increasingly difficult to worship God in the atmosphere of the Enlightenment. There was involved in the whole resulting situation an aching frustration with reference to the most elementary need of man, namely, the need to be alive to God's guiding Presence.

Popular Mechanisms of Compensation

What may henceforth be called the great frustration further comes to light if we detract our attention from church leaders and so-called representative men to consider popular mechanisms of compensation in the much neglected popular literature of the age.

The gothic,[3] shadowy character of that literature was predominant in the popular novels of Horace Walpole, who may be said to have hunted up the most terrifying elements in the medieval atmosphere of mystery. All that was left of the God-bathed landscape of reality was a pathetic setting of old castles and haunted towers which provided the proper mystery for the horrors and crimes in which the readers of the day found an increasing delight. We refer to such books as Horace Walpole's *The Castle of Otranto* (1764);

[2] *La Crise de la Conscience Européenne (1680-1715)* (Paris: Boivin, 1935).

[3] Cf. William C. Holbrook, "The Adjective *Gothique* in the XVIIIth Century," *Modern Language Notes*, November, 1941, pp. 498-503.

Clara Reeve's *The Old English Baron* (1777), Mrs. Radcliffe's *The Mysteries of Udolpho* (1794), *The Italian* (1797); last, but not least, *The Monk* (1795), by M. G. Lewis.

The English taste for somber and sepulchral literature spread to the Continent where it immediately appealed to a popular imagination which had been repressed by the aristocratic, authoritarian tone of preceding ages. Moreover, on the Continent as in England, a religiously frustrated public delighted in playing freely with forbidden themes, to delight in an orgy of strange and mysterious practices. Toward the end of the eighteenth century, the *Sturm und Drang* movement brought in its wake visions of brigands and outlaws destined to replace knights in armor. At about the same time the anti-Catholic tendency of the period, recalling the Inquisition, suggested Spain and Italy to be the refuge of crafty and perfidious monks, whom they delighted in presenting in their dungeons and somber monasteries.

The appeal was essentially to a frustrated sense of the invisible. Let us insist on this. We detect in the furor created by this type of popular literature a weird mechanism of religious compensation in a funereal context of wonder. The most widely read stories would tell of nocturnal apparitions, frightful dreams, mysterious offenses, terrible phenomena, historical crimes, moving corpses, bleeding and animated heads, atrocious revenge, and combinations of crime.

Of the widespread character of such popular literature, bibliographical indexes leave no doubt. Imitation on the Continent followed rapidly upon exhaustive translations. So much so that as early as May, 1798, the *Spectateur du Nord* printed a popular "recipe" for the novel of terror. Here are the ingredients which were said to enter into the laborious preparation of a black novel: An ancient castle half in ruins; a long corridor with many doors, several of which must be secret; three corpses still bleeding; three skeletons well wrapped up; an old woman hanged, with several dagger slashes in her throat; a few robbers and plenty of bandits; a sufficient dose of whispers, stifled groans, and horrible crashes.

The vogue of this type of literature was further spread by parodies

201

and satires. Such, for instance, was *La Nuit anglaise* published in Paris in 1799 under a pseudonym. The hero is cured of his craze for the fashionable literature by being doped, then being transported to an old castle where he awakes among horrors lifted straight out of the popular works of the day. He escapes from this farce by signing a pact with the devil to the effect that he will never touch another English novel, save those by Richardson, Fielding, Miss Bennett, and their future imitators.

Some 130 titles of the popular terror type may be counted in France alone during the early nineteenth century. It is further noteworthy that practically all the French Romantic authors began by writing in that somber vein, since this was the thing to do for anyone who wanted to attract attention. This is especially true of such writers as Nodier, Balzac, Hugo, Dumas, and George Sand, to name only a few.

In Germany the popular taste for this type of literature was even more strongly marked. Tieck and Jean Paul Richter insisted upon a supernatural setting in stories which speak of the beyond. Ideas are far more impressive when spoken by a mouth "that is not human." After the groups which gathered around Tieck and Richter a place should be given to Chamisso, author of *Peter Schlemihl*, the man who sold his shadow; to La Motte-Fouqué, author of *Undine;* to Achim von Arnim, Novalis, and above all to E. T. A. Hoffman whose *Fantastic Tales* were so real to him that, seized with terror, he would awaken his wife from her sleep. Ever patient she would arise, pull out her knitting, and seat herself close by to reassure her husband.

It is hard for us today to realize that to the Romantic generation Hoffman was a synthesis of that which all Europe wished to admire in Germany. We have ample evidence of this. Be it sufficient to see a man like Victor Hugo class Hoffman among the greatest geniuses of all times. While it may be objected that Hugo was given to overenthusiasm, his attitude is characteristic of a type of feature, real or imagined, which would appeal to the public. Byron, for example, was certainly one of the most exalted figures of the age. But then, he was painted with horrible vices, depicted as an evil genius descended upon earth, killing a mistress and drinking from her skull. A polluted nature was shown to be the source of that bitter voluptuousness with which Byron describes all agonies of body and soul.

Admittedly such features are not particularly pleasant to investigate. Yet current histories of literature and civilization are likely to throw the true perspective out of line by ignoring them. Such studies will slight, for instance, a recrudescence of interest in magic during the eighteenth and nineteenth centuries, fostered by a sense of religious frustration as well as by a new interest in history ascribable mostly to Chateaubriand and Sir Walter Scott. Or they will pass by an enormous amount of literature on occultism more especially found in the philosophical novel. Yet the same includes some of the greatest names, from Balzac to the Belgian Huysmans.

The last two centuries have seen the birth of the strangest cults and weirdest practices, leading to mesmerism, animal magnetism, and modern spiritualism. Hence there has grown another large area of literary and pseudoscientific production on supernatural themes, which reveals a high degree of fever in a public estranged from the old Christian norm.

Metamorphoses of the Devil

All that has been said in this chapter thus far tends to characterize the Age of Enlightenment as one of religious frustration. A humanity which found it increasingly difficult to answer its primordial need for worship, sought its gratification in ease, lawlessness, corruption, as well as in the weirdest mechanisms of compensation. Yet, as the deeper religious need remained unsatisfied, estrangement from God progressively yielded to a transference of allegiance. Never was the peril of a vacuum better illustrated than in those days, unless it be in our own. Our own day is but the aftermath of those days. Or rather the great Revolution "marches on." Only it appears more and more as a revolt of man against his Maker.

Milton saw the writing on the wall. His Satan truly embodied the perversities of those men who plunged England into mourning and

203

desolation. This Britannic and puritan Satan is in essence the anti-God in whom we increasingly identify an incarnation of an age discarding its allegiance. Henceforth men will be led to see an evil power at work in their midst and will focus their attention upon him more and more. Such seems to be the case at times of great upheavals. It was true of Dante and of Luther in their day. What strikes the observer, however, is to witness the amazing recrudescence of interest in Satan issuing from such a period as the Age of Enlightenment. Is not belief in the devil generally frowned upon by a rationalism of naturalistic implication?

To be sure, the tendency was first to treat the devil as a convenient allegory for literary purposes. The Germans, headed by Goethe, stressed the human side of the devil, showing little concern for his angelic nature. From the rather heavy Germanic Mephistopheles, the French first tended to create a national "Mephisto," who was light, fashionable, artistic, and slightly Bohemian, with touches of Don Juan, Gavroche, d'Artagnan and Cyrano. But the English, being more matter-of-fact, had gone to the bottom of things from the first.

Just as Milton's Satan inspired Chateaubriand, Byron's *Heaven and Earth,* as well as Byron's own legend, released a host of deceived angels over the Continent. The youthful Romantic groups fell in love with this Satan, this superhuman Manfred who had everything to charm them. In the garrets of 1830 the countenance of Milton's Satan was hung on the wall, while on the table were spread out all the books dealing with the vicissitudes of the revolted angel: the *Bible,* the *Divine Comedy, Paradise Lost, Faust,* and *The Genius of Christianity.*

The Romantics were proud rebels; they readily considered themselves to be misunderstood geniuses. One finds an affectation of nihilism among these malcontents who refused to yield to law, discontented with their time because they were discontented with themselves. In Satan they found some of their own fatalism, their own aborted ambitions. From thence arose the poetic meaning of the bandit, the outlaw personified with such success in *Ruy Blas* and

Hernani. Like themselves, their Satan deserved sympathy. A cursed, suffering being, he was worthy of pity. Hence the consoling discourses addressed to him in Vigny's *Éloa* and by the angel Liberty in Hugo's *End of Satan.* Perpetual banishment of the Damned One seemed excessive to the Romantics. Under various titles they reviewed his case and made over *Paradise Lost.* Painted in flattering colors, Satan was all the more irresistible to them because of his cryptic nature with its quality of beautiful Byronic somberness. The mystery of his soul had the delicious lure of an abyss whose dizziness one feels tempted to experience.

One can imagine what this Rousseauesque romantic sentimentality saw in Satan's moral constitution. His suffering is without joy because he suffers through hate rather than through love, and because the evil he causes others to suffer is added to his own. This agony is without respite because it is without tears. Satan himself is the cause and the instrument of his anguish. He must—an impossible task—escape from himself. The sentimentality of *Werther, René, Obermann, Adolphe,* and other *enfants du siècle*[4] would have difficulty finding a more fitting subject for lamentation. Satan is a romantic hero, only grander than the others. A more subtle Mephistopheles, a more fatalistic Manfred, a more impatient Hernani, a more bitter René, a more somber Lara, he embodies them and surpasses them all by his immensity. He finally outdoes himself and fades into the universe as a tremendous symbol of human woe.

Man's quest for salvation during the later Romantic period became sublimated in the strange theme of Satan's salvation. Vigny proposed to write on this very theme in continuation of *Éloa;* Gautier dealt with it in *The Devil's Tear* (1839); Soumet in his *Divine Epic* (1840). Hugo liked to symbolize man's deliverance and emergence from darkness through Progress. And so a whole generation took pleasure in contemplating Satan's pardon and regeneration. Meanwhile, groups would meet on a Sunday to celebrate the new cult,

[4] Goethe, *Die Leiden des Jungen Werthers* (1774); Chateaubriand, *René* (1805); Senancour, *Obermann* (1804); Constant, *Adolphe* (1816); Musset, *Confession d'un Enfant du Siècle* (1836, 1840).

THE CHRISTIAN APPROACH TO CULTURE

invoking the ruler of the underworld. Each of the participants in turn read his verses glorifying the "Most Low."

In the long run, this Satan, so strangely representative of the eighteenth century version of Enlightenment, became an immense symbol of cosmic evil in league with the forces of nature, as it were. The aching heart of contemporary man became aware of a fatality inherent in the universe, in the brutal dynamic quality of matter, in the sobbing wind as in the raging tempest of romantic fame, in falling night and in coming death. There was on every side an experience of bitterness at the very bottom of joy, nay, that kind of sensation that sometimes comes to us out of nothingness. It was found in those empty promises that lie, in happiness that ends in tears. In the words of Victor Hugo, then an old man,

> It is the shadowy depth, the mournful weight. . . .
> It is the nether force binding all with its chains.

We are reminded of John Bunyan's characterization of the Slough of Despond in the opening pages of *The Pilgrim's Progress*, with the difference that the story seems to be told in reverse, as if by a backsliding Christian just coming out of the Wicket-gate and on his way back to the City of Destruction: "This miry slough is such a place as cannot be mended; it is the descent whither the scum and filth that attends conviction for sin doth continually run, and therefore it is called the Slough of Despond." For again as the sinner goes back to his filth, "there ariseth in his soul many fears and doubts, and discouraging apprehensions, which all of them get together, and settle in this place. And this is the reason of the badness of the ground." What an introduction this, to the understanding of our day and age!

A Modern Version of Dante

Now that the relative remoteness of the last century allows a better perspective, we should not be far from the truth in pointing to Baudelaire as the one in whom the aching heart of modern man found its most stirring expression in our time.

206

Baudelaire depicted himself in one of his early short stories, *La Fanfarlo* (1847), in the character of a poet who presents his book in homage to a beautiful and melancholy young woman. When she reproaches him for the despondency permeating his poetry, "Pity me," he replies, "or rather pity all of us, for I have many brothers of my kind. It is hatred of us all that has led us to these lies. It is through despair at not being able to be noble and beautiful by natural means, that we have painted our faces so strangely." The poet further admits with pleasure that he possesses a depraved imagination. He delights in artifice and deceits, and if God had confided nature's plan to him, he perhaps would have spoiled it all. Two years after Baudelaire wrote this, he had made a timid attempt at suicide. The fear of madness haunted him. The tragic death of Gérard de Nerval in 1855 frightened him. The *Flowers of Evil* were written in 1857. The connection of these dates speaks for itself. In a letter written on January 23, 1862, one finds this confession. "I have cultivated my madness with joy and terror. I now suffer dizziness constantly. I felt the wind of imbecility pass over me." And so a contemporary psychiatrist would probably dismiss the whole case by saying that from the artificial we have now passed through the morbidly temperamental into the realms of pathology. Yet this explanation will not easily satisfy many of us.

The plain truth is that we must reach deeper into these roots of human misery. The *Posthumous Works*[5] are filled with confessions which allow us to touch Baudelaire's naked soul with our own. He postulates in each one of us two simultaneous tendencies: one toward God—spirituality, which urges man toward the heights; and the other toward Satan, or bestiality, which Baudelaire calls "a joy in descending." A few entries suggest tremendous insights into this second tendency. "The unique and supreme delight of love lies in the certainty of doing wrong." "What is boring about love is that it

---

[5] Cf. Crépet ed., *Journaux Intimes* (Paris, 1938). The editor shows that *My Heart Laid Bare* refers to the period 1859-66 (p. 125); he points out (pp. 132-33) that this title was suggested by Poe's *Marginalia*. Crépet further publishes pages of a personal diary kept between 1861 and 1864, and containing lists of friends and enemies. See also Conard ed., *Juvenilia, Oeuvres Posthumes, Reliquae* (Paris, 1939).

is a crime in which one must have an accomplice." Who better than Baudelaire has described the maliciousness of perverse love? "Do you hear these sighs, prelude to a tragedy of dishonor, these wails, these cries, these rattlings in the throat? Who has not proferred them, who has not irresistibly extorted them? Is there anything worse in the cross-examination of torturers? These reversed sleep-walker's eyes, these limbs, whose muscles tremble and stiffen as beneath the action of a galvanic battery. Drunkenness, delirium and opium in their most violent reactions certainly do not furnish such frightful and curious examples. And the human face, which Ovid believed to be made to reflect the stars, there it is with no more than an expression of mad ferocity, or distended in a sort of death. Certainly, I should commit a sacrilege to apply the word 'ecstasy' to this kind of 'decomposition.' "

This author knows of nothing more powerfully suggestive of the profound disturbance of the soul of modern man than such passages. That is the true vein of *The Flowers of Evil* in which we may acknowledge the sophisticated and genial sum of the human aberration and misery of our time. The true theme at the bottom of it all is a sort of unhealthy sensuality which delights in death, while screened behind a false mysticism which glorifies in the sacrilegious. A sort of reversed Grace is here invoked. A mysterious presence makes itself known in a steel-like coldness which grips the very bottom of the soul, as if we descended into some Dantesque funnel with the nine steps, and exclaimed:

> How icy-chill I then became and weak,
> Ask not, O reader, for I write it not.
> All words that I could use would nothing be;
> I did not die, nor yet remain alive;
> Picture in thought, if you have aught of wit,
> What was my state, neither alive nor dead.[6]

Truly *The Flowers of Evil* echoes Dante's *Inferno* at this, our end of history. Only, Dante's marshlike, dolorous realm has become

[6] Dante's *Inferno*, Canto 34, as done in English for this author by his late friend Professor George F. Cole, of the University of Pennsylvania. Let this footnote be a homage to the memory of a gentle soul.

the heart of modern man. Let one read the pieces entitled "The Vampire," "The Possessed," "The Irreparable," "Foretaste of Nothingness," "The Litanies of Satan," "Damned Women," "The Metamorphoses of the Vampire," and many others, in the light of *My Heart Laid Bare,* and make his way to a deeper understanding of this age.

To disclaim the shrewd, uncanny diagnosis of Baudelaire will simply not do. The last line of the dedication of *The Flowers of Evil* would more than take care of the attempt: "Hypocritical reader— my fellow man—my brother!"

CHAPTER FOURTEEN

A WESTERN WORLD WITHOUT RADIANCE

S EISMOLOGY has taught us how strains of increasing intensity may bring about in the crust of the earth a fault along which earthquakes are likely to occur. So also psychology tells us that increasing tensions may disrupt the human organism. There is a limit to the strains man and society can bear, and our modern world is only too familiar with earth-shaking revolutions.

In drawing attention to the character of modern frustration, the preceding chapter has brought us to the point where we may ascertain the true nature of our problems—even of our political problems. They all are spiritual problems, that is to say, primarily metaphysical and theological.[1]

However paradoxical this may seem, the present-day disruption of our world between East and West is increasingly found to have been brought about by the unbearable spiritual tensions which we are now probing. How the breaking point was reached will be suggested in the present chapter by the consideration of some characteristic instances. What makes these instances "characteristic" is that they occur along the main lines of the development our in-

---

[1] Among all the patients over thirty-five Carl Jung has treated over a long period of years, "there has not been one whose problem in the last resort was not that of finding a religious outlook on life. It is safe to say that every one of them fell ill because he had lost that which the living religions of every age have given their followers, and none of them has really been healed who did not regain his religious outlook." (Carl G. Jung, *Modern Man in Search of a Soul* [New York: Harcourt, Brace & Co., 1934], p. 264.)

quiry has revealed. There is nothing arbitrary about the selection implied in our presentation except the necessity of the selection itself which is the very soul of history.

The "breaking point" toward which we are headed is the point *where the "fault" developed which today separates a Western world without radiance from an Eastern world with a false radiance.* That a more catastrophic disruption yet threatens our contemporary world has by now come within the realm of the possible.

Man cannot break the order of God, but defying the order of God will surely break man. "The Lord reigneth."

The Aching Heart of Modern Man

Leo Tolstoy, who was one of the last great Russian "Westerners," suggested in *Anna Karenina* a permanent aspect of the plight of modern man. Ever since that moment when, as he sat beside his dying brother, Levin had caught an insight into the problem of life and death, in the light of the new convictions, as he called them, which had progressively displaced his childhood beliefs during the last fourteen years, life appeared to him more terrifying than death.

Where did it come from? What did it mean? Our organism, its destiny, the indestructibility of matter, the laws of the conservation and develop- ment of forces, these words and the scientific theories connected with them, were doubtless interesting from an intellectual point of view, but what would be their use in the face of real life? And Levin suddenly felt in the position of a man who, in cold weather, had exchanged a warm fur coat for a muslin garment. He felt, not with his reason, but with his whole being, that he was naked and destined to perish miserably.[2]

The normal reaction to such an experience so characteristic of the contemporary climate, may be described as one of stoicism, with the added feeling that it might be better in many cases not to disclose the truth indiscriminately. Taine went as far as to suggest that the most subversive forms of scientific truth be published in Latin. Miracles may well have become obsolete, Renan himself used to comment, but let a Voltaire suffice for the menial task of disclosure.

[2] Part VIII, ch. 8.

Another typical reaction was, "If those things must be said, let those say them who find pleasure in saying them." Still another typical comment was, "Let the lowly souls take care of this." Reluctance in the face of the inevitable seems to have been the current attitude. Daudet, the French Dickens, who was once characterized as "a dealer in happiness," left this entry in his posthumous *Notes on Life:*

I must acknowledge the sadness, the dismay, of my big boy who just began his senior year in philosophy and started reading Schopenhauer, Hartmann, Stuart Mill, Spencer. Terror and disgust of life; the doctrine is dead; the teacher in despair, the conversation between classes disheartening. The vanity of everything comes to the awareness of these kids and devours them. I spent the whole evening reviving my son, and giving a rub to his soul. Without my attempting to do so, I warmed myself up as well. Pondered over this the whole night. Is it a good thing to initiate them so bluntly? Would it not be better to continue to lie, to leave it to life to take away their illusions, and remove the stage-sets piece by piece? [3]

The total impact is one of pessimism as seen, for example, in the Wessex novels of Thomas Hardy, dominated by a sense of relentless fate, or more exactly of an uncompromising determinism. Men, in these novels, are slaves to their environment, to their instinct, to their heredity; most of them are destined to live a life of utter misery, without any hope of redemption, during their brief transit through this sorry world. Still more tragic is the note of despondency one hears in the verse of James Thomson, whose poetry is that of sheer, overmastering, inexorable despair. In *The City of Dreadful Night* the author proclaims that:

> . . . every struggle brings defeat
>   Because Fate holds no prize to crown success;
> That all the oracles are dumb or cheat
>   Because they have no secret to express;
> That none can pierce the vast black veil uncertain

[3] As translated from P. Martino, *Le Naturalisme français* (Paris: Colin, 1923), pp. 160-61.

Because there is no light beyond the curtain;
That all is vanity and nothingness.[4]

One of the main characteristics of contemporary life is that it has
developed tensions heretofore unknown, were it only because of a
rapidly increased rate of new information. For it is access to fresh
information more than anything else which causes a man to change
his mind. There is for example the fact that the known world has
increased in scope and in complexity. Subjects unheard of during
the Age of Enlightenment forced themselves upon the new syntheses
of knowledge: Brahmanism, Buddhism, Confucianism, Sanskrit,
Egyptology, mythology, linguistics, philology, archeology, exegesis,
etc. Biblical criticism became bolder and more effective, undermining the traditional views familiar to the believer. In physics the
formulation of Maxwell's equation representing the structure of
the field paved the way for relativity and quanta, that is, for the reconsideration of classical physics associated with the Newtonian
frame of reference. Hardly had individuals begun to adapt themselves to the notion of a clocklike universe where phenomena could
be simply explained in terms of attraction and repulsion, than the
notion of relativity crept in, all the more upsetting because it was
difficult to understand. The last props henceforth seemed to fail
man. Progress in science meant new advances in technology, and
vice versa. The very structure of society was being profoundly altered. Just at the time workers needed more protection in the new
order resulting from the industrial revolution, old guilds were wiped
out. Industrial organization was mostly unheard of, except in the
wild dreams of romantic Utopia. The machine was rapidly becoming
the master of man. The threat of uncontrolled or ill-controlled power
became a reality. Soon violent forms of ideologies would fill the
great vacuum left in the wake of modern negations.

It is not merely to Heracleitus that modern man is reverting, but

[4] Stanza xxi.

to the Homeric notions of fate and apportionment. Or should we say to the sacred horror of *Oepidus King?*

"Is the Universe Friendly?"

The trouble with chance is that it behaves like an intention. Hereditary flaws helping, as well as the fast rate of modern life, physical excesses, intellectual overwork and, perhaps, a resulting abuse of stimulants and narcotics, modern man takes an increasingly grim view of his utter dependence upon elusive forms of energy. At the dawn of the century, F. W. H. Myers said that the question he would like to put to the Sphinx was, "Is the universe friendly?" This, we are afraid, is the question in which the tensions of modern life are now being summed up.

A tragic note is struck where the individual breaks under such tensions. Statistics would be sadly eloquent. But it is sufficient to illustrate a whole aspect of contemporary uneasiness with the case of Maupassant who devoted some thirty of his stories to the suggestion of fear and anguish. These works of finished artistry are for the most part confessions wherein one may trace the progress of his nervous afflictions and his anxiety about the invisible world. To object that we are dealing here with a pathological case would amount to missing the point. The whole point is that Maupassant's "climate" is typical of our age, just as that of Baudelaire.

From 1881 onward, Maupassant was interested in what was then called animal magnetism. Later on, an atrocious fear crept into his works, which naturally resulted in tales such as *On the Water* (1881), *Fear* (1882)—note another *Fear* in 1884—*The Inn* (1886), where the climax is reached with the shepherd's madness. In *A Madman* (1886) we are confronted with a combination of magnetism and the phenomenon called by spiritualists the transfer of objects at a distance. The hero's hands have the strange power of drawing objects toward him, especially when the atmosphere is charged with electricity. "Madmen attract me," confesses Maupassant in *Madame Hermet* (1887). And indeed one may say that he presents us a whole

214

gallery of mad people whom he studies by transferring to them some of his own sensations—madmen disordered by excess, enervated by the search for strange sensations. Certain of Maupassant's mad people end in suicide; others are devoured by their philosophical hatred and the obsession of death. We also find macabre tales of violated tombs where phantoms appear.

In the meantime, Maupassant followed Dr. Charcot's courses at the Salpêtrière hospital on the ailments of the nervous system. He was deeply impressed. The contemporary philosophical theories about the unknown that surrounds us, in reaction to the scientific pretensions of the preceding generation, were to become mingled in Maupassant's works with the doctrines of modern spiritualism which he was likewise studying. Aided by his own mental disorder, this unknown became animated. The unfortunate Maupassant, progressing toward madness, sensed hostile powers roaming about. His hallucinations multiplied and now and then threw him into atrocious fright.

Toward the year 1884 he began to feel a being (*He?*) take shape near him, whom he saw without being able to touch. The hero of his tale marries to end a solitude that frightens him. In 1886 Maupassant attempted a first version of *The Horla*, which he revised in 1887, complicating it with the substance of recent readings on hypnotism. This formidable story—the adjective is not exaggerated—constitutes a minute and anguished diary in which Maupassant has translated his own experience, more especially his resistance against an ineluctable hallucination which became increasingly real. The hero of his story firmly believes himself mad, and then to be under a hynoptic spell. His efforts towards clarity are pathetic. At night he seals a carafe of water, which he finds empty in the morning, though he is certain of not having left his bed. Then there is further revealed to him the existence of a being determined to ruin him. It is "Horla" whom he feels ever-present behind him. Finally one day the hero succeeds in shutting this being up in his house, which he sets on fire. But the obsession again takes hold of him. Horla is not dead. "Then, then I must kill myself!" There could be nothing more humanly tragic than this autobiography of a writer whom insanity was gradually overcoming, and was finally to conquer toward the end of 1891. On January 1, 1892, at Cannes, Maupassant tried to kill himself, like the hero of *The Horla*. After eighteen months of agony during which he failed to recover his reason, the unhappy writer was delivered by death.

Baudelaire's "Fellow-men"

Our contemporary man is no longer of a piece. He has become a monster of uneasiness. Young Dostoyevsky went as far as the place of execution for having been imbued with the new socialistic dreams, ranging in his case from the emancipation of the serfs to the abolition of censorship. The penalty having been commuted at the last minute, he was driven back on himself during long years of exile. As he dissected his past life to the pettiest detail in the light of the only book available to him, the New Testament, he found himself to be a hotchpotch of the most contradictory tendencies. And so were his fellow-prisoners. Later, some of this experience found expression in the character of Raskolnikov (in Russian, "The Dissenter") in *Crime and Punishment*. Why should not an idealist put out of the way "a stupid, senseless, worthless, spiteful, ailing, horrid old woman, not simply useless but doing actual mischief, who has not an idea what she is living for herself, and who will die in a day or two in any case." Of course she does not deserve to live, "but tell me, would you kill the old woman yourself?" The thing once done, however, by a young student who had just absorbed Fourier and Darwin in the same breath, why should he brood endlessly over it and sit in his room "like a spider"? Why should he be estranged from his sister, his mother, nay, his best friend, as if "something awful, hideous" had slipped between them? It is poor consolation to hear one of the police explain, "It's as well that you only killed the old woman. If you'd invented another theory you might perhaps have done something a thousand times more hideous." [5] What, then, is that *thing* that will crouch at the door if a man does not do well?

Again and again, as his misery becomes unbearable, Raskolnikov is shown to turn to the wall, just as that other would-be revolutionist Rubashov, the hero of Koestler's *Darkness at Noon,* is said to notice that an old tooth has started to throb again. The strange fact about this latter case is that nothing mattered to Rubashov as long as he was allowed time to develop a new theory. Henceforth his toothache was gone. But then, should the former Commissar of the People be reminded of a lie which proved decisive for the passing of the death sentence on an innocent girl, the throbbing in his tooth would not only begin to bother him again, but would soon prove unbearable. "Rubashov had the feeling that the whole right side of his face was drawn into a cramp. His head became duller and heavier, it was with difficulty that he prevented it from sinking on his breast." [6]

What is the meaning of all this? Physiology may well be on its way to replace psychology, even to displace Christian ethics. Yet it is aggravating, to say the least, to find such an "obsolete" mechanism of conscience transferred to a rotten tooth. Moderns have done away with "superstition"; yet the wages of sin still imply a ransom, only a cruder form of ransom. Not even Schopenhauer's prospect of a Nirvana of extinction could relieve this situation.

Most certainly the conscience of our day needs the good offices of what the scholastics used to call a *scientia rectrix* to interpret rightly the discoveries and hypotheses unceasingly blossoming in a climate of intellectual anarchy. With Nietzsche we become further aware of the contagious nature of modern iconoclasm. Before we denounce him as a "blond beast" and the anti-Christ, however, we should realize that what he was saying had admittedly been made out of what he had heard by questioning and listening at a variety of conversations among his contemporaries. In this connection the real clue to Nietzsche is to be found in *Beyond Good and Evil.* Why Atheism nowadays? he asks. All he can find in the so-called modern religious

---

[5] Dostoyevsky, *Crime and Punishment* (1866), I, 6; IV, 3; VI, 2.

[6] *Darkness at Noon,* "The Third Hearing," 3, copyright 1941 by The Macmillan Co.

mind is a profound distrust of the theistic satisfaction. "The father" in God is thoroughly refuted; equally so, "the judge," "the rewarder." Also his "free will": he does not hear. Nay, the whole burden of modern philosophy is that an *attentat* has been made on the old conception of the soul which was the basic presupposition of Christian doctrine. "The path to the fundamental problems" has now become psychology. In this light, then, we may read a tale of disillusionment in the history of Western man's thought. All philosophy is "a confession, a sort of 'involuntary and unconscious auto-biography.'"

Partially under the influence of Darwin,[7] Nietzsche sees life in terms of self-assertion on the part of living things seeking above all to triumph over weakness by discharging their strength through sheer will power. Thus the "gospel" of adjustment which has such wide appeal in our day may be said to have its climax in the gospel of the Superman. "The Superman is the meaning of the earth. Let your will say, the Superman *shall* be the meaning of the earth."[8]

Not only do we reach here the apex of will to power, but we are faced with a transvaluation of values in the disorganized soul of some of our contemporaries. That is, a new process of crystallization is in the making whose residue must be the sum total of Christian values. There is found in Nietzsche an abhorrence for any interpretation of cultural values and their development according to a Christian scheme, for any effort at rediscovering and justifying the ways of the Hebrew-Christian God.

Thus what Baudelaire called "reversed Grace" finds another tragic expression in a pessimism partly born of megalomania and fear. A form of *Weltschmerz* far more pernicious than the romantic melancholy of an earlier age, henceforth contaminates a whole people of literary and artistic culture, everywhere bringing a disheartening

[7] Nietzsche, *Jenseits von Gut und Böse* (1886), Engl. trans. *Beyond Good and Evil* (1907). Par. 23; par. 6; par. 13 for this and preceding quotations.
[8] Cf. Nietzsche, *Der Wille zur Macht* (1888). Engl. trans. *The Will to Power* (1909, 1910); *Also Sprach Zarathustra* (1882). Engl. trans. *Thus Spake Zarathustra* (1909), Prologue, par. 3.

fruitage of human misery or mere cynicism. We need only point to such characters as those of Hemingway. Worshipers of brute force in this, our contemporary wilderness, they "discharge their strength," as Nietzsche would say, in lust, rape, sensuous love, and meaningless killing. There is a steel-like coldness in their hearts, and for all their activism they know that they are doomed to frustration.

A Great Divide Is Reached

A great divide has thus been reached in our day and age. There are, on the one side, those "drunk with the sight of power" who have developed a cold-blooded master mentality; and there are, on the other side, multitudes of those whose sensitivity has become benumbed, their will stultified, and whose destiny threatens to be one of slavery to some new master race. They have given in to what their unnatural voice calls "the vanity of it all" in a sophisticated tone which painfully tries to hide a tragic undertone. Like Figaro they hasten to laugh at everything for fear they might have to cry.

"Give me liberty, said Patrick Henry, putting his straw hat on the first day of May, or give me death. And he got it." So Jimmy Herf was laughing to himself as he was walking west along Twenty-third Street. The nonacademic man who read *Manhattan Transfer* by John Dos Passos may recall the passage in one of the very last pages of the book; how, some time later, Herf "sits smoking happily. He can't seem to remember anything, there is no future. . . . Perhaps he's gone crazy, perhaps this is amnesia, some disease with a long Greek name. . . ." Sunrise finds him walking between dumping grounds full of smoking rubbish piles, hungry and with blisters on his big toes. His last quarter is carefully spent on breakfast in a lunch wagon opposite a gasoline station. He asks a red-haired driver for a lift.

"How fur ye goin'?" asks the man at the wheel.

"I dunno. . . . Pretty far."

This is the end of the book and the beginning of a new era.

219

Jimmy Herf was going pretty far indeed: where? He did not know. Others would do the knowing for him.

Ours is no longer the era of the middle-of-the-road man. We now live at a time when we are forced to make a decision at each point in our life. Either man will let himself go like Jimmy Herf or in *some* way recover a sense of power and purpose.

CHAPTER FIFTEEN

An EASTERN WORLD
with a FALSE RADIANCE

THERE is today a tragic split between East and West. The crisis lies much deeper than most people think. It is a spiritual crisis— a crisis involving on the one hand hopeless, aimless Western populations which can still work and give away but can no longer believe; and, on the other hand, professionally led revolutionaries, Communist dominated trade unions, intellectuals excited by new possibilities, colonial people awakened from resentment to self-assertive power. The West is old and feels old. It is slowly disintegrating, perishing for lack of vision. The East is set afire by the false radiance of a new paganism. This enthusiasm is not the blind emotionalism of an ephemeral outburst, moreover. It is under the control of shrewd psychologists who have well-outlined goals and time tables, and well-tested tactics; men who know exactly what they must do and precisely when they must do it. The scientists have been enrolled in the service of the new faith and made to wear the uniform. And because the new faith demands much, it *is* a faith. Men die for it. However much our wishful thinking may cherish the thought of populations longing for Western liberation in Asia or behind the iron curtain, the over-all picture of Communism on the march is in many ways comparable to that of early Christianity out to conquer the Hellenistic world.

It is a fatal error to believe that our contention is with atheism. Our contention is *with pernicious forms of substitute religion* which

221

have developed in areas weakly held by the church. These last words are not to be interpreted in terms of authoritarianism or want of it. Any true authority flows from a power to persuade and inspire, in a world of men whose primary need is the need to worship, as we have previously been made to realize. Worship in turn implies a vision: "Where there is no vision, the people perish."

When I speak of areas weakly held by the church, I mean areas where the people who sit in darkness and in the shadow of death are not shown what the church sees when she looks at the world of nature and of man. Because the Christian landscape of reality is what it is, it constitutes the vision that can guide the feet of men into the way of peace. Yet the church seems increasingly unable to communicate her vision. It is the loss of that vision and of the first love born of that vision in the faithful, which has caused the church to lose ground and influence.

When Albert Schweitzer was confronted with the question, "Is religion a force in the spiritual life of our age?" he answered, "No!" He qualified this negative answer as follows: "There is still religion in the world; there is much religion in the church; there are many pious people among us. Christianity can still point to works of love and to social works of which it can be proud. There is a longing for religion among many who no longer belong to the churches. I rejoice to concede this. And yet we must hold fast to the fact that religion is not a force." That religion *was* defeated in our time is only too obvious to Albert Schweitzer. "For it lifts up its voice but only to protest. It cannot command. The spirit of the age does not listen. It goes its own way." [1]

[1] "Religion in Modern Civilization," *The Christian Century*, November 21 and 28, 1934. Copyrighted by Christian Century Foundation and used by permission. My quotation is from reprint in George Seaver's *Albert Schweitzer, the Man and His Mind* (New York and London: Harper & Bros., 1947), Appendix III, p. 335.
Later in his article Albert Schweitzer gave the following characterization of what he called "the spirit of the age": It "dislikes what is simple. It no longer believes the simple can be profound. It loves the complicated, and regards it as profound. It loves the violent. That is why the spirit of the age can love Karl Barth and Nietzsche at the same time. The spirit of the age loves dissonance in tones, in lines, and in thought. That shows how far from right thinking it is, for right thinking is harmony within us." (*Ibid.*, p. 338.)

By "religion" Albert Schweitzer means "Christianity." This clarification is essential to our present development, inasmuch as man remains today the "religious animal" he has always been, even in the Eastern half of our world. Therefore when Schweitzer states that "the spirit of the age" no longer listens to the church but goes its own way, we should realize that the new way is still a religious way.

This is the crux of our argument in this chapter. Any man in a position of influence who has not in this day and age acknowledged the religious nature of ideologies in general and of Communism in particular, is but a blind leader of the blind.

Communism, a Substitute Religion

Communism is a heresy using Christian categories so as more effectively to dispose of Christianity. Only that which has been replaced may be truly said to have been destroyed.

In the course of Ecumenics he gives in Princeton Seminary, President John A. Mackay brings out a point by point parallelism between Christianity and Marxist Communism.[2] The materialism of Marxist Communism is no longer the old-fashioned materialism, but a dialectical materialism teeming with life which has become an equivalent for God. The new religion has its sacred writings. Its scriptures are *The Communist Manifesto* of Marx and Engels (1848), *Das Kapital* of Karl Marx ([1859], 1867, 1873), as well as the writings of Lenin and Stalin. It has a holy people also, the world Proletariat. The "prisoners of starvation" are led out of "Egypt" and destined to rule the nations with a "rod of iron." "Holy Mother Russia" is the "first fruits" and agent of the revolutionary process. The Messiah is Lenin, who, having come out of exile and led the Proletariat out of "Egypt" now lies embalmed in the Kremlin, an object of virtual adoration. The Apostles are Joseph Stalin and the Politburo, with Leon Trotsky cast in the role of Judas. The church is constituted by the Communist Party which gathers the faithful. A militant monastic order, moreover, it makes upon its members an absolute demand, one of utter

[2] I am indebted to Dr. Mackay for allowing me to use in this paragraph material borrowed from his personal notes.

223

commitment to an existential kind of truth which must be "done." The missionaries of the new religion are overt Communists and "fifth columnists" also charged with the task of world revolution! This task is fulfilled by "liberation" and indoctrination. The doctrine itself is a catechism proceeding from a systematic theology, a rigid structure of Marxist ideas which must be accepted and applied with unquestioning devotion. The system involves an ethic whose only absolute is the interest of the Revolution, and an eschatology which envisages "the Day" of world revolution and the "kingdom" of a classless society. The liturgy appears in the use of songs, anthems, and dances, all of them meant to produce a sense of liberation and exultation.

Practically every point of this characterization of the religious nature of Marxist Communism could be illustrated by Arthur Koestler's already mentioned *Darkness at Noon*,[3] the most powerfully suggestive book inspired thus far by a genuine realization of the situation that confronts us today. The novel constitutes a synthesis of the lives of men personally known to Koestler who were victims of the so-called Moscow trials. The reader is awed from the beginning by terrible suggestion of the new generation rising under Communist inspiration. The whole plot develops within the walls of an up-to-date prison where purges are consummated after trial by torture, the final scene allowing the reader to take part in the very experience of death. Throughout Koestler's story, the Party casts its shadow upon the relentless succession of events. Lives are caught in the ineluctable, uncanny machinery set into motion by shadowy hands, invisible yet present to the point of being actually felt as if through some repulsive contact. Men stutter for fear at the approaching doom. The Party cannot be mistaken. An individual can make a mistake, not the Party. "The Party is the embodiment of the revolutionary idea of history. History knows no scruples and no hesitation. Inert and unerring, she flows towards her goal. At every bend in her course she leaves the mud she carries and the corpses of the drowned.

[3] Available in Modern Library Books (vol. 74). Exact references for the following allusions or quotations may be found on pp. 43, 56, 75, 81, 103, 152, 157, 212, 213. Copyright 1941 by The Macmillan Co. Used by permission.

History knows the way. She makes no mistakes. He who has not absolute faith in History, does not belong in the Party's ranks." Here predestination becomes the most ghastly fatality uttered in the ever-recurring assurance that "I shall pay"—pay for the one and only crime, the counterpart of our sin against the Holy Ghost, namely, political divergence. The individual is nothing, the Party is all. "The branch which broke from the tree must wither."

Instead of chapters and parts, the book is divided into "hearings." How can one endure such a rhythm? It is all "a question of constitution." In the Party death has no mystery, no romantic aspect. It is a logical consequence, a factor with which one reckons and which bears rather an abstract character. Needless to insist, pity becomes a vice in this sublimated Nietzschean context. "There are only two conceptions of human ethics, and they are at opposite poles. One of them is Christian and humane, declares the individual to be sacrosanct, and asserts that the rules of arithmetic are not to be applied to human units. The other starts from the basic principle that a collective aim justifies all means, and not only allows, but demands, that the individual should in every way be subordinated and sacrificed to the community—which may dispose of it as an experimentation rabbit or a sacrificial lamb. The first conception could be called anti-vivisection morality, the second vivisection morality." Nothing could be clearer than this.

What grips the Christian reader of *Darkness at Noon* most is a confrontation with the incarnation of the "vivisection" type of morality and religion, the character called Gletkin, "who never showed signs of fatigue, never yawned, never smoked, seemed neither to eat nor to drink, and always sat behind his desk in the same correct position, in the same stiff uniform with creaking cuffs."

We would seem to be living in a day when it takes more "nerve" to be a Communist than a Christian.

The False Front of Communism

The way to appraise Communism is to view it and judge it first of all on what it claims to be, namely the equivalent of an infallible humanitarian church, grounded in immutable scientific laws. We should, for good measure, take the word "claim" to mean what it says: the Communist propaganda is summed up in a *proclamation* corresponding in our time to the *kerygma* of Apostolic Christianity. There comes to the observer's attention one essential difference which works to the advantage of the new proclamation: while the Apostolic preaching challenged the wisdom of this world, the Communist proclamation presents itself as being in line with human thinking at its best. It involves a landscape of reality integrated as a whole in such a way as to appeal to factory workers, peasants, and intellectuals alike. In the manner of all institutionalized authoritarianism, it says to the unlettered, "Ask the well informed: *they* know!" The well informed to whom this and similar appeals are made constitute the mainstay of Stalinian ideology. Theirs is a living tradition of high intellectual quality, one which has influenced a modern European literature of humanist inspiration for almost a century. This tradition was strong in Germany. It meant nothing short of rebirth to the French "Party of National Renaissance" after the last war. Yet it seems to have developed more fully in Italy than anywhere else, as witnessed by such powerful thinkers as Antonio Gramansci who spent the last ten years of his life in the jails of Mussolini; the contemporary historian Emilio Sereni, his disciple; Palmiro Togliatti, a humanist whose appeal to intellectuals is particularly strong. We who like to exalt the liberalism of a Benedetto Croce hardly realize that his message today pales into insignificance as compared to that of an Emilio Sereni.

This, then, is what makes for the prestige of Communism: it presents itself as the new faith, an enlightened faith grounded in a perennial humanism now buttressed by a scientific substructure; a faith which brings to focus the immutable laws of the world of nature and of man, and provides its devotees with the most complete and coherent landscape of reality available anywhere; a faith, finally, which promises national freedom to the captives, liberation to the downtrodden, and land to those who have tilled it by the sweat of their brows from time immemorial.

226

Now the plain truth is that this totalitarian pattern of claims cannot stand an objective consideration. To show that this is so is the only honest and effective way of countering Communist propaganda, while getting on our side an intelligentsia of humanistic leanings.

It is hardly necessary to insist on the fallacy of promises of national freedom. The only nationalism thriving behind the iron curtain today is the Russian nationalism of Stalin himself. Any form of local emulation becomes a crime, as was the case for Dimitrov in Bulgaria, Gomulka in Poland, and Tito in Yugoslavia. Recent happenings in Czechoslovakia only add new evidence to the record of the last ten years. Any velleity of national resistance amounts to betrayal. Titoism is the name for such deviations from the rule of Russian nationalism.

Now for some of the corollaries. The interests of the workingman behind the iron curtain are measured solely in terms of whatever happens to be the interest of the Russian totalitarian state. The same is true of scientific interests, as witnessed for instance by the Lysenko controversy and the liquidation of geneticists. Artistic interests fare no better. Specific patterns of composition are forced upon music or any other form of expression. In other words, the humanism of Karl Marx has to all practical purposes yielded to dictatorship.

An honest consideration of the record will show that Stalin knows only the one principle summed up in the word "opportunism," and he is perfectly cynical about it. H. R. Trevor-Roper, a history don at Oxford, puts it this way:

Both Lenin and Stalin changed their tactics with vertiginous cynicism, professing absolute doctrinal consistency, and denouncing as heretics those whose changes did not keep pace with their own. The only difference is that Stalin, having lasted more than three times as long as Lenin, has had time for three times as many changes. Having liquidated the generals who planned a German agreement in 1937, he made one himself in 1939; having disposed of Trotsky for preaching international class war in 1927, he is preaching it himself now; having equated communism with national resistance in 1941, he is now denouncing national independence as petty bourgeois deviation; having wooed the prosperous

227

peasants in France and Italy in 1945, he is now suddenly denouncing them as reactionary kulaks.[4]

Opportunism, then, is the only principle which links Stalin to Lenin. There is however a difference between the two men with regard to opportunism. To Stalin opportunism is not only a means to an end, but it is an end in itself. To Lenin opportunism was a means of maintaining party discipline. In this connection the true successor of Lenin was Trotsky. The accentuation towards opportunism pure and simple took place when Communism veered towards Lenino-Stalinism instead of toward Lenino-Trotskyism. What was further discarded in this new orientation was Lenin's intellectual persuasion which made allowance for humanistic speculation. In other words, Lenin was still a convinced Marxist in both his interpretation of history and his analysis of society. His opportunism was in a way a necessary concession to the realities of the moment; nay, an indispensable corrective to the Marxian ideology which was mostly speculative. As the more practical man, Lenin knew that a revolution does not take place in a vacuum. It must not only proceed from the actual situation, but make the best use of available resources, however imperfect. Take the peasants, for instance. Living in close touch with the soil within a horizon restricted in every way, they are conservative everywhere. They are about the worst material a revolution has to cope with. Their incurable conservatism discouraged Karl Marx in 1848. And so he pronounced them beyond hope. Not so Lenin. He was too realistic for that. He knew that nothing lasting could ever be realized without the help or, at least, the benevolent neutrality of the peasants. And so he started them burning down the mansions of landlords. When this was done, he helped them divide up the estates. Or take the fact of existing parties. However unorthodox they may be, they hold the unique advantage of being in power. So Lenin realized the best solution is to use them while they last, and

[4] "Stalin Would Have Liquidated Marx," *The New York Times Magazine,* January 30, 1949, p. 42. Used by permission. The present section is based on this penetrating study.

rule behind the shield their façade provides; then to force them out in the name of the orthodoxy of the Party. That all this is opportunism cannot be denied; yet it is the opportunism of a practical reason which had to bring down to earth visions born of pure reason.

Before the inquiry is carried further back in this direction, let us conclude this present section. It has become clear that the Communism proclaimed by Soviet Russia in our day is a far cry from the original Marxist doctrine. Stalin has little in common with Marx, and it is true that he would probably have "liquidated" him. The actual disruption between the two came about when the true succession Lenin-Trotsky was displaced by the Lenin-Stalin line of inheritance. Once Lenin is left out of the picture, the sordid contrast stands exposed. On the one side, and whatever further reservations we may have to make on Karl Marx, we see a tolerant and in many ways generous humanism; on the other, a ruthless, cynical opportunism bent on sheer nationalistic power—the power of Russia.

What must first be exposed, then, is the lie of the religious façade behind which the Russian leaders carry on their own business; the false profession of a hallowed Marxian faith and doctrine meant to cater to whatever humanitarianism and genuine intellectualism may still be alive today. The proclamation of the Stalinian gospel constitutes as brazen an effrontery as the world has ever known.

The Rise of Cosmic Impiety

The Communist Manifesto (1848) in which Marx and Engels set out their view of historical and social development provides essentially two things, namely a landscape of reality and a theoretical method of proceeding upon it. Our modern world stands in dire need of both. Hence the appeal of Marxism.

Ever since Kant eliminated the higher realm from valid intellectual inquiry, a sense of the resulting vacuum haunted the heart and mind of man. A certain amount of compensation was found by Kant's followers in the fact that the mind itself had henceforth been enhanced to full status as a maker of reality. The Absolute was then drawn by Fichte (1762-1814) into the realm of the mind's creative activity to

229

which Kant had already traced everything else in human experience. Thus Fichte's "absolute self" became the one source of power. This Ego which posits itself was called upon to provide the foundation of German hegemony in the *Addresses to the German Nation* (1807-08). A philosophy of totalitarianism was the natural outcome of the belief that "to have character and to be a German undoubtedly mean the same thing." Once the individual mind became the measure of all things in a modern world where the absence of God was taken for granted, there appeared *ipso facto* a tendency to use its pseudo-creations to satisfy one dream of power after another.

The ultimate result was bound to be a prostitution of the life of the mind. Bertrand Russell senses at this point a grave danger of *cosmic impiety*. Once all checks upon the concept of truth have been removed, he explains, every element of that genuine humility which is essential to human thinking at its best, is also removed. "When this check upon pride is removed, a further step is taken on the road towards a certain kind of madness—the intoxication of power which invaded philosophy with Fichte, and to which modern men, whether philosophers or not, are prone." And Bertrand Russell concludes in a truly prophetic vein, "I am persuaded that this intoxication is the greatest danger of our time, and that any philosophy which, however unintentionally, contributes to it is increasing the danger of vast social disaster." [5]

Such a philosophy was the philosophy of Hegel (1770-1831). Now that every form of check and balance has been removed from the philosophical scene, we are in a position to see what may be expected of a mind once it becomes at long last a full-fledged pseudo-maker. Plato's idealism had been submitted to the Aristotelian critique; Augustine's had been restrained by Aquinas. The idealism of modern man, reasserted in principle by Descartes' *Cogito,* came to unrestrained expression with Hegel. Now that mind had become *the* maker, the Platonic paradox of the reality of the intelligible was finally resolved in total surrender to the intelligible. "Whatever I

[5] *A History of Western Philosophy,* p. 828.

think is, and whatever is, is right," may be said to have become the sinister implication of philosophy once Hegel had completed his task.

Fichte's Ego required an obstacle to overcome in order to sharpen its powers. And so it postulated another self to exercise itself. With Hegel, this dialectical process took on cosmic significance. Of Plato's world of Ideas there was but one Idea left—left, that is, to embody itself in the material world. This was done through a process of struggle henceforth identified as the ultimate stuff of history. The dialectical process of thesis to antithesis, led to a synthesis destined to similar contradiction and conflict. In each case, the challenge of the opposite led to a new clash out of which another view arose, one pronounced to be more adequate to the facts than either of the original positions. This dialectical struggle of the Idea striving to embody itself in the natural world was both history in the making and the attempted expression of it.

Granted that Hegel was a genius with an astounding erudition at his command and that his works present a profusion of rich insights, it is nonetheless true that the cosmic process he visualized was a pseudo creation of his own mind. What impressed young Kierkegaard was that this man Hegel was given to a highly pleasurable type of intellectual juggling. His was the aesthetic attitude of the uncommitted man.

Hegel's new Trinity of Thesis, Antithesis, and Synthesis was more than a gratuitous postulation of the process according to which the Idea or Spirit comes into its own. Prussia turned to her own use the resulting Idea of the State to justify every form of internal tyranny and external aggression. Thus a new faith principle which found expression in "Deutschland über alles."

Either Christianity or Marxism

Karl Marx retained the Hegelian pattern, but he also used it in his own way. He made material process the means of producing a philosophy to end all philosophies by allowing the Leader to control this same process. Reality was no longer "Thought—moving—matter," but "matter-in-motion-producing-useful-thought." Hence the two dogmas of Marxism: historical materialism and economic determinism. Thought became the by-product of matter in motion. The key to cultural growth was the study of the material environment and of its improvement. Only by changing the fundamental structure of a cultural pattern could one compel a change of mind in man. Free decision was an illusion. And so the question "why?" had no meaning. A "scientific" analysis of the patterns of history would reveal that they actually work out according to a dialectical process which is the mere reflection of class struggles. Hence the fundamental *and* historical dogma with which *The Communist Manifesto* opens: "The history of all hitherto existing society is the history of class-struggles." Capitalism was doomed. A victorious revolution of the workers would establish a socialist new order under the dictatorship of the proletariat. The State would "wither away," to make room for a classless society truly democratic in character and communistic in economy.

That a communistic economy per se does not challenge the Christian view in the least will be freely granted by those who remember the original status of the first church according to the Acts of the Apostles (2:42-47). The early Christians "had all things common; and sold their possessions and goods, and parted them to all men, as every man had need." It must be acknowledged that the failure of a Christian society to remember those early standards of value and put them to use may be partly responsible for the rise of a new order which claims them as its own. The candid reader of Karl Marx will further admit that a true spirit of brotherhood inspires many of his pages.

The challenge to Christianity lies also in the fact that churches have been increasingly patronized by those exposed as "exploiters," whether kings or capitalists. The otherworldliness of the Christian proclamation, the corresponding promise of a compensation of the ills of this world order, and subsequent appeals to resignation, have actually played into the hands of the ruling classes. Religion has been in this connection what Charles Kingsley was the first to call the

232

"opium of the people"—or, as the current saying has it, "pie in the sky when you die." The churches have been rewarded by the rich man's patronage. As a result, many a workingman keeps away from the pew because too many ministers seem to live in a world different from his own.

Yet it would seem that many in the ministry today are part of the proletariat, and poor relatives at that. The danger that the ministry could in some ways be influenced by Marxism may become greater than that of its falling victim to the enticement of capitalism. The same is increasingly true in the teaching profession. This is why it is so important for the Christian to view Marxism aright.

It is preposterous to place side by side the passages of the Acts of the Apostles presenting scenes of early Christian communism, and selections illustrating the concern of Karl Marx for the welfare of the common man. Only the *context* of both will yield the truth. The characterization of the first Church in Acts 2:42-47 is immediately preceded by Peter's sermon on the lordship of Christ and its implications in the apostolic proclamation. It is immediately followed by an account of the first mighty work wrought by Peter and John in the name of the Lord, and Peter's second sermon on the fulfillment of the covenant. The context of the Marxist welfare state, on the other hand, is an uncompromising materialistic interpretation of the world of nature and of man, forced upon the Christian landscape of reality and challenging its very relevance at every point.

The Wider Context

Reduced to its normal proportions, Marxism constitutes but one of the many ideologies which have characterized our modern age, although some manifestations of ideology appeared in ancient times. In other words, there is a wider context to be taken into consideration if our survey of Communism is to yield adequate information.

Such is the vastness of the subject involved, however, that I must reluctantly depart from the policy of not quoting myself. During the last war I published in the series of the American Philosophical Society, a volume on the literary tradition of Ideology from Lucretius down to our day.[6] The immediate object of the inquiry was to trace the sources and appraise the impact of the liberal thought of the American and French founding fathers. I would at this time present some of the conclusions impressed upon me by the study of that long record, in so far as they bear upon Marxism. I leave it to the persons who are interested to turn to the larger treatment for justification and further bibliographical references. In the same spirit and for the same reason, I have avoided loading this chapter with necessarily sketchy footnotes.[7]

What is of immediate interest here is the perennial mechanism found to be at work wherever a new form of ideology appears. The word "ideology" is confusing. According to Webster's New International Dictionary its meaning suggests "visionary speculation; idle theorizing." Utopias are said to be "social romances, or ideologies." We may well understand the outburst of John Adams on receiving the chief work of Destutt de Tracy, as witnessed by his letter of December 16, 1816, to Thomas Jefferson: "3 vols. of Ideology. Pray explain to me this theological term! What does it mean?" The rest of the letter almost defies quotation.

Yet the term "ideology" as Destutt de Tracy used it, simply meant the science of ideas, the study of their origin and nature. This study which was at least as old as Epicurus, had somewhat narrowed down when Tracy characterized it in his *Elements d'Idéologie*. Its reference was to a theory according to which all ideas are derived by sensations. The theory itself traced its main origin in modern times to John Locke. Locke's fundamental presupposition in turn was a mere restatement of the Stoic axiom, *Nihil est in intellectu quod non prius fuerit in sensu*—nothing is in the mind which was not previously in the senses.

[6] *La Tradition Littéraire des Idéologues,* with an introduction in English by Professor Gilbert Chinard, of Princeton University (Philadelphia: The American Philosophical Society, 1943).

[7] A sixteen-page bibliography will be found in *ibid.,* pp. 284-99.

What actually happened is that a perfectly normal and respectable form of psychological inquiry turned into vague yet enthusiastic forms of mysticism with revolutionary tendencies. Thus the sober "analysis" which Cabanis was anxious to derive from physiology became a wild upsurge of romantic apocalypse.

But the mechanism of the deviation *also* was as old as Epicurus, or at least as old as Lucretius who gave such a splendid poetic expression to the views of his master. To Epicurus, the origin and development of ideas was but one aspect of the atomism of his day. He borrowed from Democritus a theory of ideas according to which objects constantly emit in every direction small material images which in turn impress their likeness into the brain. Hence mechanically produced sensations developed those over-all concepts we characterize as truths. These are but the outcome of the workings of nature within human nature. So far, so good. We are still dealing with a scientific concern leading to scientific conclusions. With Lucretius, however, this emergence takes on a new significance. Since truth is found to belong in the natural realm, Nature—with a capital N—*is* the Principle to be exalted. And so, from the beginning of his poem, *De rerum natura*—Of the Nature of Things—Lucretius celebrates the victory of Epicurus over religion. *From an object of scientific investigation, nature has now become a faith principle called upon to account for all available data.* As a result, we already find in Lucretius the main antireligious themes of some modern ideologies: religion leads to crime;[8] it is a lie, and truth must be substituted for it,[9] etc. The principle of the "new" wisdom is that "nothing is ever created from nothing through the agency of a divine power." [10] As for the eulogy of philosophy on which the second book of Lucretius opens, it might well have been used as a motto for the Age of Enlightenment, after having been borrowed from Ennius who himself owed it to Homer. We refer particularly to the outcry "Do you not see

[8] *De rerum natura* I. 80-101.
[9] I. 102-45.
[10] I. 149-50.

what nature barks [at you] . . . ?"[11] The very notion of Providence appears to Lucretius as the mere opinion of an ignorant philosopher.[12] What an error to believe that the world was created for us by a divine will! [13] Everything happens in nature without the intervention of the gods.[14]

This, then, was already the way "ideology" as a normal scientific investigation became "ideology" as a new religious enthusiasm bent upon displacing religion altogether.

The same mechanism reappeared during the Age of Enlightenment when, through a curious coincidence, the poem of Lucretius enjoyed a renewed popularity. Then Baron D'Holbach, the eighteenth century challenger of religion, adopted as a motto for the second volume of his *System of Nature,* this quotation from *De rerum natura:* "These truths once known and securely in thy possession, henceforth nature appears free to thee, exempt from proud masters, accomplishing everything by herself, spontaneously and without constraint, without the participation of the gods." [15] The antireligious frenzy of the French Revolution found one of its main sources of inspiration in D'Holbach's book which was the eighteenth century replica of the poem of Lucretius—minus the genius of Lucretius.

With all necessary reservations we may see similar "deviations" following upon the scientific formulation of modern times. This happened in the case of the notion of progress originally worked out by political scientists; also to the perfectly legitimate notion of Darwinian evolution. It is stranger still to find these two notions which had emerged from entirely distinct realms, merge into one and become the faith principle of Evolution-Progress. But surely a limit was reached when this same faith principle was called upon by a liberal Christianity to provide a new framework for the reinterpretation of

[11] *Nonne uidere nil aliud sibi naturam latrare, nisi . . . etc.* (II. 16-17).

[12] II. 167 sq.

[13] II. 180-81. Repeated in V, 198-99. This same Book V opens on a new exaltation of Epicurus just as did Book IV, where Epicurus' glory was identified with that of Athens (IV. 1-42).

[14] II. 1090-1104.

[15] D'Holbach's reference to *De Rerum Natura* II. 1158, is inaccurate, however. The exact reference of his quotation is to II. 1090-93.

biblical material. Thus the Bible message was recast according to a principle entirely foreign to the data at hand. And so, even the history of the Israel of God was turned into an ideology!

Reverting to Marxism in the light of this wider context, we may realize that its rise was but one more instance of the same mechanism at work. Whatever their validity, the speculations of Hegel still constitute a scholarly interpretation of the world of nature and of man. Yet we saw how, at the hands of Prussian imperialism, this same interpretation gave rise to the ideology of "Deutschland über alles." And so, in similar manner, at the hands of Karl Marx it was turned into the ideology of Communism. The present chapter has further revealed that this happened in successive stages. There was still much of a candid historian and analyst in Karl Marx. Lenin disposed of this speculative aspect of the doctrine. Yet it was left to Stalin to transform and turn the whole into a virulent pseudo religion. The frightful thing about Stalinism is the cold-blooded way in which it took under control the mechanism detected in our previous paragraphs. Henceforth this mechanism was made to animate a sinister Punch and Judy show.

The Radiance, a False Radiance

What has been said makes it clear that the faith principle which transforms a normal scientific or philosophical pursuit into a pseudo religion is of an essentially naturalistic nature—whether the nature exalted be nature in general or human nature in particular. Whatever scientific undertone may linger after the transformation has taken place, can only impress the unsuspecting.

In every instance of transformation, the creature or some part of creation is exalted in the holy place instead of the Creator. In the case of milder types of ideology such as those referring to naturalism pure and simple, progress, evolution, evolution-progress, or even scientism in general,[16] our contention is merely with patterns de-

---

[16] The positivism of Comte is a further development of the ideology of Progress given the status of a scientific dogma in the Law of the three stages (cf. ch. 1 of *Positive Philosophy*).

veloping in a social order where a regime of check and balance remains in control. But let the control of check and balance weaken, nay, let a shrewd cynicism get the upper hand, and a whole order of reality will be overturned, made to stand upon its head as it were. This was doubtless the deeper implication of the Nietzschean *Umwertung aller Werte*—transvaluation of values. The fullness of time was at hand when Zarathustra uttered his prophecy, "The Superman *shall* be the meaning of the earth" [17]—a *new* type of prophecy, inasmuch as the *"shall"* here expresses a will to power strained to the uttermost.

As this part of our inquiry comes to a close in the midst of the great apostasy of modern times, we realize more than ever the necessity of an effective Christian approach to culture as conditioning an effective Christian leadership for culture. A better understanding of the mechanism involved in the pseudo leadership of ideologies vindicates the view that our need is for the adequate biblical faith principle that will allow a comprehensive metaphysical interpretation of the lanscape of reality.

[17] F. Nietzsche, *Thus Spake Zarathustra* (1882), Prologue, 3.

PART FIVE

The Christian Approach
to Culture

CHAPTER SIXTEEN

The PATH of APPROACH

E VER since we proceeded from Socrates to Plato we became aware
of what has in these pages been called "the ontological deviation." Yet the sense of a deviation implies that another path of approach to culture was available to Christian philosophy. Let us now
explore this aspect of the subject as we set out to formulate the
Christian approach to culture. It was said in the Introduction that it
would be a strange thing to deal with culture without ever learning
anything from culture. The time has come for us to reconsider the
Christian approach in the light of past experience.

The Path That Was Shunned by Christian Philosophy

An inquiry into the Platonic paradox of the reality of the intelligible pointed to a possible confusion between reality and intelligibility.
We were then well on our way to the Scholastic formulation.

A strange passage in Francis Bacon's *Novum Organum* draws attention to the fact that this later emphasis on Plato and Aristotle may
well have thrown the development of philosophy out of line:

The common notion of the falling off of the old systems upon the
publication of Aristotle's works is a false one; for long afterward, down
even to the times of Cicero and subsequent ages, the works of the old philosophers still remained. But in the times which followed, when on the
inundation of barbarians into the Roman empire human learning had
suffered shipwreck, *then the systems of Aristotle and Plato, like planks*

241

of lighter and less solid material, floated on the waves of time, and were preserved.[1]

A better perspective on this history allows us to appreciate the depth of Bacon's insight. We know that the Heracleitean view of reality as developed by the early Greek atomists had the future for itself. Yet these forerunners were forced into the background by Plato and Aristotle. Subsequently, the static world of Scholasticism was ushered in. It was in terms of the resulting grammar of concepts that Christian thought was translated. Deep affinities appeared between a static world view and grammar of concepts on the one hand, and a static church on the other.

A striking illustration of this, with special reference to the present chapter, is the "infallible teaching" of Rome on transubstantiation. According to the Council of Trent, this word should be understood as "the wonderful and singular conversion of the whole substance of the bread into the Body of Christ and of the whole substance of the wine into the Blood, the species of bread and wine alone remaining." [2] This means further that both the *matter* and *form* of the respective *species* of the bread and wine cease to *be* as the Body and Blood begin to *be* in a new way, the species being the common bond between these two pairs of terms. The conversion implied here has no parallel in nature in that the whole *substance, matter,* and *form* is involved in this singular eucharistic *transubstantiation.* What takes place in the order of nature, on the other hand, is either *accidental* change, as involved in the temperature of water heated on the fire, for instance, or *substantial* conversion, when bread eaten becomes something else. In this case only one part of the *substance* is changed, namely the *form;* the *prime matter* remains. I have italicized the Scholastic terms. Were I to present the subject more fully, the next task would be to show how the medieval doctors of the Church, especially Aquinas, adopted Aristotelian categories only to "adapt"

[1] I. lxxvii (italics mine).
[2] Council of Trent, Sess. xiii, can. 2.

them. This is especially true of "substance,"[3] the first of the ten Aristotelian categories.[4] While we may detect new motives for the Roman advocacy of such Scholastic concepts even today, it must be admitted that these same concepts have become hopelessly meaningless to the modern mind. Even elementary particles retain neither permanence nor identity, as far as the contemporary physicist is concerned. While the Thomist conception of this universe as a hierarchy of creation to be interpreted through analogical knowledge is relevant, a new grammar of concepts is essential to the adequate transcription and useful communication involved.

Reverting to the Baconian intuition, we may further realize that when the Aristotelian stagnation came to an end with Galileo, the new approach to scientific thought was on its way to Newton, Einstein, and Max Planck—that is, to a restoration of the original Heracleitean-Democritean perspective now freely yielding its potentialities.

Once science recovered its true lineage, then, its tradition proved to be one of great weight and consistency—one that cannot be ignored in vain, still less broken. And yet, while the Reformation was meant to develop a good neighbor policy towards that tradition, it actually reverted to Scholastic ways of thinking in its theology, and discarded philosophy. No wonder the Christian landscape of reality ceased to make sense! As for the modernistic wing of the church, it became lost in a frigid eighteenth century deism. Later in the post-Kantian world, it turned into forms of religious "liberalism" which amounted to integration by surrender.

The task at hand, then, is to restore the true perspective which had already been somewhat thrown out of line when Christianity began to make its way into the world of thought. The ruling philosophers of those bygone times were indeed largely responsible for many of

[3] Cf. esp. *Contra Gentiles* I. 25; *Summa Theologica* III, Qq. 73-83, with special attention to 75 and 77.

[4] The other nine being: quantity, quality, relation, place, time, position, state, action, passion. All of these refer to *modes of being* that may be asserted in predication.

the ills that befell the new faith, and yet not in the way evangelicalism from Tertullian to Karl Barth has viewed the situation.

Professor Hartshorne on "Divine Relativity"

Summing up the case, it may be said that the deviation considered in the previous section began with the Platonic paradox of the reality of the intelligible, that is, with a Parmenidean identification of ultimate reality with an Absolute conceived of as immutable. Hence there came a unique category of impassibility later transmuted into a designation of the God of Exodus 3:14. This resulted in the conception of a motionless, self-contained, ab-solute Entity. That the Personal Living God of Exodus 3:14 could not possibly "fit" into that man-made Procustean notion has by now become obvious. The same is true of the God Socrates dimly apprehended in the context of general revelation.

We should therefore pause when the Yale University Press offers a scholarly contribution to this, the basic problem.[5] The study under consideration is based upon a series on religion in the light of science and philosophy, delivered at Yale University under the Terry Foundation.

The presentation of Professor Hartshorne's argument is objective. No other concern comes to light on his part than a compulsion to state as clearly and as forcefully as possible the truth as he has come to see it. In its negative form, the thesis is that the traditional doctrine of God as a divine Substance wholly nonrelative toward the world, *does not provide for the "personal" character of Deity*. The author then argues that "A personal God is one who has social relations, really has them, and thus is constituted by relationships and hence is relative." [6] In this manner the personality of God so essential to the knowledge of faith is reconciled with the requirements of philosophic reason.

[5] Charles Hartshorne, *The Divine Relativity, a Social Conception of God* (New Haven: Yale University Press, 1948). Quotations are used by permission of the publisher.

[6] *Ibid.*, p. viii.

244

The structure of the book is naturally determined by the dialectical character of the approach. God is considered as supreme, yet related to all. The divine attributes may therefore be approached as types of social relationship. As a result, not only does such logical absurdity as was involved in the customary conception of Deity disappear, but religious values as expressed in terms of worship, ethics, and culture are fully restored.

The somewhat technical character of many a page is relieved by the realization that what actually emerges from such exacting scholarship is nothing short of a revolution in theological outlook wherein true piety may be reconciled with keenness of intellect. Having duly credited Thomas Aquinas for having left us an admirable chart showing at least the location of the rocks (!) Charles Hartshorne departs from his academic composure to decry as truly unworthy "the rotten foundation" of the basic medieval postulate of an absolute God. Why is it, he asks, that so many of us do not cease our unconscious obeisance to such a postulate? In the last part of this chapter,[7] the author attains to what Pascal called "veritable eloquence," namely, the natural eloquence of truth.

As the argument progresses, it appears that far from detracting from the lofty values we have acknowledged in the classical view, the relativity of God both transfigures and enriches such values. The Relative is now seen to include the Absolute and so we are on our way to a re-evaluation of the idea of Creation.[8]

The last chapter diagnoses some of the deficiencies of inherited religions, such as otherworldliness, power worship, asceticism, moralism, optimism—last but not least, obscurantism, "the theory that we can best praise God by indulging in contradiction and semantical nonsense."[9] It appears to Professor Hartshorne in the last analysis that both theology and Christian philosophy have been on the wrong track for some two thousand years. What actually happened is that men fell down and worshiped their own concept of the wholly

[7] *Ibid.*, pp. 48-49.
[8] *Ibid.*, pp. 86-94.
[9] *Ibid.*, p. 149.

245

absolute or immutable. It would have been more pertinent, and much wiser, to proceed in Christian thought from the manifest necessity of divine social relatedness to the world, and thus to seek the supreme excellence of Deity, its unfailing adequacy, in a conception of divine social relativity.

If modern science has taught us anything, it is that absolutism is a disease. It is so in the political realm, it is so in the realm of thought, and still more so in the realm of religious thought. Philip Frank, who succeeded Albert Einstein in the Chair of Physics at the University of Prague, showed in a recent book that whatever truth the absolutist has, he can actually hold it by virtue of its relatedness alone.[10]

No wonder scientific men of good will become immediately aware of unbearable tensions when their attention is drawn to a theology of Aristotelian inspiration. The main reason for this may be ascribed to the sublimation of God as the Absolute. What should be said is that God is the Absolute only in the realm of abstraction, and the reason for this is that he is the Supreme Relative in the realm of concreteness. If words mean anything, moreover, they say that there is a world of difference between making God the sum total of the Cosmos, as would a pantheist, and seeing him to be the Pattern of interrelated particulars and One independent of it, as is the case for Professor Hartshorne. The resulting view is emphatically not pantheism, but *panentheism*, as he puts it. In so doing, he rightly points out that the view "agrees with traditional theism on the important point that the divine individuality, *that without which God would not be God*, must be logically dependent, that is, must not involve any particular world." [11]

Bringing to a head the whole gist of a potent argument, Professor Hartshorne may very well prove to have provided for theological thought in our time the equivalent of the Planck-Einsteinian revolution in physics:

[10] *Relativity, a Richer Truth* (Boston: Beacon Press, 1950).
[11] *The Divine Relativity*, p. 90 (italics mine).

God orders the universe, according to panentheism, by taking into his own life all the currents of feeling in existence. He is the most irresistible of influences precisely because he is himself the most open to influence. In the depths of their hearts all creatures (even those able to "rebel" against him) defer to God because they sense him as one who alone is adequately moved by what moves them. He alone not only knows but feels (the only adequate knowledge, where feeling is concerned) how they feel, and he finds his own joy in sharing their lives, lived according to their own free decisions, not fully anticipated by any detailed plan of his own. Yet the extent to which they can be permitted to work out their own plan depends on the extent to which they can echo or imitate on their own level the divine sensitiveness to the needs and precious freedom of all. In this vision of a deity who is not a supreme autocrat, but a universal agent of "persuasion," whose "power is the worship he inspires" (Whitehead), that is, flows from the intrinsic appeal of his infinitely sensitive and tolerant relativity, by which all things are kept moving in orderly togetherness, we may find help in facing our task of today. . . . If even God thinks enough of the least and worst of us to permit us to form, with all that we are, integral self-determined members of his present reality, rivulets poured into his "ocean of feeling," it ought not to be beneath our human condescension toward each other to accord that "respect for the human individual" (or still better, that Reverence for Life—Schweitzer) which contemporary thought acclaims as the universal ethical standard.[12]

And just as the Planck-Einsteinian views supersede the Newtonian view while safeguarding the general frame of reference it provides, an amended view of "divine relativity" may be said to supersede the Thomist ontology while acknowledging all its true insights.

A New Reading of Exod. 3:14

A further conclusion directly bearing upon this aspect of the problem is that in the particular case of the ontological interpretation of Exodus 3:14, the biblical text appears to have been somewhat solicited by Thomism. What was essentially a matter of *personal identification* was made to become the foundation for ontological speculation. He, who was meant to be conceived as *HE WHO IS*, became not only HE WHO *IS*, but an Absolute Self-contained Principle, the very thought of Whom—or Which—is sufficient to dry up

[12] *Ibid.*, pp. xv-xvi.

the springs of prayer in the human soul. When he disclosed himself to Moses as I AM, the burden of his revelation was that he is not only the One Who *IS*, but the One Who says *"I."* [13] Once this is understood, even general revelation becomes clearer as we trace it through ancient cultures down to Socrates.

The immediate knowledge we have of the Supreme, Prior Act of Existing, then, is that it refers to a Person of whom personality in us is but a most inadequate image. Person in God, or rather, God the Person may only be referred to as the Absolute in that we must strain our faculties of knowing beyond any possible thought that may be called adequate at all before we begin to think of him. Absolute, also, in that in him we find to an *infinite* degree the faculty of response to any virtue or influence that may be abroad in a universe which depends utterly upon him for its existence. In this context, and in this context only, does prayer take on full meaning and significance, because it is a prayer to One who is Providence indeed, One by whom the very hairs of our head are all numbered. In this context also does the whole realm of creation become truly sacramental. The source of all true poetry is that we actually live, and move, and have our being in a world where God clothes the grass of the field and takes thought of the lilies which neither toil nor spin.

To designate this Beginning of all beginnings, this efficient Principle of all that has any degree of existence, the prologue of John used the luminous word *logos*. Heracleitus had first applied it to the cosmic reason which gives order and intelligibility to a world of change. The notion was more fully developed by the Stoics. They understood it as designating the creative source and purposive concern which make of the universe a living unity in which the parts are adapted to one another and to the whole. They carried these conceptions as far, or rather, as high as is at all possible to mortal man, gaining access to the very notion of providence *(pronoia)* in a world of nature *(physis)* characterized as an ordered course of

[13] Or, as suggested by Ras Shamrah texts, "the One who speaks"—the *same* God who has made himself known to the Patriarchs.

events. The transition between this wonderfully prepared concept and the Hebrew modes of scriptural teaching was made by Philo of Alexandria.

The revealed element which transformed the concept of *logos* while freeing it from all materialistic and pantheistic dross, was that of the Word embodying the divine Will, and personified in Hebrew poetry. Marvin R. Vincent in his *Word Studies in the New Testament* adds an extremely precious pointer. I italicize the passage by reason of its importance to us at this point. *This personification,* he writes, *"is based on the thought that wisdom is not shut up at rest with God, but is active and manifest in the world."* [14] And so we arrive at the meaning of *Logos* in the prologue of John, that of the Revealer and Interpreter of the One who was at the beginning, the Organ of all his manifestations in the world, which depends upon him for its existence. The name *Logos* finds its expression in Jesus Christ in whom God was reconciling the world unto himself.

[14] New York: Charles Scribner's Sons, 1889. Reprint, Grand Rapids, Mich.: Eerdmans, 1946, II, 27.

CHAPTER SEVENTEEN

The STRUCTURE of TRUTH

THE ontological type of approach which the preceding chapter has shown to be inadequate with reference to Exodus 3:14 represents the very type of metaphysical thinking condemned by Kant's *Critique of Pure Reason*—whatever the further developments of Kantianism may have been. Now that a new reading of Exodus 3:14 further interpreted in an adequate philosophical context has disposed of the unsatisfactory construction placed upon it by Scholasticism, we may hope to secure relevant insights into the structure of truth.

The plain fact is, further, that metaphysical thinking should emphatically not be equated with the type of ontological realism condemned by Kant. *Metaphysical thinking has a status of its own.* It appears whenever analogical symbols are used with transcendent reference in such realms as those of sensory knowledge, scientific or political theories, and, above all, philosophical thought. Dorothy Emmet takes great pains to show that metaphysics is always "in some sense an analogical way of thinking." She further points out that the reason we are lagging in constructive thought, more especially Christian thought, is that we lack the proper organizing faith principle. We lack "relating ideas in terms of which some co-ordination of thought and experience might be achieved." [1] As a result, a culture without an ultimate reference lacks the principle which would provide it with meaning and orientation.

[1] *The Nature of Metaphysical Thinking*, pp. v, 216.

Clearly, the key to a regulating Christian metaphysics in particular, and in general to a relevant approach to culture, is an adequate analogy.[2]

Our Knowledge of God

The One who *identified* himself to Moses as *I AM*, IS in every part of a universe which utterly depends upon him for its existence. He is there very much as "ego" is in every part of the human organism. He may be called absolute with reference to the extreme character of our abstract concepts of him; also because he is perfectly responsive to his relatedness to all. Keeping in mind the conclusions reached thus far, there is left to us one pertinent concept to characterize him, and that is in the statement that he is *the Cosmic Self*.

Can we say more than that?

An answer has already been suggested in the use of "ego" to refer to the self of natural man. While saying that God is perfectly responsive in his relatedness to all means that, in some way, he is in every man, yet surely we have not the least right to infer that when man says "I" he says in effect *Deus factus sum,* "I have become God." To emphasize this crucial distinction, then, just as "Cosmic Self" was used to designate God, it is better to use "ego" to designate the proper way for man to refer to himself. This admittedly leaves open the question as to the real relationship between man and God. Let us pause here. What is meant is that natural man living in alienation from God goes through life with a false "ego." How does this come about, may we ask? Now that preliminary considerations of a necessarily technical character have brought the matter to a head, we will try to clarify it with yes or no simplicity.

Every one who has had opportunity to observe an infant knows

[2] Turning almost at random to contemporary religious books, one may find such statements as: "If, as can hardly be questioned, the nineteenth century interest in the historical Jesus has waned, one reason may be that there was no adequate philosophy to sustain it." (R. W. Stewart, *An Introduction to Jesus for the Twentieth Century* [New York: The Macmillan Co., 1947], p. 117.) Or again: "The kind of philosophical presuppositions which are behind the classical dogmas are by no means necessary." "I agree with Bishop Barry that we need a Christian metaphysic which will do justice to the status of personality of existence." Etc. (W. R. Matthews: *The Problem of Christ in the Twentieth Century* [London: Oxford University Press, 1950] pp. 36, 27.)

that it is headed for a laborious discovery of its body, of which its toes seem to be the most remote, yet somehow the most accessible part to investigate. This may explain why they retain the baby's attention. The time arrives when the infant has become aware of a body which is not the rest of the world. At first the little child speaks of himself in the third person. "He does not want this," "He wants that." Having finally taken full control, "I" becomes his most used and abused word. "I don't want this," "I don't want that," "I don't want to." "I" becomes possessive and self-assertive in the most amusing as well as in the most ugly ways. "I" develops as "ego" and this "ego" becomes an end in itself. "Ego" is gradually inflated to extremes of egotism.

The next distortion appears where a parental egotism, extended to include the child and accentuated in possessive attitudes, forces itself upon the offspring's own "ego," inflicting a false "superego"[3] upon this already false "ego."

Education will attempt to correct the results of the whole fateful process. There is first and foremost the social education which results from repeated clashes between the wee despot and his schoolmates. Then educators take full advantage of the child's spontaneity, of his love for recreation and of obvious altruistic tendencies, not to forget a natural pride which is to be turned into self-respect. This entire educative process, whatever else it may claim to do, aims essentially at rectifying the child's behavior and at eliminating its most shocking features.

Family life, professional discipline, and an ever-widening pattern of social relationships, strengthen and complete the whole procedure. Yet education at best "presses out" the pre-existing "ego," as well as it "presses in" features essential to a minimum of decency. The "ego" is not changed. It is at best restrained, with a good polish to boot.

[3] "The long period of childhood, during which the growing human being lives in dependence upon his parents, leaves behind it a precipitate, which forms within his ego a special agency in which this parental influence is prolonged. It has received the name of *superego*." (S. Freud, *An Outline of Psychoanalysis*, tr. J. Strachey [New York: W. W. Norton, 1949], p. 16. Originally published in Germany under the title *Abriss der Psycho-Analyse*, 1940.)

The point is this: the status natural to such a false "ego" is one of enmity with God. In order to commune with God, it is in dire need of *at-one-ment*—and this implies far more than mere rectification and surface polishing. Jesus had to make this very thing clear to the puzzled Nicodemus. The man had come to the famous Rabbi for a "question period" of his own; and he was told strange things, such as, "Except a man be born again, he cannot see the kingdom of God." This did not make sense to the "ego" of Nicodemus. How could these things be? Could a man enter the second time into his mother's womb? Yet the Rabbi insisted, "That which is born of the flesh is flesh; and that which is born of the Spirit is spirit. Marvel not that I said unto thee, Ye must be born again. The wind bloweth where it listeth, and thou hearest the sound thereof, but canst not tell whence it cometh, and whither it goeth: so is everyone that is born of the Spirit." And Nicodemus still did not understand. "How can these things be?" he kept on repeating. *A classical scene, this, between "I" and "ego."*

And so we are now ready for further clarification. God is the Cosmic Self, Redeemer in Christ of our false "ego."

What, then, is the meaning of this? What is to be the outcome of the "at-one-ment" through the new birth? The answer is not hard to find. It is implied, in fact, from one end of the Bible to the other, and confirmed by thousands of years of religious experience; it is a corresponding assurance of that quality of life known as *eternal life*, calling forth a tremendous awareness of being truly alive.

In what he called "A Plea to Theologians" [4] Walter Lowrie insisted that the original gospel was a *simple* gospel. What made it so pregnant was that it was essentially a message of eternal life. Jesus "spoke of eternal life as precisely equivalent to the Kingdom of God." The way Paul the Apostle made the gospel intelligible to all men was to present it with this same emphasis. Forty times do we find him referring in his letters to young churches, to eternal life—

[4] Cf. Walter Lowrie, "The Simple Gospel: A Plea to Theologians," *Theology Today*, July, 1950, pp. 159-68.

or to life simply and emphatically, along with the verb "to live." Following him, the author of the Johannine writings spoke of eternal life, or of being alive, ninety times. "In this way the Gospel was endeared to all men, and especially to the Gentiles, who, as St. Paul justly described them, were 'without hope and without God in the world' (Ephes. 2:12)." And what shall we say of Christian art or of the toilsome effort to define the nature of Christ? It was not made in the interest of intellectual curiosity, far from it, but in the interest of finding assurance for the eternal life of the Israel of God. If any doctrine can properly be called catholic, it is the gospel of eternal life.

We are now ready to complete in conceptual terms accessible to us, our transcription of the supreme Act of Existing, which the Bible designates as God the Creator. He is THE COSMIC SELF, REDEEMER OF OUR FALSE "EGO" IN THE LIVING BODY OF THE ONE CHURCH. Not only did Jesus Christ for our sake take his stand within full view of the Living Reality involved in our tentative characterization, but he identified himself with it unto the most ignominious death. Referring to him who could say, "I and the father are one," Paul the Apostle summed up eternal life in the pungent statement, "No longer I ('ego'), but Christ liveth in me," thus bracketing God the Creator with his Christ to be worshiped and obeyed in spirit and in truth—a strange kind of truth which is to be *done*.[5]

I agree with Walter Lowrie that "if the Gospel were rightly understood as the promise of life, of life more abundant, without money and without price, and if it were universally proclaimed in this sense, nothing in secular life could compete with it, and no man without poignant regret would turn away from the promise."

For to those who set their face against an evil day in the awareness

---

[5] Cf. E. J. Goodspeed, *A Life of Jesus* (New York: Harper & Bros., 1950), p. 226, on the fundamental conviction of the early Church with reference to this very point. Also W. R. Matthews, *The Problem of Christ in the Twentieth Century* (Oxford University Press, 1950), secs. 3 and 4, esp. pp. 76 sq.; and John Knox's admirable book *On the Meaning of Christ* (New York: Chas. Scribner's Sons, 1947), ch. 8, and esp p. 58.

of the kingdom within, physical death will be but the blinking of the eyes which does not interrupt vision.

Analogy of Personality

My goal has been the formulation of an adequate key principle relating concepts to be used in analogical thinking in such ways as to speak to the condition of modern man. Such a key idea now appears. Whereas Scholastic thought detected in Exod. 3:14 the principle of an analogy of Being, it is possible to perceive in the same text an analogy of Personality. It is clear that no revolution is involved in this but merely a change in emphasis, the analogy of Personality being anchored, as it were, in the same biblical disclosure. The contention here is that *the analogy thus revised is truer to Him who is infinitely responsive to every single element, influence, or virtue, in a universe utterly dependent upon him for its existence; truer also as a key to understanding a dynamic world of change culminating in life and personality.*

I have just said that the clue to the difference involved between the two forms of analogy is essentially one of emphasis in the interpretation of the One who revealed himself to Moses as I AM. The Scholastics were induced by their Aristotelian frame of mind to emphasize the concept of *Being* implied in the verb. My position, justified by the historical context of the event at Horeb, is that the notion of Being *per se* remains indefinite and becomes easily tautological unless further clarified. We were led to see in an earlier chapter that the text of Exod. 3:14 expresses essentially an *identification.* Hence my emphasis upon the subject, *I* AM. The analogy implied in any attempted metaphysical transcription, then, is more than an analogy of Being. While it is of crucial importance to know that God *is,* it is far more important still to know that he is he who says *I.*

The Analogy Applied

At the higher level of religious life, where the "ego" is transformed and the individual becomes a real person, the New Testament char-

255

acterizes his salvation by saying that the new man in Christ has *become* a child of God. At this higher level the analogy of Personality is raised to one of Fatherhood—truly an analogy of faith.

At a lower level the individual "ego" is subject to the analogy of Personality because of the image of God the Person which remains, however imperfect and defaced. He is still intellect and will, these two aspects characterizing personality in him.

At the lower level of mere organism, life has been characterized [6] as proceeding upon an order-from-order principle. The marvelous faculty through which a living organism feeds upon "negative entropy" to delay the decay into thermodynamical equilibrium (death), assures the maintenance of a fairly high level of orderliness. Metabolism frees the organism from the atomistic disorder it produces, while literally sucking orderliness from its environment. Thus the living cell presents an orderly and lawful behavior of matter and keeps it up. In its own way it also has a personality. This is again the case for the structure of cells making up an organism. But further, these cells exhibit in their own way a "will" to live. This they do while taking account of each other (as Whitehead would say). In other words, there is also a dim intimation of personality at the mere organic level.

This is so true that Alfred North Whitehead not only made of such realities the starting point of his philosophy of organism, but he also generalized their significance. To him every single element in the universe is sensitive to the presence of all others, "perceiving" them and "taking them into account." This is all the more impressive as the laws found to be at work in the structure of living matter, far from eluding the laws of physics, merely involve other laws, superphysical laws as it were—yet physical laws just the same. The scientist should not divide "the seamless coat of the universe." The advance proceeding from the realm of physics promises to continue

[6] By Erwin Schrödinger in his book *What Is Life? The Physical Aspects of the Living Cell*, based on a series of lectures delivered under the auspices of the Institute for Advanced Studies at Trinity College, Dublin, in February, 1943 (Cambridge: at the University Press, New York: Macmillan, 1945). See esp. ch. 6, "Order, Disorder and Entropy" and ch. 7, "Is Life Based on the Laws of Physics," pp. 76-86.

through biochemistry to genetics and the biological sciences in general.

The interdependence of all things in a continuous process of world-building was already suggested in a passage from Francis Bacon which Whitehead himself was very fond of quoting:

It is certain that all bodies whatsoever, though they have no sense, yet they have perception: for when one body is applied to another, there is a kind of election to embrace that which is agreeable, and to exclude or expel that which is ingrate; and whether the body be alterant or altered, evermore a perception precedeth operation; for else all bodies would be alike one another. And sometimes this perception, in some kind of bodies, is far more subtle than sense; so that sense is but a dull thing in comparison to it: we see a weatherglass will find the least difference of the weather in heat or cold, when we find it not. And this perception is sometimes at a distance, as well as upon the touch; as when a loadstone draweth iron; or flame naphtha of Babylon, a great distance off. It is therefore a subject of a very noble enquiry, to enquire of the more subtle perceptions; for it is another key to open nature, as well as sense; and sometimes better.

What is felt to be at work in such a universe consisting of *events* and their correlations is the agency of a divinity whose power "flows from the intrinsic appeal of his infinitely sensitive and tolerant relativity, by which all things are kept moving in orderly togetherness." [7]

And so even in that "lowest" of all realms where the natural tendency of matter to go over into disorder comes to its own, there is still a sense in which so-called "material" things are being upheld. At the fringe of events thus interpreted in the light of contemporary science, there is found a vindication of the ancient view according to which matter borders on nothingness. Yet the whole interpretation of the universe involved is no longer inert or static, but dynamic— that is, in line with the best scientific tradition developed since the days of Heracleitus.

In the measure as this tradition of science becomes amenable to the support and stimulus of a new philosophy in our day, the biblical analogy of Personality provides a unique key of interpretation. It

[7] Charles Hartshorne, *The Divine Relativity*, p. xv.

257

provides clarification and understanding of the togetherness of a world of change. Not only does it make allowance for the universal ethic of "reverence for life," but also for an infinitely poetic view of a world where the humblest things speak to us as would a smile on a human face, or a friendly light in a window when the night is cold and dark. In the words of Charles Hartshorne who freely acknowledges his indebtedness to Whitehead, "There is no presupposed 'stuff' alien to God's creative work; but rather everything that influences God has already been influenced by him, whereas we are influenced by events of the past with which we had nothing to do." [8]

The structure of the truth thus finds its meaning, value and significance in the eminently responsive divine Personality. The divine Personality is actualized in the individual states, characters, and events to which God is related in unique ways. They all depend upon him. He depends upon them. If it were not so, to speak of prayer and providence would be empty, meaningless verbiage.

[8] *Ibid.*, p. 30.

CHAPTER EIGHTEEN

The PEACE of a GREAT DAWN

IT should not surprise anyone, even in these dark days in which we live, to see a book such as this end with a note of joy. Indeed Christianity has been so much caricatured that one may well be excused to forget that it is

> good, mery
> glad and joyfull tydings, that maketh a
> mannes hert glad, and maketh hym synge,
> daunce and leepe for ioye.[1]

Nay, because Christianity is what it is, it may view the future with a glowing confidence.

A few years ago some of the leading Protestant theologians of this country were called together in one of our great American centers of learning to be constituted as the editorial board of a new review. The editor-in-chief, who was also the founder of the review, made it clear that his aim was to restore theology to its former rank and dignity as "the Queen of the Sciences." The boldness of this statement overwhelmed the group. There was a hush, then a murmur in which timid wonder became articulate. "How can this be brought about—nay, how can this even be uttered in our day?" Many a listener evidently would have been satisfied with less, with some kind of recognition for theology as a science in our day. All the editor

[1] William Tyndale, *Prologue to the New Testament* (1525). (I owe this reference to Dr. Hugh T. Kerr, Jr.)

would concede was that if true theology is queenly in rank and dignity, its superiority must become manifest not by arrogant claims to veneration, but by the validation of its worth in humble, effective service.

The discussion had now become lively. Some kind of opposition was crystallizing, the gist of the objection being that an immediate claim to her lost throne by theology might be somewhat unwise, at least for the present. For on the true status of theology in rank and dignity everyone seemed to agree. The area of disagreement was merely around the messianic secret: was it or was it not advisable to reveal it at the outset and proceed without any more ado to call theology "the Queen of the Sciences"? The "nays" seemed to have it, although there was not as yet any motion on the floor. A theologian need not have any motion on the floor before he starts arguing.

Then something happened. A quiet, retiring man, who had been increasingly drawing the attention of everyone because he had thus far kept his peace, gently cleared his throat as if to speak. There was a silence. For everyone had by now recognized Walter Lowrie, the Kierkegaardian scholar. Yet Walter Lowrie was evidently not in a hurry to have his mind known. He took time for a deep puff from his pipe and then, with an infinitely conciliatory tone, while a spark of light brightened the twinkle of his left eye, he suggested meekly:

"Gentlemen, could you not at least call her the First-Lady-in-Waiting?"

While meant as a joke calling for a sense of humor in its interpretation, the sally goes to the heart of the situation that confronts us in the last analysis. We have been advocating the Christian approach to culture only to be made aware of the fact that Christian thought is far from having clarified its views with anything approaching scientific precision and near unanimity.

Theology Comes of Age

The eternal fallacy which may still hide this fact to many of us has been brought to our attention throughout these pages, namely, an ever-recurring confusion between *reality* and *intelligibility*. The point is that just as man lived with nature and from nature long before there was any physical or natural science on his horizon, he has lived, and moved, and had his being in the life-giving Creator down to our day when he is still without an adequate theology. It is perfectly relevant, therefore, to stress the reality of a vital Christian experience while suspending judgment on premature theological pronouncements in the realm of *intelligibility*.

Once this essential distinction between *reality* and *intelligibility* is realized, two corresponding connotations of the designation "theology" come to light. The one which most naturally occurs to us is that of "sacred knowledge"—and "sacred" meant originally "untouchable." The immediate reference here is to the elementary proclamation involving the *reality* of God and of things Christian. Those who devote themselves to the discipline involving these forbidding realities are called Doctors of Divinity, or Doctors of Sacred Theology. Their function amounts to a priesthood, their teaching to a solemn authoritative disclosure. Even at such lofty heights, however, the pointed question arises whether the proclamation involved would not gain in potency by being communicated in thought patterns more congenial to the mind of our day. At this point the second connotation of the designation "theology" is already involved.

As the proclamation breaks in upon the realm of history, calling out individual persons from social groupings into the Israel of God, historical, psychological, and social factors are immediately implied. The various sciences claim jurisdiction over their human aspects. At this level of human apprehension and understanding theology becomes a science dealing with *intelligibility* as do the other sciences. *It is this second acceptation of theology that we have in mind when we say that theology is coming of age.*

What used to be called most improperly the "residue" of philosophy, after the emancipation of the secular branches of science, is henceforth found to constitute the lower fringe of theology. We just said "improperly" because this lower fringe, like the "tissue"

261

which lines the outer body covering, is essentially an area of growth. To acknowledge it as such is the only way of providing for the proper orientation of the hierarchy of the sciences. The further and all-important reason for this is that the area of growth under consideration is also the area of contact between the supreme Reference and a hierarchy of sciences henceforward given orientation, full meaning, and value. The relative sterility of a certain type of academic philosophy today may be ascribed to a neglect of this live area of investigation. Further carrying on our analogy with epithelial tissues, we should remember that these are the breeding ground of the glands which secrete enzymes indispensable to subsequent transformation of the body structures.

Considered in its second connotation then, theology may be defined as that scientific discipline which concerns itself with the human aspects of both general and special revelation. The supreme dignity of its object cannot detract in the least from its responsibilities to the scientific world. Quite the contrary: *because* of the supreme dignity of its object it should be second to none in the rectitude of its methods as well as in the exhaustive character of its scholarship.

And now abide the elemental theology practically identified with the *reality* of the gospel, and a philosophical theology aiming at an ever more adequate *intelligibility* of the landscape of reality involved. Admittedly the greatest of these two is the reality of the gospel. While dealing with philosophical theology, therefore, we should remain at all times conscious of the limitations and inadequacy of our human infirmity.

An Aristotelian Stagnation in Theology

Walter Lowrie's sally was to the point. Theology as a science has been the First-Lady-in-Waiting for a long time.

True, theology used to be called "the Queen of the sciences" in an age when Aristotle was supposed to have spoken the final word in practically every branch of scientific knowledge. What happened, however, is that the prolonged popularity of Aristotle actually retarded the advance of science, especially of physical science, during the Middle Ages. Physical science managed to break away from its Aristotelian stagnation in the days of Galileo and has progressed by leaps and bounds ever since. Other sciences have followed suit.

The Reformation and the advent of modern science prove to have been aspects of the same historical revolt against scholasticism, as Whitehead has shown. But then the Reformed theology reverted to scholasticism. As a result, the Aristotelian stagnation prolonged its influence in theology. This was one aspect of the situation faced by John Wesley. It goes a long way toward explaining his instinctive reticence in matters of dogma. Yet there is deeper justification for this same wariness.

As Comte saw it, the sciences should be classified in an order which is both logical and historical, in an order of decreasing generality as well as of increasing complexity. There is no doubt, for example, that mathematics is of all sciences the most general, since it studies all possible forms of magnitude and quantity. Astronomy is less general than mathematics and more complex in both its object and method. Dealing with the world of phenomena, it necessarily adds observation and some types of experimentation, or rather testing, to mathematical reasoning. This order of classification is further an order of independence and relative dependence. Each science is independent of the one which follows and dependent upon those which precede it. One can actually study chemistry without a knowledge of life. On the other hand, it is impossible to study living beings without knowing the general laws of physics and chemistry. This order, then, is a historical order. It is a matter of record that the order of fruitful development of the various sciences confirms the general structure which proceeds from mathematics, through the sciences of nature, to the human sciences. This is why we find this order convenient for the study and the communication of scientific knowledge, precisely because it is both logical and historical.

Supposing that one should try to give definite formulation to problems *and* solutions involving the higher forms of knowledge before the fullness of time is reached, he would likely become a blind leader of the blind in the intellectual realm. This has actually happened along the path of scientific progress.

Let us take an illustration from a science which matters very much to us, that of medicine. No better guide in this field could be found than the founder of experimental medicine, Claude Bernard, through whose impetus a scientific medicine came into its own, *only as late as the middle of the nineteenth century*—a fact that should constrain us to pause at this point. The scientific concept of medicine had been held back by endless controversies between "vitalists" and "antivitalists" so-called, the bone of contention being that science ended where the consideration of life began. At this point, it was felt, a "vital principle" intervened which caused all possible predictions to go astray, thus rendering experimentation fruitless. Just as a walking man disposed of Parmenides' and Zeno's denial of the possibility of movement, the vitalist controversy was simply ignored by Claude Bernard, who thereupon proceeded with what proved to be an extremely successful series of experimentations in biology. The vicious circle had been broken, the role of clever but empty dialectics had come to an end. It would be an understatement to say that such dialectics had their day. They had been anybody's sport for centuries, the only limitation to such feats of logic being the amount of imagination of the talker in question, also the fact that as a rule such dialectics were practiced in Latin— a good way, doubtless, of hiding their emptiness. In one of his comedies, Molière shows such an impressive confabulation breaking up with the doctors all leaving together. To a questioner wondering where they were going, one of them answered solemnly that they were going to see a man who had died the day before. This, of course, made the questioner wonder still more, until his query was silenced by the doctoral pronouncement that they were going to see this dead man in order to find out what should have been done in order to prevent his death.

When we pause and think about this comical answer, we realize that there is a great deal of truth involved in it. The trouble with these seventeenth century doctors was that they were unable to provide for a given situation because they were unable to foresee such a one—because they did not know enough. So they ventured all sorts of explanations in the form of gratuitous systems which led nobody anywhere. A survey of eighteenth century literature in philosophy would uncover the growing awareness of this fact in a number of works written on, or rather against, such systems. The case of medicine is but an illustration of what was true and will ever be true in every branch of knowledge, including theology. Far from being an indictment, such an admission amounts to rendering justice to necessary preliminary efforts at investigation.

The Human Sciences Lay the Groundwork

To say that God is in every way in the beginning is not the same as contending that theology was at the beginning.

The candid observer who asked what Christianity is would rightly be told that it is a historical religion. This being the case, then, its ultimate formulation depends upon the constitution of truly scientific methods in history.

Similarly, Christianity would have to be characterized, especially for Methodists, as a religion of experience. As such, it raises the deepest and the most complex problems on the part of another young group of sciences, namely, the psychological sciences. Yet, at this point again, the theologian is confronted with unsolved and even unformulated problems. The growing realm of psychoanalysis alone is rapidly forcing drastic reformulations upon him.

It is not necessary to insist any more than has been done in these pages that biblical truth is essentially truth to be done. To grasp the principle in its essential is simple enough; but we, in our day, have come to realize that a course in social science will go a long way to help even an itinerant preacher. To the thoughtful theologian the very sight of "starvation in the midst of plenty" should betray a technical inability to provide, symptomatic of an inability

265

to foresee as well as of a lack of adequate knowledge in social and political science. In this phase of its investigation, theology will more and more see it as part and parcel of its task to reach its problems through those related to production and distribution, the function of labor leaders, the technique of charity, and many others.

This is emphatically not to say that the theologian should be a universal "Jack-of-all-trades," but that his discipline is bound to reflect the interests and concerns of the whole edifice of human knowledge of which it is called upon to become the cornerstone. If the task sometimes appears a hopeless one today, it is precisely because theology can only proceed efficiently upon the groundwork laid down by the human sciences. These, however, are as yet in various formative stages. They cannot be viewed in their unity. Neither can the threads of their essential conclusions and methods be gathered in a clear, coherent whole, easy to grasp and to use for higher pursuits.

In the light of these conclusions we may henceforth appreciate the infinite wisdom of a conservative attitude with regard to evangelical Christianity.[2] The simplicity of the gospel once apprehended in its reality, however, the Christian would keep aloof from all forms of theological isolationism and obscurantism, as well as from stringent theological systems. Systems are not found in nature, but merely in the mind of man. Were they allowed to have precedence they would prove to be stumbling blocks across the path of a genuine Christian enlightenment and resulting leadership.

The Transition Period Ahead

In conclusion, let Christianity safeguard its original gospel in its vitality and in its integrity for fear it might degenerate into moralism, mere activism, or a pseudo liberalism. Having made sure of the

[2] On this crucial issue see John Knox, *Criticism and Faith* (New York and Nashville: Abingdon-Cokesbury Press, 1952): "It is one of the major purposes of this book to show . . . that biblical historical criticism not only has no stranglehold on Christian faith, but does not have it in its power to destroy one jot or one tittle of the gospel" (p. 21). For an immediate elaboration of this statement, turn to the second chapter, "The Security of Faith," pp. 26-42.

immediate realities involved in this gospel, the One Church will remain in a unique position to face the prolonged period of transition ahead, with an open mind and a forward look, within the framework of ecumenicity.

Only a painstaking elaboration of the Christian landscape of reality will allow the Ecumenical Church to formulate a consistent long-range program. Such an elaboration and resulting formulation will help our secular order out of this wilderness in which it is now losing its soul.

As the previous section has shown, however, time is hardly ripe for the constitution of theology as a full-fledged scientific discipline. The human sciences from which such a discipline will have to draw a varied and extensive amount of information, as well as a consistent, comprehensive view of the universe, of history, and of man, have themselves hardly reached a scientific status as yet. A frank acknowledgment of the resulting situation will go a long way towards a realistic evaluation of the difficulties that confront our day and age.

One of the most pressing needs of the One Church today is an Ecumenical Institute for Advanced Study. Its main task should be to encourage research and the subsequent preparation and co-ordination of monographs assigned to the most qualified Christian scholars all over the world, with a view to formulating a Christian approach to culture. Neglecting no valuable contribution from the humble, it would mostly operate as a clearinghouse for the well-assessed contributions of the scientific world. Only through such an enlightened, wholehearted co-operation with the secular order may the Ecumenical Church hope to hasten the day when a genuinely scientific theology will become the cornerstone of the hierarchy of human knowledge—under God the Creator. Mental convergence being thus increased, more adequate theological views will bring denominations closer together and promote the cause of Ecumenicity. No longer will every individual theologian worth his salt feel that he must write from beginning to end a voluminous treatise of dogmatics of his own and all his own. As is now the case in the scientific world, the task of theology will proceed on a judicious division of social labor making for an ever closer organic solidarity under the auspices and benevolent guidance of the Ecumenical Church.

Such a day is still far away, yet an awareness of some of its promises should help us prepare for it more intelligently and more lovingly. Meanwhile we should realize that one of our worst mistakes would be to believe that we have solved the problems involved, while the truth is that these same problems have hardly been formulated.

It is not that theology is obsolete, then, but that it still is, and for an unpredictable length of time, in the embryonic stage. Let it be added more forcefully still that such a lag should under no circumstance be taken as an excuse for theological isolationism or defeatism, especially in a day like this. Let rather the experience of the pre-Hitler type of "ivory-tower" Lutheranism in Germany be a constant reminder and warning to us. Such misunderstanding, moreover, would only make for more theological stagnation and resulting sectarianism.

We should find a source of comfort in the growing realization that the misfortunes and aimless wanderings of our secular order must, in part, be ascribed to the theological immaturity of our age. Our culture has grown unevenly, in distorted or even monstrous ways, for want of that proper guidance and integration under God, which only a well-established theology could give. There is profound meaning in the fact pointed out by George S. Hendry, that "the faith in God the Creator has given rise to no major controversy within the Church, except perhaps for the episode of Marcion." [3]

Light on Our Upward Trail

The fact that theology has not as yet reached a genuinely scientific status goes a long way to explain the lack of a firm leadership on the part of the church today. It helps us understand why, as a result, we have to contend with futility on the one hand, and on

[3] *God the Creator* (Nashville: Cokesbury Press, 1938), p. 11.

the other with a wild growth of ideologies henceforth identified as so many forms of substitute religions. As far as the cultural aspects of our plight are concerned, we must once more acknowledge that we are unable to provide for new situations because we were unable to foresee them; and that we were unable to foresee them because we did not know enough—above all, because our scientific transcriptions of available clues were not always read in the right perspective.

In this frank admission we may find reason for both a charitable estimate of the handicaps inherent in the task of the theologian and a committed reassessment of our destiny in terms of our heritage.

Let theologians, therefore, be reconciled with the idea that more than once during the long period of transition ahead they may be likened to those seventeenth-century physicians wearing long robes and carrying on confabulations in Latin. Yet let also a Christian fortitude be the best of their counsel, in the joyful assurance that the fullness of time lies ahead for those who know themselves to be "labourers together with God."

The peace of the church is not the peace of the grave, but the peace of a great dawn. Theology is not a musty, obsolete, empty logicism, playing in the areas abandoned by science, but a vigorous discipline in the making, destined to become the keystone of the edifice of human knowledge—under God the Creator.

INDEX

270

273

283